MUSICK FYNE

D. James Ross

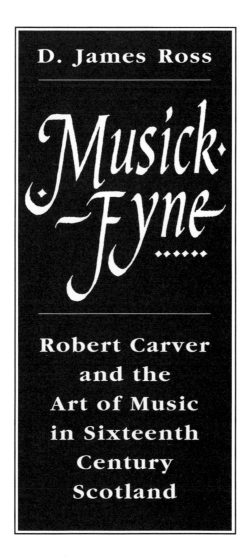

Musick·Fyne

Robert Carver
and the
Art of Music
in Sixteenth
Century
Scotland

THE MERCAT PRESS
EDINBURGH

First published in 1993 by Mercat Press
James Thin, 53 South Bridge, Edinburgh EH1 1YS

© D. James Ross, 1993

ISBN 1873644175

The publisher acknowledges subsidy from
the Scottish Arts Council towards the
publication of this volume.

Typeset by Hewer Text Composition Services Ltd, Edinburgh
Printed by Butler & Tanner Ltd, Frome and London

SCOTORUM TERNA NOMEN CUM LAUDE TRIUMPHA;
SIT GENS PRO TITULIS NOBILITATA SUIS.
VIRIBUS INDULGET, MULTOQUE INFRACTA LABORE
DURA SUBIT, VERBIS PARCA, SED ALTA CUPIT.
SUBDOLA SI SIMULET FRAUDES INIMICIS, AMICUM
PLURIS HABET REBUS, PATRIA CARA MAGIS.
DURATURA DIU CRESCAT SUB SIDERE FAUSTO
SCOTIA, CRISTICOLIS TERRA BEATA VIRIS.
O SUA SEMPER AMES JACOBUM SCOTIA QUARTUM,
QUO DUCE TE CELO FAMA SECUNDA FERET.

Triumph with threefold praise, O name of Scots:
May thy folk for their own merits honoured be!
Proud of their strength, unbowed by heavy loads,
They endure; few their words, yet they seek the heights.
Though to foes it may seem they use deceit, yet their friends
They value more than any thing, even than their native land.
Long may Scotland thrive, beneath a favouring star,
And lasting be the blessings on this folk that worships Christ.
O thou, his Scotland, shouldst love James the Fourth
By whose aid fair fame will carry thee to heaven!

(From a 'carmen elegium' written in July 1512 by James Foullis,
procurator of the 'Scottish nation' at the University in Orleans.
Translated into English by Jamie Reid Baxter.)

Contents

Illustrations

Plates

Musical Examples

Editorial Method

My intention in providing substantial musical examples is to give readers an accessible representation of the music under discussion rather than to derive definitive and copiously annotated scholarly study editions, which are in many cases already available elsewhere and described in the text. As most readers will be interested in reading musical examples at a glance or performing them instrumentally, I have therefore simplified the editorial method in several respects. Editorial accidentals (including minimal *musica ficta*) appear in brackets above the relevant notes, and obvious errors in the source have been corrected and missing sections restored, both without comment. Underlay has been included only where it has a direct bearing on the purpose of the example. Where only selected parts from a complete score are represented, this is clearly indicated (e.g. 'Bass parts only'). With these reservations, the examples represent a direct transcription into modern terms of the stated source, rather than a distillation derived from a number of sources, where several sources exist. This latter method may indeed provide some sort of *Urtext*, but if we assume that the sources were used for performance (as for example the appendix to the *Wode Part-books* almost certainly was), presumably the singers and instrumentalists performed and were satisfied with the version of the music in front of them. I have also presented all the examples at the pitch at which they appear in the stated source. (Muriel Brown has attached a note to her edition of *Gaude flore virginali* to the effect that the nature of the text and the curiously low tessitura of the voices would suggest that the piece should be performed a perfect fourth higher—I have stated my opinions on performance pitch on pp 58–60.) I am indebted to Muriel Brown for her kind permission to use extracts from her complete edition of the works of Robert Carver.

Foreword
by Dr Jamie Reid Baxter

It's soon', no' sense, that faddoms the herts o men,
And by my sangs the roch auld Scots I ken
E'en herts that hae nae Scots'll dirl richt thro',
Als nocht else could—fur here's a language rings
Wi' datchie sesames, and names for nameless things![1]

When Hugh MacDiarmid wrote these words in 1925, he was not to know that half a century later the Glaswegian Tom Leonard would go even further, and demonstrate in one of his poems that the claim 'In the beginning was the word' should, in all honesty, read 'In the beginning was the sound'.

Music, Carl Nielsen once observed, is living sound. James Ross's book marks a first stage in a process which should have begun decades ago. It attempts to place a great composer in his living context—the Scotland of the sixteenth century Stewart Renaissance, to which MacDiarmid looked when launching his twentieth century renaissance with the battle-cry 'Not Burns—Dunbar!' Since 1960 and the 400th anniversary of Knox's Reformation, we have seen an ever-rising tide of brilliant historical and literary writing reappraising Scotland's past. Our perceptions are being radically altered. But amid all these thousands of pages the reader will seek almost in vain for any reference at all to the art of music. Yet, as this book persuasively argues, the music of Scotland's golden age has its own light to shed on the long-hidden European kingdom of the Stewarts, and its own life to infuse into its personalities and events. The writers of today are not at fault; they have not overlooked this musical treasure-trove. Music is not to be looked at. It is to be heard. Its sounding life does indeed dirl right through human herts, providing human lugs can perceive it, and the delay in restoring this repertory of living sound to its place in our hearts and minds is only now beginning to be made good—it was as recently as 1982 that a sustained effort to perform and publicise the music of Robert Carver began.

Appropriately enough, that effort began at Eastertime, and in the mediaeval precincts of Bishop Elphinstone's university in Old Aberdeen. As students there, James Ross and I had been much involved in exploring the byways of 'British music', in the concerts and recitals of the resoundingly named 'Aberdeen University Havergal Brian and British Music Society'. The English composer Havergal Brian had been chosen as a symbol of unwarranted neglect—ironic indeed, given the unsuspected wealth our own country's past had to offer. I myself first encountered it not in the printed pages of Kenneth Elliott's *Music of Scotland 1500–1700* (1957), but on the BBC. On 29 September 1978 a reconstruction of Mass for St Michael's Day as it might have been sung in early sixteenth century Scotland was broadcast. It used Carver's ten-part Mass, and the first few moments of the *Gloria* constituted one of the key experiences of my life. The shattered fragments of St Andrews Cathedral were suddenly restored to shining, sounding life, and a music that rang with secret passwords and names for nameless things threw open a whole lost world, as vibrant as it had been the day the gates had slammed shut.

But music, in Busoni's phrase, acknowledges no frontier posts: I have seen this same reaction of awestruck wonderment and recognition in listeners who have no interest at all in the troubles of a small kingdom in the northern ocean. It was the quality of Carver's music, not its nationality or historical significance, that overwhelmed James Ross, when I finally persuaded him to listen to it in January 1980. So impressed was he that by 9 November he had organised a whole concert of Scottish Renaissance music for voices and instruments. The centrepiece was the *Gloria* from the Mass *L'Homme Armé*, the only Carver Mass published. A year later, having taken up his first teaching post at Nairn Academy, he was asking me to reconstruct an entire mediaeval service to frame a complete performance of the Mass *L'Homme Armé*, to be given under his musical direction by the Inverness choral group Musick Fyne and the Clerkes of Old Aberdeen.

And thus, on a beautiful Spring evening, 17 April 1982, Robert Carver's music was heard surrounded by plainsong in a Scottish Cathedral for the first time since the Reformation. Music by John Blak, sometime Maister of the Aberdeen Sang Schule, preceded the *Introit* for the Saturday after Easter, *Eduxit Dominus*—'The Lord hath led his people forth in rejoicing, and his chosen ones in gladness'. The enthusiasm that greeted this event led the rejoicing down the coast to St Andrews that same autumn, when through the good offices of Musick Fyne's founder, Neil Price, the Renaissance Group of St Andrews University sang the Mass *L'Homme Armé* under the late Douglas J Gifford and recorded it in 1983. The Aberdeen and Inverness singers gave a further performance of the Mass *L'Homme Armé* in the same year, establishing a tradition of singing Eastertide presentations of Carver's Masses in Old Aberdeen which would last until 1989 and include first modern performances of three further Carver Masses. Difficulties in obtaining performance editions of the music were overcome when one of Muriel Brown's piano students, Alan Gyle, found out that she had transcribed Carver's complete works some twenty years before, and was delighted to have them sung. The Carver Choir of Aberdeen sang her edition of the five-part Mass in St Andrew's Cathedral, Inverness, and in the ancient St Athernase Kirk of Leuchars in November of the same year, and gave the six-part Mass its first modern hearing on the eve of Pentecost 1986; première recordings were made of both works. In 1987, now based in Luxembourg, I persuaded the Saltire Society to mark what we then believed to be Carver's Quincentenary by bringing the composer's music to the Edinburgh International Festival—at last.

The Renaissance Group rose to the occasion, and a Carver Mass in liturgical reconstruction became a feature of the closing days of the Festival until 1991; all of Carver's signed works bar the Mass *Pater Creator omnium* were sung before vast audiences, while I chanted the part of the celebrant—some of the more keyed-up experiences of my life. In 1988, the Renaissance Group sang the ten-part Mass in Luxembourg on Easter Day and recorded it in July.

But the year 1982 had also, quite coincidentally, seen the birth in Glasgow of that most necessary element, a fully professional choral ensemble. Founded by Alan and Rebecca Taverner, Capella Nova have made a huge impact on Scottish musical life, and they took up Carver's Mass *L'Homme Armé* in 1983. By 1990, they were packing Glasgow Cathedral for a whole week with liturgical reconstructions featuring 'the complete Carver', and the ensuing recordings have won merited international acclaim.

All of the performances and recordings recalled above, however, accompanied as they were by a solid and constant publicity campaign, have helped to create a growing awareness that here is a music that fathoms the hearts of men, truly an 'open sesame' to unsuspected worlds. A single performance of a Carver Mass is enough to demolish the hoary myth about Scotland the barbarous wasteland, that long in darkness mourned, until John Knox came to prepare the way to Union with England and hence, the dawn of civilisation.

It is good to see Carver mentioned in the same breath as James IV's towering master makar, William Dunbar, in the latest one-volume history of Scotland (1992). It is equally moving to see a page from the *Carver Choirbook* exhibited as one of the glories of Scottish culture in the National Trust for Scotland's 'Kingdom of the Scots' display at Bannockburn. But a vast amount remains to be done. James Ross's book—commenced, like so much else, in 1982—is intended above all to stimulate. There is a dearth of recordings, let alone regular performances, of most of the other music and composers he surveys. One major work he discusses, Andro Blakhall's five-part setting of Psalm 101, was given its first modern performance on 8 December 1992, to mark the 450th birthday of Mary, Queen of Scots. Mr Ross has written his book to enable readers to place these composers and the living sound of their work in time and space, as part of the life of the Stewart Renaissance. The insights of a cultural historian and connoisseur of the literary splendours of that age are here combined with those of the practising musician; Mr Ross is a singer, conductor, instrumentalist, editor and arranger. As director of the first modern performances of the five- and six-part Masses of Robert Carver, he is uniquely qualified to write this first major study of the composer and his world. He has done so with wit, passion and verve, qualities which characterise the man quite as much as they do his performances—both as musician and accomplished actor.

This book is for everyone. Its author sees history as the living past, of which the present, that is, ourselves, constitute the sum and product. Especially relevant, therefore, are his comments and thoughts on the actual performance of the music—this is a book about real life. Gawain Douglas's forthright words at the end of his Scots translation of Virgil's *Aeneid* spring to mind:

Go, wlgar Virgill, to every churlich wycht!
Say I avow thou art translatit rycht;
. . .
Nou sall thou be every gentill Scot be kend,
An to onletterit folk be red on hycht
That erst was bot with clerkis comprehend.[2]

Mr Ross has written to enrich our appreciation of a moment in human history, in the hope that proliferating performances of Scotland's Musick Fyne will ensue, and detailed research and publication continue apace, so that all can share, exchange and benefit. This book chronicles a dark tragedy—it surveys the apogee, decline and death of a culture—but in its author's hands, this tale of self-destruction has become a thing of life and light, an illumination of the past that creates a source of inspiration for the present and future.

Luxembourg, 25 January, 1993

Acknowledgements

I would like to thank principally my dear friend Dr Jim Reid Baxter, who first introduced me to the music of Robert Carver and who has continued to encourage, assist and cajole my ensuing efforts. I am also grateful to the members of Musick Fyne and Coronach, The Clerkes of Old Aberdeen and their director Dr Andrew Morrisson, The Carver Choir of Aberdeen and Dr lain Marr and the Rev. Alan Gyle, as well as the accomplished soloists and valued friends who have made possible so many performances of sixteenth century Scottish music, in particular to Gordon Tocher who never once threw a tablature back at me, and to Muriel Brown, without whose editions and kind permission to perform them Carver's music may well have remained the fruitless preserve of musicologists.

I am indebted to Professor Ian Cowan, Dr Isobel Woods, Bruno Turner, Professor Lionel Pike, Sally Dunkley, Alan Buchan and especially Martin Anderson for their advice, and I would also like to acknowledge the kind interest and support of John Purser, Richard Turbet, Neil Price, the late Professor Douglas Gifford and the members of his Renaissance Group, the Scottish Music Information Centre, Edinburgh University Library, the National Library of Scotland, the Music Department (ob. 1992) of Aberdeen University and Mike Spiller, who first opened my eyes to the workings of the Renaissance mind.

Deame fill a drink and we sall sing
Lyk mirrie men of Musick Fyne.

(Nou let us sing)

Introduction

Thirteen years into the sixteenth century, King James, the fourth Stewart of that name to rule over the Scots, crossed the River Tweed into neighbouring England at the head of the largest and most splendid army ever raised in Scotland. The glittering company in their prestigious French white plate armour included all the dignitaries of the nation—bishops, earls, abbots, a host of knights and a contingent of loyal Highlanders.[1] The entire country had supplied soldiers for this long-awaited assault on an arrogant and increasingly overweening 'auld enemy', seemingly bent on destabilising a Europe in urgent need of unity. The inexorable political spiral which had induced James IV to invade England reveals much about sixteenth century Scotland.

As an independent kingdom with a long and distinguished history, Scotland commanded a position of considerable respect in Europe, with a political influence frequently far in excess of its limited resources. This international status was due almost entirely to the efforts of the Stewart dynasty which had held the Scottish crown since the late fourteenth century—a series of extraordinary monarchs working from a restricted power base, who employed a blend of opportunism and natural talent to rein the wilful groupings and factions of the 'Thrie Estaites' of Scotland into the mainstream of European affairs: and after an unpromising start, they enjoyed considerable success.

James IV had succeeded in uniting Scotland to a degree unparalleled before or since. This was a monarch rightly claimed as 'the glore of al princely governing', and the campaign in northern England in the autumn of 1513 was merely one part of a vast strategy carefully built up over the preceding years and designed to seal Scotland's status as a European power—she did after all possess the finest navy in the north and one of Europe's most impressive collections of artillery. James' invasion in late August 1513 had been co-ordinated with France, under attack from England, and the avowed result of the successful defeat of the brash young Henry VIII was to be a pan-European crusade against the Turkish menace in the eastern Mediterranean.

By the turn of the fifteenth century, Scotland had established a valuable network of political alliances throughout Europe, and James set about unifying the continent's mutually antagonistic factions into a credible European commonwealth. His first priority was to set about removing that perennial thorn in Scotland's flesh—the constant threat of military interference from England. In 1502 this new political initiative reached a satisfactory outcome in the form of a Treaty of Perpetual Peace between the two nations, ratified by

Pope Alexander VI and cemented in 1503 with James' marriage to Margaret Tudor, sister of the future Henry VIII.[2] For centuries Scotland had enjoyed a special relationship with France, the Auld Alliance, and now in a daring gamble, always the hallmark of Stewart diplomacy, James sought to reconcile treaties with the ancient rivals, England and France.

The pivot of James' plan was a projected crusade in which he envisaged the united powers of Europe dealing a co-ordinated pre-emptive strike against the Turks, whose growing influence in the Mediterranean was an ominous warning of territorial ambitions to come. To this end he had commissioned the building of a massive flagship, the *Great Michael*, which was intended to spearhead a naval challenge to Turkish supremacy in the Mediterranean. It is possible that James was simply using the Turkish threat as a device to unite Europe and draw attention to his own kingly status, but it is much more likely that as a man of vision—alone it would seem among the European monarchs—he could see the very real threat that Islam posed to Christendom. He undoubtedly also regarded himself as the rightful heir to the mantle of the would-be crusader Dukes of Burgundy, the European power brokers of the fifteenth century.[3]

Feigned interest on the part of his peers, springing largely from opportunistic expediency and petty motivations,[4] ensured that James continued to devote himself to his ambitious plan for Scotland and Europe, but with the accession of Henry VIII to the throne of England in 1509 and that monarch's commitment in 1512 to the Papal and Austrian Holy League against France, it became clear that the military defeat of England might be a necessary prerequisite for the success of that plan. Meanwhile, the cynical and self-seeking manoeuvring of Pope Julius II, the 'Warrior Pope', dramatically counterpointed James' wider European vision.

The two countries to whom James had tied Scotland with irrevocable treaties, France and England, were at each other's throats and James was faced with a stark choice: join the Holy League and turn on the Auld Ally, France, or renew the Auld Alliance and provoke the wrath of the Pope and Scotland's formidable neighbour England. James sought the terms he thought most advantageous to Scotland. Alliance with his arrogant and headstrong brother-in-law promised nothing either financially or politically, whereas Louis XII of France offered a package which included enhancement of Scotland's status in Europe and a not inconsiderable sum of money. Furthermore, Henry VIII had no heir and James IV and Margaret Tudor stood next in line to the English throne. To James in 1512 it must have seemed that the crown of England was within his grasp. In the summer he renewed the Auld Alliance with France.

In the dying months of 1512 (and of his own life) Pope Julius II threatened to excommunicate James for his breach of the Treaty of Perpetual Peace with England and his defiance of the Holy League. In June 1513 Henry invaded France and on 16 August helped his Austrian allies to inflict a heavy defeat on the French in the Battle of the Spurs. James' invasion of England, envisaged as a *coup de grâce* to be delivered to a demoralised enemy fighting on two fronts, commenced therefore under less than auspicious circumstances.

However, the Scots invasion of Northumbria was highly successful in its primary objective, the destruction of the massive English stronghold of

Norham Castle, unsuccessfully besieged three times before, which fell in only five days on 29 August. An English army was already speeding northwards, and reached James IV's impregnable position on Flodden Edge on 8 September. Inexplicably, James did not attack the numerically inferior English force while it was still manoeuvring, but waited until the following day, when he was compelled to change position to Branxton Hill, thereby denying himself use of his splendid artillery, and obliging his state-of-the-art military technology (in this case, long pikes wielded by packed phalanxes of moving infantry) to operate on entirely unsuitable terrain. This single disastrous miscalculation on the part of the Scottish monarch served to snatch utter defeat from the jaws of almost certain victory.

Within two hours, James IV lay dead in the English mud, mutilated beyond recognition by the vicious billhooks of the enemy, around him the butchered bodies of two abbots, a bishop, an archbishop, nine earls, fourteen lords, the ruins of his chivalry and their discarded armour, magnificent in appearance but in practical terms a deadly hindrance in the Northumbrian mud.

It was a catastrophic opening to a century which, superficially at least, gives the impression of limping from one catastrophe to the next. The infant James V, who was crowned shortly after Flodden, would himself die less than thirty years later, after the humiliating defeat of his army by the English at Solway Moss in 1542. And the minority of his daughter Mary, who would also find a violent death at the hands of the English, was marked by a series of devastating English invasions and a further crushing defeat, inflicted at Pinkie Cleugh in 1547.

But this apparent procession of national disasters masks the considerable

The crown of Scotland is symbolically presented to the Earl of Surrey as the English celebrate their unexpected victory at Flodden (*The Hulton Deutsch Collection*).

diplomatic and political successes engineered by the Stewarts. That Scotland was sitting on the 'inner council' of Europe at all was itself an astonishing achievement, and even if the volatile stuff of power politics occasionally blew up in the face of the monarch, Scotland derived palpable advantage from its international status.

A century which presents an initial impression of profound national disruption proves on closer examination to have been a surprisingly secure and prosperous period, punctuated by moments of disaster. The isolated set-backs of the sixteenth century seemed to be the unavoidable consequence of Scottish prominence in international affairs, and in the long intervals between them, the kingdom enjoyed an independence of action unparalleled before or since. Scotland was playing for high stakes at the table of European politics, well aware of the risks and able, on occasion, to sustain crippling losses without throwing in the hand dealt to it.

The Church, a very substantial institution in Scotland, was the most powerful single force maintaining and constantly renewing Scotland's links with the European mainland. Since 1472, when St Andrews had been chosen from among the eleven episcopal sees to be erected to metropolitan and archepiscopal status, the Church in Scotland had enjoyed a considerable degree of autonomy from Rome, and this was confirmed when, at the instigation of James IV, Glasgow also attained archepiscopal status in 1492. Authority for the Scottish sees was divided between the two archbishops, and Glasgow became responsible for Dunkeld, Dunblane, Galloway and Argyll, while Ross, Caithness, Moray, Aberdeen, and Brechin remained under the jurisdiction of St Andrews. Church revenues, raised largely from the extensive tracts of land in its possession, supported eleven cathedrals, a growing number of important collegiate churches (by 1560 forty-two had been given this enhanced status) and countless parish churches and smaller establishments, as well as financing the lavish staffing necessary for their day to day functioning. The Sang Schule, which was an integral part of many of these establishments, ensured a reliable supply of musically literate choirboys, and in return supplied the boys with a broad education in a range of other subjects. A number of monastic orders were represented in Scotland, with important and influential abbeys at Scone, Cambuskenneth, Dunfermline and Arbroath, with further communities on far-flung Iona and, despite the menace from the south, at Melrose, Kelso, Dryburgh and Jedburgh, while Franciscan, Dominican and Observant friars were present in large numbers in all major centres of population, preaching, teaching and ministering to the sick.

This large and powerful body of opinion was represented as 'Spiritualitie' in the 'Thrie Estaites', the King's Parliament, which also drew upon the two other major groupings of his nation—'Temporalitie', the nobility and landed gentry; and the 'Burgesses', representatives of the merchants, the rising 'middle classes' and, in theory at least, of the common man. Throughout the fifteenth and sixteenth centuries the 'Thrie Estaites' busied themselves with enlightened political and social measures. The political agenda consisted largely in translat-ing the more manageable schemes dreamt up by their monarch into practical terms and in averting the consequences of the more hare-brained Stewart notions. The social measures included genuine attempts to rid the system of abuses and to improve the lot of the 'pwr cowmonis'.

Occasionally the 'Thrie Estaites' came up with advice which united the dual aims of security at home and prestige abroad, as when they counselled James III to 'travel throw his Realme and put sic Justice and polycy in his awne realme that the brute and the fame of him mycht pas in utheris contreis'.[5] It was at his own peril that James failed to implement this sound advice, and later Stewarts were quick to learn from the mistakes of their predecessor. James IV and his successors travelled widely and frequently through the kingdom, extending the reach of law beyond the important cathedral towns of Glasgow, St Andrews, Elgin, and Aberdeen, and the chief centres of population such as Perth, Dundee, Edinburgh and Stirling, which were largely concentrated in the prosperous central belt, out into the northern and western fringes of the kingdom. The sixteenth century also marked an increased centralisation of administrative activity in Edinburgh, and it is really from James IV's building of the palace of Holyroodhouse in 1501, in preparation for his forthcoming marriage to Margaret Tudor, that Edinburgh's definitive rôle as capital city can be dated. The residences at Falkland, Stirling and Linlithgow also received their share of royal attention, and remained important centres of court activity.

The considerable self-confidence of the Kingdom of Scots during this period is reflected in its cultural achievements, flamboyant but at the same time worldly-wise; and complementing the dazzling military panoply of the Scottish kingdom which invaded England in August 1513, we have the far more enduring splendour of the work of poets, theologians and historians.

As the 1513 campaign commenced, Gawain Douglas (1474–1522) had scarcely laid down his pen after completion of his great *Aeneid* in Scots, and William Dunbar (c. 1460-c. 1520), court poet *par excellence*, was ranging with impressive flexibility across the whole spectrum of poetic activity from the scurrilous 'flyting', a form which poets employed to rail abusively at rivals and critics, through lyrics both secular and religious to the stylised nobility of his *Lament for the Makaris*,[6] which records a further galaxy of extinguished stars, among them Robert Henryson (c. 1436-c. 1503)[7] and the father of poetry in Scots, John Barbour (c. 1320–1395).[8] Many of the other masters whom Dunbar ranks with Barbour have left nothing by which one can judge their greatness. The Scots term 'Makar' is usually equated directly with the English epithet 'poet', but something of the uniqueness of the Scottish masters has attached itself to the terminology, making a direct translation impossible.

Sir David Lyndsay (c. 1486–1555) of the Mount was the elegant jewel of the court of James V, a gem which could cut as well as sparkle, as his drama *Ane Satyre of the Thrie Estaitis*[9] amply illustrates, while in Alexander Scott (c. 1515–1583), in whom the talents of composer and poet were combined, the court of Mary Stuart[10] possessed a lyrical and ceremonial voice of superlative quality.[11] Probably the finest of this procession of Makaris, though, graced the court of James VI in the figure of Alexander Montgomerie (c. 1550–1598), a poet of outstanding gifts, whose use of the literary Scots tongue is quite simply exemplary.[12]

As with these great literary figures, the outstanding scholars who enriched the intellectual life at the Stewart courts are also accorded much of the recognition they deserve. The quality of work executed by the historians Hector Boece (c. 1465–1536) and John Mair (1467–1550) during the reign of James V has long been acclaimed, while the status of such towering intellectual giants as Bishop William Elphinstone (1431–1514) and George Buchanan (1506–1582) has never been in doubt. Resident communities of Scottish intellectuals in all the most prominent centres of European scholarship ensured a continuous intellectual ferment in the Scottish universities in Glasgow, Edinburgh, St Andrews and Aberdeen. With James IV at Flodden field fell his illegitimate son, Alexander the 'boy priest', Archbishop of St Andrews, who had studied at universities in Scotland and on the Continent, and whose untimely and cruelly inappropriate demise was lamented by no less a figure than Erasmus of Rotterdam.

But what of the cultivation of music? The term generally used in Scotland at this time for music in more than one voice, serious part-music as opposed to folk music, was 'Musick Fyne', and in this sphere too Scotland excelled. The Auld Alliance with France and trade links with the Low Countries and the traditional propensity of Scots scholars to travel abroad offered the kingdom lively cultural links with the Continent, giving Scottish musicians direct access to the main centres of late Mediaeval and early Renaissance composition, Paris and Flanders. This contact was assiduously cultivated by the Stewarts, who recognised the value of keeping a finger on the musical pulse of Continental Europe.

From the reign of James I, apparently a remarkable composer as well as a major poet,[13] the Stewart dynasty produced a series of monarchs who were themselves gifted practical musicians and who understood and appreciated the very finest and most modern trends in music. James III and James IV lavished attention on their Chapel Royal and the latter also played the lute. James V was an excellent sight-reader, although the quality of his voice seems to have left something to be desired, in contrast to his daughter Mary, whose sweet singing, possibly of her own compositions, delighted foreign ambassadors. At the instigation of these discerning monarchs, Scottish musicians were sent to the universities and courts of France and Flanders, centres of musical theory and practice, where they came into contact with stimulating and challenging new ideas, to be integrated into their flourishing native musical styles. Indeed, such was the commanding position of Scottish composition in the early sixteenth century that it could even borrow without fear of saturation from the distinctive insular English school, represented by the collection of music which arrived with James IV's bride Margaret Tudor in 1503.

Even as the all too brittle Perpetual Peace snapped and the nation was swept up in the surge of self-confidence which led to the campaign of 1513, there emerged arguably the greatest of these musicians, Robert Carver alias Arnat (1484/5-after 1568) whose distinctive works are preserved in a single choir-book. Carver probably worked with the Chapel Royal, a virtuoso choral group based in Stirling which provided the King's church music and which in 1501 James IV had taken time to elevate to a standard worthy of a Renaissance prince. Contemporary accounts[14] record that as refounded by James, the

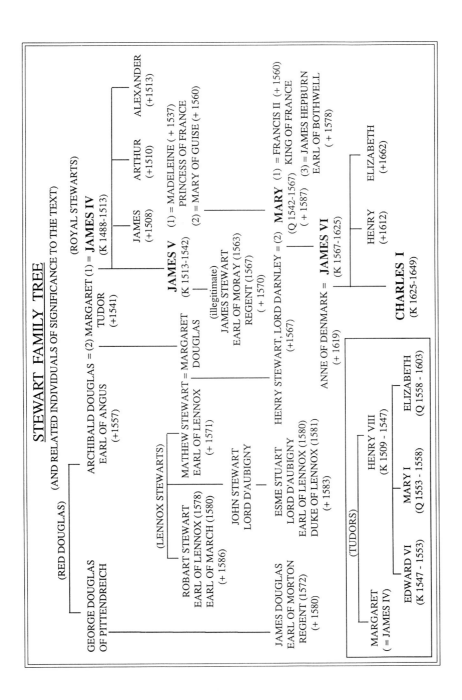

STEWART FAMILY TREE
(AND RELATED INDIVIDUALS OF SIGNIFICANCE TO THE TEXT)

Chapel Royal boasted a dean, a subdean, sacristan, sixteen canons (provided with the financial support of the same number of prebends), and six choirboys, as well as three organs and a magnificent music library. In 1505 this contained four antiphoners with gilt lettering (possibly along the lines of the English Old Hall or Eton Choirbooks) and upwards of twenty further manuscript and printed collections of music.[15] What all this music was like, and how much of it was Scottish, will never be known: not one of these splendid choirbooks survived the sacking of the Chapel Royal in 1559 by Protestant mobs, the subsequent holocaust of the Chapel's 'Mass buikis' undertaken by James Stewart, Earl of Moray (soon afterwards to be Regent to James VI) and the ensuing decades of neglect occasioned by the banning of the celebration of the Mass. But one choirbook, which was probably added to the library shortly after the 1505 inventory was taken, miraculously escaped almost unscathed the clutches of the fanatics, and survived the neglect and misguided 'restoration' of subsequent centuries. It contains the complete surviving works of Robert Carver.[16]

On the death of his father, the infant James V was crowned with due ceremony, and the Regent Albany ensured that French interests were upheld, despite a brief pro-English interlude led by the Earl of Angus, when Henry VIII was even offered the throne. Under the refining influence of the Franco-Flemish and Paris schools musical tastes on the Continent had shifted, and a suave High Renaissance style of composition came to dominate church music. Scottish composers such as Robert Johnson (c. 1500-c. 1560) and David Peebles (c. 1510–1579) responded with motets which avoided epic scale and virtuosic display in favour of flowing lines and modest textures. The visit to France in 1536 by James V and his return in 1537 with the first of two French wives undoubtedly gave this movement further impetus, and by the middle of the century the new style was completely integrated. But the early years of the minority of James V had been marked by events outside Scotland which would eventually be of more lasting significance for Scottish culture than the High Renaissance.

In Germany, Martin Luther had completed his break with the Catholic Church and, borne down the same arteries as the latest trends in High Renaissance culture, these Protestant ideas were not slow to reach Scotland. The vigorous response of the Crown and the Church to the threat of heresy was not alas matched by the internal reform that would have addressed the many obvious abuses rampant at the time. Furthermore, the Church was reeling under the financial exactions of the Crown, whose nomination to major posts of eminently unsuitable candidates degenerated latterly into the disgraceful phenomenon of granting abbeys '*in commendam*' to absentees who might not even be clerics. The venality and corruption is tellingly depicted in David Lindsay's *Satyre of the Thrie Estaitis*, but the personal greed of those from the king downwards who were bleeding the Old Church white, prevented the implementation of the remedies which many within the ranks of the clergy were calling for. The repressive measures enacted by the Scottish government merely drove the early Lutheran reformers underground and abroad, whence few returned. Those who did come back in the late 1550s were of a Calvinist stamp, and they proved vastly more inimical to musical life than the Lutherans.[17]

In the meantime James V had emerged from minority in 1528 and embarked on a political career every bit as brilliant as his father's but, if anything, more uncompromising. His court, too, was as splendid as his father's, and a number of part-songs, similar in style to the French chanson, reflect a court life of considerable vigour and cultivation, flourishing under a true Renaissance prince, high-minded and bawdy, ruthless and carelessly brilliant.[18]

There is a horrible inevitability about the way in which this mercurial monarch was drawn into and fell victim to the continuing rivalry between France and England. Condemned as a heretic by the Pope and intimidated by his Catholic neighbours, the ageing Henry VIII arranged to meet his nephew James in York in September 1541 to discuss their religious differences. James was initially enthusiastic, but he was eventually dissuaded by his more cautious advisers and failed to keep the appointment.[19] Henry's enraged response was an invasion, accompanied by floods of Protestant literature. James' personal avarice and ruthlessness had alienated his nobles, and it was a reluctant, if large, Scottish army that was totally routed at Solway Moss late in 1542, while Henry prepared to issue resounding proclamations of his rightful overlordship of Scotland and denounced the kingdom's very existence.[20] James V died in December, a broken and disillusioned man, and Henry saw the chance finally to abolish Scotland altogether by marrying the newly-born Mary, Queen of Scots to his own infant son, Edward.[21] When this offer of 'free and equal union' was rejected, Henry inflicted on Scotland the dreadful 'Rough Wooing', which did enormous damage to church properties—and which the greatly impoverished church establishment could do little to repair.

Meanwhile, French influence continued unabated in the persons of Cardinal Beaton and James V's widow, Mary of Guise. It was to France that Mary, Queen of Scots was sent for her immediate safety in 1548, the Dauphin having been chosen as her spouse as the first part of a policy designed to lead to the creation of a unified Catholic super-state, comprising Scotland, France—and England.[22] To this end, the single-minded Queen Dowager watched with equal dedication over the fortunes of the daughter whom she had borne to James shortly before his death, and those of the nation the girl would one day rule. It is during the minority of Mary, Queen of Scots, that mention is first made of Alexander Scott, the courtly poet-composer who would dominate the secular stage until the reign of James VI.

But in 1559 another upheaval erupted in Scotland. Mary of Guise had endeavoured to hand over to her daughter the same nation that her husband had left in 1542, but in order to stem the drive for change she resorted increasingly to foreign support—and the Scots reaped the whirlwind as Scotland itself became the chessboard of European ambitions. While the French propped up the crumbling Catholic status quo, the English supported and fomented growing demands for Reformation. By 1560, when Mary of Guise died, an English invasion on behalf of the Reformed nobility had precipitated the country from a state of social disruption into the full throes of Reformation, and an orgy of smashed stained glass and destruction of 'popish idolatry'.[23]

Into this uproar returned the young widowed Queen Mary,[24] an ardent Catholic herself but determined to exercise religious tolerance, a policy which the many powerful Protestants amongst her courtiers did not reciprocate. For church music, the ramifications were immense and far-reaching. The dismantling of the great institutions of the Old Church—physical as well as organisational—meant that there was no money for the upkeep of the Sang Schules essential to the future of the art of music, and the more restricted rôle afforded to music in Protestant services ensured that Scotland would never again produce religious composers of the standard of Robert Carver, or of the masters of the High Renaissance style, Robert Johnson and David Peebles. A number of composers, such as John Buchan (fl. 1560–1608), John Angus (fl. 1543–1595), Andro Kemp (fl. 1560–1570) and John Blak (fl. 1546–1587) did embrace the New Faith, and seem, albeit reluctantly, to have learned to live with the severe restrictions placed on their compositional powers of invention.

While the Reformation brought sacred and secular music to its knees, the court remained largely aloof from Calvinist strictures. Mary encouraged and participated in much secular music-making, in emulation of the French court where she had spent her formative years, and some fine music for consort survived her fall in 1567, the result of her political ineptitude and her disastrous second and third marriages. Her forced abdication marked the end of any form of liturgical activity requiring great works of artistic creativity.

Once the Calvinist Reformers had decided on the extremely limited rôle music was to play in their services, it left precious little scope for compositional skill. The court however never dispensed with its musicians, a characteristic difference of attitude symptomatic of that conflict between court and kirk which would one day erupt into the National Covenant and all the subsequent tragedies of the seventeenth century. The fourth and last Regent for James VI, the formidable Earl of Morton, was pro-English in his politics and virtually Anglican in his religious beliefs, and in 1575 the General Assembly of the New Church criticised the court for its luxury and display—one of Morton's sins being, no doubt, the employment he gave to so many musicians.[25] He certainly made extensive and shrewd use of the services of the outstanding composer of the time, Andro Blakhall (1536–1609).

French influence returned again in September 1579 with Esmé Stuart, Seigneur d'Aubigny, who improved the lot of the young king considerably, not least by arranging the execution of Morton. Wrested from the influence of his French cousin, James was kidnapped by anti-French Calvinists in 1582,[26] but escaped the following year and was finally able to restore some sense of national political autonomy—hitherto, all of his Regents had acted virtually as managers of Scotland on behalf of Elizabeth I of England. This liberation was accompanied by the cultural flowering of the Castalian Band, nurtured by their intellectually brilliant monarch, who was a not inconsiderable poet in his own right. The members of this artistic circle, who included the virtuosic Montgomerie, wrote in Scots according to guidelines laid down by their royal patron, and raised the part-song to new pinnacles of perfection. With the assistance of Esmé Stuart, James had restored the Sang Schule system, and now he felt confident enough to regenerate the Chapel Royal.

Then in 1603 came the gentlest of national upheavals but paradoxically the one which marked the end of Renaissance Scotland. In an ironic reversal of the fate of his three royal predecessors, James VI was called upon by the English to be their monarch. What England had frequently attempted by invasion was eventually achieved by diplomatic negotiation. The sixth James Stuart, King of Scots, became the first monarch of Great Britain, the United Kingdom of which he had long dreamed and which would eventually spurn the high-handed brilliance of the Stuart dynasty.

In the absence of the focal point of the court, the neglect of the arts in Scotland advocated by the Calvinist Reformers and then consolidated by the Presbyterians rapidly gained ground and a treasury of Musick Fyne fell from use, quickly tarnished in the national memory and was forgotten. The die was cast for subsequent centuries when the predominance of a dynamic folk culture seemed to satisfy most Scots that this was the only culture their country had ever possessed. Isolated attempts by composers such as Sir John Clerk of Penicuik (1676–1755), Thomas Erskine, Earl of Kellie (1732–1781), and John Thomson (1805–1841) to re-introduce Scotland into mainstream European musical culture were doomed to failure. They no longer had access to an indigenous stock onto which they could graft the styles of composition they had encountered on the continent.

Eventually, folk music in turn was domesticated and pressed into service as the art music of the Victorians, and Scotland was furnished with a ready-moulded synthetic culture, which was seen to fit the bill admirably. In most minds the romances of Sir Walter Scott became Scotland's history, the harmonised waulking songs of the Hebrides its artistic legacy. The relatively recent rediscovery of Scotland's alternative legacy of Musick Fyne, genuine

The charismatic Esmé Stuart, Seigneur d'Aubigny (*National Galleries of Scotland*)

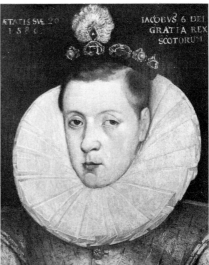

James VI, already worldly wise at the age of twenty (*Falkland Palace, The National Trust for Scotland*)

indigenous art music of the highest quality, means that this myth can no longer stand unchallenged. More significantly it has given performers and composers access to the very roots of the art music of Scotland for the first time in over three centuries.

The worthy attempts of nineteenth and twentieth century Scottish musicians to revive a tradition of large-scale musical composition were made in complete ignorance of the existence of musical giants such as Robert Carver. The contrast with the situation in England is striking and instructive. In playing a leading part in the twentieth century musical Renaissance in England, Ralph Vaughan Williams naturally built upon the national music of the previous generation, but more innovatively he returned to the more remote past, to folk music and to the Tudor church music of the sixteenth century. Of these two sources of inspiration, the latter proved the more fundamental—his compositions may trace the rustic steps of folk music, but they live and breathe the spacious world of the Tudor masters. His first great masterpiece was his *Fantasia on a Theme by Thomas Tallis* of 1910.[27]

Modern Scottish composers have either not attempted any kind of engagement with the Scottish tradition at all, or have drawn exclusively upon the wealth of Scottish folk music (and in many cases superficially and artlessly). The most significant period of Scottish musical history has on the whole remained a closed book to them—and as a result, the twentieth century Renaissance in Scottish music has remained strangely rootless and lacking in direction.

But the long-delayed dialogue between gifted native composers of present day Scotland and the great masters of her musical golden age has at long last been set in motion by Ronald Stevenson's 12-part motet *Domino Roberto Carwor*, composed in 1988 on a poem by Jim Reid Baxter,[28] which explores the implications for modern Scottish composition of the rediscovery of its true ancestry. In a setting of the 23rd Psalm, completed in 1992 and using Alexander Montgomerie's brilliant Scots translation, he makes further reference to the Carver legacy and includes two sections of psalm tunes in reports. It is to be hoped that younger generations of Scottish composers will follow the impressive pioneering work of this remarkable Scottish universalist. The priority for the moment must be that a forgotten century of Musick Fyne become familiar through performance and recordings, a process which thankfully after some four hundred years of silence is at long last well underway.

In 1513, scarcely two weeks after the catastrophic Battle of Flodden, the Scottish Chapel Royal sang a lavish work which is arguably the finest treasure of this entire musical Golden Age. The surviving Scottish courtiers did not deem it appropriate, as one might have expected in the wake of such a national calamity, to call for a work of mourning and brooding introversion, but rather for a musical cornucopia brimming with confidence and optimism. This performance of Robert Carver's monumental Mass *Dum sacrum mysterium* was not intended to lament the passing of a dead king, but to celebrate his many achievements by gracing the Coronation Mass of the little boy who succeeded him, his infant son, James V. Of all the events surrounding Flodden, this joyous affirmation of continuity is perhaps most symptomatic of the resilience of sixteenth century Scotland and its culture.

Part One

CHURCH MUSIC

(Previous page) A representation of a singer issues from an initial letter C in the *Carver Choirbook* (*by courtesy of the National Library of Scotland*)

1

Chosen Chantour Full Cheif in the Cannonry

The *Carver Choirbook* and Robert Carver in Context

Simply listed under the number Adv. Ms. 5.1.15 in the National Library of Scotland in Edinburgh is the finest surviving gem in the crown of Scottish Renaissance culture, a large, incomplete manuscript volume of sacred polyphony. Just how this one choirbook, out of all those known have been housed in cathedrals, abbeys and collegiate churches, had the sheer luck to survive long enough to turn up in the Advocates' Library (founded 1682) is not known. But thanks to this miracle, the complete verifiable work of one of Scotland's most outstanding creative talents was saved for rediscovery this century.

The manuscript, once referred to as the *Scone Antiphonary*, is now known as the *Carver Choirbook*, in acknowledgement of the composer who enjoys such a monopoly over its contents. For the most part meticulously copied, the *Choirbook*'s spectacular initial capitals were originally executed in scarlet ink, many of them aged now to the colour of dried blood, the letter-shapes themselves merely the departure point for a variety of caricatures which recall the grotesque insights of Hieronymus Bosch or Pieter Breughel: monkish gargoyles with elfin ears, bulbous noses, stubble beards, many with protruding tongues, one with gryphon feet, another spewing fire. By analogy with contemporary English practice, it is possible to entertain the thought that these could be fanciful representations of Carver's ecclesiastical colleagues or even of Carver himself, but at any rate they demonstrate a delight in decoration on the part of the copyist which provides a graphic foretaste of the composer Carver's riotous imagination and obsession with embellishment. Less arcane in its significance is a letter A, fashioned into a naive representation of the crucifixion, while a number

A stylised portrait of the English composer John Taverner decorates a letter E at the beginning of his Mass *Gloria tibi trinitas* (*The Bodleian Library, University of Oxford*)

of doodlings and practice letters lend parts of the *Choirbook* the appearance of a well-kept scrapbook.

This impression is reinforced by the marginalia attached to a number of the works. Indeed very little is known about Robert Carver apart from the scraps of information which he himself appends to his compositions: isolated details, dates and, tantalisingly, Carver's own signature, the latinised Robertus Carwor—an evocative point of contact with this most elusive personality.

Despite the work of J A Fuller-Maitland[1] in the early part of this century and that of Dr Kenneth Elliott over the past thirty years[2] the manuscript long lacked the wider attention it deserves, but more recent study by Dr Isobel Woods[3] has confirmed much about Carver that was previously only speculation, and has unearthed much more. The details, which can now be regarded as factual, may be summarised briefly.[4] In addition to signing his name to seven compositions in the *Choirbook*, Carver marked two of them with the dates 1513 and 1546 respectively, referring in each case to his age at the time of completion and the number of years that he had been in holy orders. This would seem to be very obliging until it is realised that the dates do not tally, and, indeed, in the first inscription, the date of completion seems unaccountably to have been altered.

The anomalous information declares that Carver wrote the first work in his twenty-second year, in his sixth year in orders, placing his date of birth in 1492, while the later work was written in his fifty-ninth year, indicating 1488 as his date of birth. Isobel Woods[5] has proposed that 1513 originally read 1508, a year during part of which a man born in 1488 would indeed have been in his twenty-second year. She also provides an ingenious explanation of the necessity for this change of dates.[6]

However, documents unearthed in the Aberdeen City Archive by Dr John Durkan of Glasgow University[7] seem to indicate that Carver was born as early as 1484/5. This suggests that the first date in the *Choirbook* should read 1506 (in Scotland throughout the sixteenth century the year began only on the 25th March), which is indeed very plausible, but leaves unresolved the problem that in the second inscription Carver states that in 1546 he was in his fifty-ninth year and his forty-third in orders. As both these dates suggest a completion date of 1542/3, rather than the apparent 1546, we must assume that the obvious haste with which Carver copied the later work into the *Choirbook*, in marked contrast to the other works, led to confusion with the date. A composition date of 1543 would, as we shall see later, coincide neatly with the appearance of Carver's alias on the Chapel Royal register.

As he proudly declares in the manuscript, Robert Carver was at least nominally a canon at the Augustinian Abbey of Scone, but it is now widely accepted that the recently revitalised Chapel Royal in Stirling provided a more viable context both for the *Choirbook* and for Carver.[8] It is now recognised that the alias, Arnat, which Carver attaches to his signature in the *Choirbook* provides confirmation of this suggestion, in that it may be linked to David Arnot, bishop of the Chapel Royal between 1508 and 1526, indicating Carver's acknowledgement either of generous protection[9] or even illegitimate parentage, while the Robert Arnot who appears on the Chapel roll in 1543 and again in 1551 may well be Carver. Outwith the *Choirbook*, the name Robert Arnot appears in the personnel register for Stirling Parish Church in 1516, 1518, 1527, 1540, 1542 and 1543, while Carver's signature appears on a number of documents connected with Scone Abbey, the latest dated 1566. Further documentation suggests that he was still alive in 1568 and as Carver would then have been an extremely old man in his eighty-fourth year, he must have died soon after this date.

It should come as no surprise that Carver had associations with Aberdeen. In 1495, when Carver was ten, the outstanding churchman of his time, Bishop William Elphinstone, had founded his University in Aberdeen and had invested great efforts in the expansion of the Parish Church of St Nicholas, already one of the largest collegiate churches in Scotland, which by 1491 had a choir of sixteen and a Sang Schule. He then turned his attention to St Machar's Cathedral and as part of a wide-ranging programme of expansion he arranged finance for an enlarged choir of no fewer than twenty vicars choral, with two deacons, two sub-deacons and two acolytes, and a Sang Schule master to train six boy choristers—a choral group intended ostentatiously to rival the Chapel Royal! Carver may have received his early musical training at the Sang Schule and sung in the choir of one of these great establishments.

Isobel Woods provides another piece of the jigsaw with her identification[10] of an entry at the Flemish University of Louvain in 1503/4, registering one 'Robertus de Sto Johanne in Scotia' as referring to Carver ('St John's' was the customary name for Perth in the sixteenth century). This suggestion is made enticingly plausible by the fact that the entry appears in conjunction with the enrolment of 'Johannes Grant', a name which appears along with Carver's on all of the Scone documents. She also draws attention to the fact that that one David Kervour was associated with joinery work undertaken at the Chapel Royal in Stirling between 1497 and 1504, by which latter date he has acquired the epithet 'ald', but definitive evidence of a family link between 'ald David' and young Robert is lacking.[11] Another Carver appears in the Treasurer's accounts for Linlithgow Palace of 1512, where mention is made of a payment for seventeen weeks' work done 'at the Kingis organis' by one James Carwour and 'tua servituris'.[12] Although James Carwour is described elsewhere as a ship-wright, it is tempting to think that such a protracted period of employment for three men would have involved more specialised work than standard joinery. Having a close relative with the skills necessary to set up and possibly even tune an organ might well have given the young Robert the impetus and context for the decision to devote his life to the art of music.

Isobel Woods has speculated further[13] as to Robert Carver's activities in the Burgh and Parish Church of Stirling under his alias Arnat/Arnot, but her proposal that he may be identified with the Robert Arnot, Burgess of Stirling, whose dynamic career as bailie, master of work and treasurer may be charted in the town records, must for the time being remain obscured by a surfeit of Arnots and Roberts, two of the most common Scots names at this time. Although further biographical details will undoubtedly emerge, it is clear that Carver's employment at the Chapel Royal and his contribution of music to its repertoire mark the high-point of his career.

In all, the *Carver Choirbook* contains five settings of the Mass signed by Carver: the four-part *Pater Creator omnium* and *L'Homme Armé* Masses, the Mass *Fera pessima* in five parts, a six-part setting and the spectacular ten-part Mass *Dum sacrum mysterium*, as well as two of his motets:[14] *Gaude flore virginali* in five parts and *O bone Jesu* in no fewer than nineteen. In addition to these works by Carver, the manuscript contains a copy of the Mass *L'Homme Armé* by the Franco-Flemish master Guillaume Dufay (c. 1400–1474), along with a number of anonymous Masses and a selection of *Magnificats, Salve Reginas* and motets, some of which are also to be found in the *Eton Choirbook*, a roughly contemporary English manuscript with considerable relevance to the work of Carver.[15]

Isobel Woods[16] has identified five distinct forms of handwriting in the manuscript, two of which are found in conjunction with Carver's signature and could be viewed as two vintages of his own hand. Exhaustive study of the scripts and foliation have allowed her to arrange the compositions in the *Choirbook* into approximate chronological order of copying, clarifying in the process details about possible musical influences on Carver's composition. The English settings of the *Magnificat* and *Salve Regina* seem to constitute the earliest entry in the manuscript, probably copied around the time of James IV's marriage to Margaret Tudor in 1503. Around 1506[17] Carver and one of his colleagues wrote in the next group of works, including all of Carver's Masses (except the Masses *Pater Creator omnium* and *Fera pessima*) and his motet *Gaude flore virginali*, the anonymous Masses *Deus Creator omnium* and *Rex virginum* in four parts, Dufay's Mass *L'Homme Armé*, the motets *Eternae laudis lilium* and *Ave Dei patris filia* by the English composer Robert Fayrfax (1464–1521) and other fragments. Around 1513 further additions, including Carver's motet *O bone Jesu*, sections of his ten-part Mass and the conclusion of the Fayrfax motet *Ave Dei patris* which had been left incomplete in 1506, were executed in a hand similar to that of Carver's colleague in 1506. After a gap of over thirty years, Carver entered his Mass *Pater Creator omnium*, which he dated 1543, and the Mass *Fera pessima*, for which Isobel Woods proposes the date 1548. Finally some time between then and the mid-1560s, Carver and another entered a Mass in three parts, while colleagues added a number of further fragments, including an instrumental treatment of the first psalm. The hiatus between 1513 and Carver's probable reappearance in the Chapel Royal in 1543 may be accounted for by a lack of activity in the Chapel Royal, for which Isobel Woods proposes convincing evidence,[18] and it is possible that Carver sought employment elsewhere, perhaps in the Parish Church in Stirling or maybe even back in Aberdeen. It seems inconceivable that such a prodigious composer would stop composing for thirty years in the prime of his life, but sadly none of his music from this period has to date come to light, while the absence of the opening page of the Mass *Pater Creator omnium* may indicate the loss of some work from the *Carver Choirbook* itself. If the *Choirbook* originally contained more compositions by Robert Carver, the quality of the pieces that survive would make this loss tragic indeed.

These are remarkable works, rich in influences and at the same time absolutely and radically unique in the way that music can be only occasionally. Carver's music is not simply European polyphony with a Scottish accent: it has an entire vocabulary of its own, a musical language silenced from the 1560s until our own century. In the early sixteenth century the refined polyphony of Josquin Desprez (c. 1440–1521) and his contemporaries of the Franco-Flemish school, namely Alexander Agricola (c. 1446–1506), Jacob Obrecht (c. 1450–1505), Loyset Compère (c. 1450–1518), Heinrich Isaac (c. 1450–1517), Pierre de la Rue (c. 1460–1518) and Jean Mouton (c. 1459–1522), reigned supreme throughout the Continent, and lively economic and cultural links with France and the Low Countries allowed some of that inexorable tide to spill even into the geographically remote Kingdom of Scotland. As early as 1473, Scottish musicians such as the lutenist John Broune were being sent to Flanders to learn from the Franco-Flemish masters, and whether or not the young Carver joined this constant stream, he must have had ready access to copies of Franco-Flemish polyphony brought back by returning Scottish musicians. Isobel Woods suggests that Dufay's Mass *L'Homme Armé* and the anonymous Masses *Deus Creator omnium* and *Rex virginum* may all have been copied from a Continental source such as Carver would have had access to, had he indeed studied at Louvain. Franco-Flemish polyphony is the basic stock of Carver's style, but the spices which he blends into it are varied beyond expectation.

The early English settings in the *Carver Choirbook*, some of which appear in the *Eton Choirbook*, are very different in style from the Continental pieces. As a result of the Wars of the Roses and the long inward-looking reign of Henry VII, whose main concern as a usurper was to stabilise his position, England had, in dramatic contrast to her northerly neighbour, adopted an increasingly insular attitude in the arts. While continental composers moved inexorably in the direction of dynamic styles of expression employing imitative counterpoint, English music became increasingly monumental and static. This conservative style is nowhere better chronicled than in the *Eton Choirbook*, that lavish collection of church music compiled towards the end of the fifteenth century and featuring the work of the finest polyphonic masters of the day: Walter Lambe (born 1451/2) and John Nesbett (fl. late fifteenth century), both represented by *Magnificat* settings in the *Carver Choirbook*; William Cornysh (c. 1468–1523) whose *Salve Regina* appears in the *Carver Choirbook*; Richard Davy (c. 1467-c. 1516), John Browne (born c. 1452) and Robert Wylkynson (fl. 1496–1515). The most lavish *Eton Choirbook* works present a distinctive combination of highly embellished vocal lines and massive block chords, an idiom which evidently impressed the young Carver, who may have participated in performances by the Chapel Royal of the works by Nesbett and Lambe in their repertoire. By 1506 he had successfully grafted the Eton idiom on to the smoother, more disciplined Continental style, to produce the distinctive synthesis of fluidity and rich decoration so characteristic of his entire output.

But to talk purely in terms of Continental and English influences fails to account for many of the distinctive elements of Carver's style, and ignores the possibility that he may well have belonged to an independently flourishing Scottish tradition of church music. The ravages of time mean that the scanty evidence for such a tradition is, to put it mildly, inconclusive. Simon Tailler, a thirteenth century Scottish musical theorist, brought back a knowledge of the latest compositional techniques of the Notre Dame school when he returned from his studies in Paris, and he wrote a number of theoretical works and most probably a body of music to complement them.[19] All of this is now lost, but won Tailler the respect of succeeding generations. He would seem to be a possible candidate for the composition of some of the works in the manuscript known as *Wolfenbüttel 677* (WI), a collection of church music from this period associated with St Andrews and in the new Notre Dame style which Tailler would have encountered in Paris. In addition to proposing that the manuscript be referred to as *The St Andrews Music Book*, John Purser[20] puts forward a persuasive case that it was copied at the instigation of David Bernham, Bishop of St Andrews, while the copyist himself secured immortality of a sort by appending the plea 'May Walter, the writer of this book, be blessed' in words and music to the end of the object of his labour. How many of the works in the manuscript were composed in Scotland cannot be definitely ascertained, but sections which may well contain native compositions boast some pieces in an unusually ornate style. This music is distinguished for 'its extraordinary virtuosity, its vast range, its demands on vocal flexibility in scale passages, its sequential phrases, repeated notes and breath control, and its frequent use of thirds',[21] and may well represent an attempt to reconcile the latest in imported French compositional techniques with a native strand of highly embellished vocal improvisation. It certainly establishes beyond reasonable doubt that thirteenth century Scotland possessed a distinctive native school of composition which drew simultaneously upon local and French elements and which already boasted a distinctive character which would have discernible resonances three centuries later in the work of Carver.

In the fifteenth century James I (1394–1437), who may himself have been a composer, is recorded[22] as bringing scholars from England and Flanders to instruct his court in the Arts, and the English influence of John Dunstable (c. 1375–1453), the most famous European master of his day, and Leonel Power (c. 1375–1445) was probably encouraged by the next three generations of Stewart monarchs. Their frequent use of thirds, so admired on the continent, would certainly have been to the taste of Scottish singers accustomed to whatever succeeded the music of *The St Andrews Music Book*, and Scottish composers, instructed in the art of polyphony, would presumably have been in a position to seize upon such innovations and integrate them into the native style in a manner established by the thirteenth-century Scottish contributors to the *Music Book*. The destruction of all but one of the Scottish Chapel Royal Choirbooks of this period reduces such theorising to mere speculation, but it is more than likely that such a native school would have continued to thrive under a series of musical monarchs, who certainly supported the vocal forces necessary to perform such music.

There is some anecdotal evidence that Walter Frye (fl. fifteenth century), often assumed to be English, but who has proved difficult to trace in any English records, may in fact have been Scots. Frye's *Ave Regina* which is portrayed in a fresco in the Chateau Montreuil-Bellay in Anjou is traditionally identified locally as the work of 'a Scots monk'. Recently (and intriguingly in the light of the Scottish/Burgundian parallels which emerge in the next chapter) Rob Wegman has shown that the manuscript containing Frye's three surviving Mass settings (BR 5557, Bibliothèque Nationale, Brussels) was probably compiled for the wedding in 1468 of Margaret of York and Charles the Bold, Duke of Burgundy. At any rate, for Carver to start writing music at the early age of twenty-one in a mature style which is still recognisable in music he composed forty years later, it is almost essential to presuppose some sort of national school of composition with a relatively up-to-date style upon which the young composer could build, while the great demands his music makes upon singers certainly indicate some tradition of virtuosic choral singing, spanning the era between *The St Andrews Music Book* and the *Carver Choirbook*.

A further element in such a putative native school of composition, and one whose influence is evident in Carver's music, would surely have been the improvised music of the Celtic minstrels, who are recorded as attending the Scottish court under the patronage of James IV. Stirling itself stands almost at the gateway to the Highlands, and Gaelic was still very widely spoken in the Scotland of Carver's youth. The King was the last of his line to speak Gaelic and played the Celtic harp, the clarsach. A debt to traditional ('folk') music may also help to account for the frequent incidence in Carver's work of a sense of two tonics, adjacent tones, dominating the harmony in regular and equal alternation. A similar phenomenon survives in much Scottish folk music in the form of a so-called 'double tonic'. Isobel Woods points[23] to the possibility that large-scale vocal improvisation in as many as ten voices at once may have been standard practice in Scotland, an appealing explanation both of Carver's penchant for music in many parts, and of his remarkable tolerance of passing dissonance, which would clearly have been an unavoidable and perhaps even a desirable feature of any such large-scale vocal improvisation. Gaelic psalm-singing in modern times, with its improvisatory dimension and *ad hoc* polyphony, demonstrates the same degree of tolerance regarding passing dissonance. By definition, such performance practices generally belong to an oral tradition, and while the transient results may be described, no other aspect of the event is committed to paper. The earliest native work in the *Carver Choirbook*, Carver's Mass in ten parts *Dum sacrum mysterium*, is already in a mature style which can only hint at its debt to such unwritten traditions.

A late sixteenth century anonymous theoretical treatise entitled *The Art of Music collectit out of all ancient Doctouris*[24] is evidence for a continuing interest in the theory and philosophy of musical composition. Compiled around 1580, probably in connection with James VI's decision to revive the Sang Schules in November 1579, *The Art of Music* contains a wealth of music, native and Continental, by 'auld musicians' from earlier in the century, whose compositions, though on the whole fragmentary, are 'haldin autentic'. Some of these pieces are duly credited to 'Doctur Josquini' and 'Doctor Fairfax', others, traced to the Franco-Flemish masters Jean Mouton, Pierre de La Rue, Jacob Obrecht, Johannes Ockeghem (c 1425–1497), Heinrich Isaac and the Scot Robert Johnson, are used without acknowledgement. Further material is thought to be the work of the Scotsmen Andro Blakhall and John Blak, and was possibly composed specifically for *The Art of Music* in the later sixteenth century. In addition to the assertion contained in the extended title, there is internal evidence in *The Art of Music* that the compiler is drawing upon earlier native treatises, indicating that a cosmopolitan interest in musical theory flourished in Scotland in the early sixteenth century, presumably tracing its roots back to the works of Tailler in the thirteenth century. Certainly, many of the techniques described, such as 'Countering', 'Dissonance' and 'Diminucioun' demonstrate a continuing fascination with virtuosity and elaborate embellishment.

These factors would indeed provide a worthy foundation for a whole school of Scottish composers, culminating in Robert Carver. Perhaps a considerable wealth of Scottish music has been lost, but Carver's overwhelming monopoly over the contents of a manuscript as prestigious as a Chapel Royal Choirbook could also suggest that he was regarded by his contemporaries not as merely another representative of their musical tradition, but as a talent such as they had not witnessed in generations, standing head and shoulders above anything else their nation had produced within living memory.[25]

Be that as it may, any consideration of the blend of diverse influences in Robert Carver's music, even one which takes into account a thriving native school, can be no more than a starting point in getting to grips with what is essentially the work of an individual genius, the creation by one great mind of a unique sound world, which is best appreciated through a closer and more specific scrutiny of the music itself.

2

Proportionis Fine and Sound Celestiall

Aspects of Carver's Style and Choice of *Cantus Firmi*

Written over a period of some forty years, Carver's works exhibit an exceptional consistency of style, which means that regardless of its vintage his music retains a marked identity, an instantly identifiable sound world which springs from the idiosyncratic use of a number of musical devices.

The most persistent and striking feature is his unusual response to the then current perception of music in terms of hexachords, a response which plays a fundamental part in the creation of 'the Carver sound' and merits closer attention. The hexachord system involved the division of the compass of each vocal part into a series of overlapping scales made up of six notes, divided in turn into two groups of three notes separated by an interval of a tone, and with a semitone interval between the two groups. As the range of the melody in each voice part changed, it was felt to pass from the realm of one hexachord to another, adopting the resultant change in relative pitches. In this way, while modern octaves build one on top of the other, starting and ending on the same note and retaining the same order of tone and semitone intervals, the hexachord system involved regular switching of this order as the vocal range passed from one hexachord with its central semitone interval to another with a differently placed semitone. In his Mass *L'Homme Armé*, Carver uses hexachords based on C, G and to a lesser extent F and B flat.[1] (See Example 2.1.)

Given that the piece has a tonal centre of G, it will be seen that there is a curious alternation in the third of G chords between B natural and B flat and that the leading note, F, is a natural rather than the sharp expected by modern ears. The predominant effect is that of the VIIth or Myxolidian mode, in essence our major scale with a flattened seventh, but with frequent alternation between a major and a minor third, the B natural/B flat alternation caused by the switching hexachord. The hexachord chart below illustrates that the bass part for example has a customary B flat in its lower range (because the hexachord it operates in is based on F) while in its upper range it has a B natural (hexachord based on G). To use modern terminology, it will depend upon which octave it is using whether it will establish major or minor tonality. This is also the case with the other voice parts.

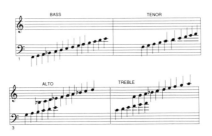

Example 2.1

This hexachordal system of music was already beginning to break down by the sixteenth century and by the end of the century it would be entirely superseded by the major/minor octave system formulated by Giovanni da Palestrina (1525–1594). At the beginning of the century though, its implications were still widely felt. Composers tended to use modality and the hexachord system with a considerable degree of freedom, and the system was made even more arbitrary by the growing influence of *musica ficta*, the practice of sharpening leading notes and occasionally thirds according to context. *Musica ficta* was the province of performers, who adapted the notes in front of them in accordance with an agreed code of practice, quite divorced from hexachordal or modal considerations. It seems to have been the result of an attempt to make melodic lines flow more naturally, at the expense of harmonic rules, which in any case were in a state of flux and in many cases no longer fully understood even by composers. Clearly, composers, who in most cases were also performers in their own right, wrote their music in the knowledge that it would be subjected to *musica ficta* in performance, and the addition of appropriate editorial accidentals to the music of this period is an essential part of the preparation of a modern performance edition.[2]

The application of *musica ficta* to Carver's music is something of a thorny issue. Muriel Brown[3] has argued convincingly that Carver's cadences need little attention from the editor, as cadential phrases where the editor may consider applying *musica ficta* are frequently simply restatements of phrases which occur elsewhere in the piece in contexts where *musica ficta* would be totally inappropriate. It does indeed seem unlikely that Carver would sanction the alteration of a melodic motif simply to diminish the modal impression which elsewhere he is so anxious to enhance.

Carver seems unusually aware of the harmonic potential of the ambiguous situation created by his use of the hexachord system, and much of the harmonic interest of his music stems from this juxtaposition of major and minor. An example from the Credo of the Mass *L'Homme Armé* considered in modern harmonic terms will help to illuminate the situation.

Example 2.2

The F major chord in the first two bars moves through A minor to G minor (alto b' flat from hexachord based on F) only to flash through G major (treble b' natural from hexachord based on G) to G minor again (alto b' flat from hexachord based on F) before G major is finally established in the tenor part (b natural from hexachord based on G). The analytical description may be ponderous, but the effect is magical, like a mirror turned in light—a harmonic device (for that is what Carver has made of it) that surpasses the realms of occasional dissonance to become a conscious trademark of harmonic manipulation. It is an approach to harmony which has laid him open to the charge of being clumsy or 'primitive', but this is to misinterpret, using alien criteria, an intentional and an infinitely subtle feature of a fully integrated technique of composition.

Carver's use of hexachords is also eminently practical. A bass singer engaged in performing Carver's Mass *L'Homme Armé* becomes attuned to singing 'in the minor' in the lower range and 'in the major' in the upper, each segment of the vocal range acquiring its own character. In the alto part the effect is the same, although the major/minor coloration is appropriately reversed—major for the mellow lower range, minor for the more strident upper range. These devices lend an essential spice to Carver's otherwise rather static harmony, a restriction dictated to an extent by the fundamental limitations of *cantus firmus* composition itself, and partly by the florid embellishment of the vocal lines which require a solid foundation on which to flourish.

In Carver's case this vocal ornamentation takes two basic forms: the running scale, filling intervals with cascades of rapid notes,[4] and the distinctive ornament which perhaps deserves to be known as the 'Carver snap'. A particularly fine example of running scales appears in his treatment of the '-mus' ending of 'benedicimus' in the treble line of the *Gloria* of the Mass *L'Homme Armé*:

Example 2.3

while 'snaps' dominate the alto cadence 'Deus Pater omnipotens' in the same *Gloria*.

Example 2.4

In the central solo section of the *Gloria* these devices come thick and fast and are occasionally blended to form a figure which recurs in solo sections later in the Mass.

Example 2.5

The quality of singers at Carver's disposal in the Chapel Royal is reflected in the way in which he liberally stretches his virtuosic vocal lines over the entire compass of each of his voices—generally an octave and a fifth—and often within the space of a bar or two.[5] Particular demands are placed upon the male altos, who are asked to demonstrate uniform agility at both extremes of their range and, indeed, over the break between their true and falsetto registers, demanding flexibility in the placing of this break point. In his six-part Mass there are three demanding alto parts and clearly the Scottish Chapel Royal boasted a fine body of alto singers. This challenging treatment of the alto voice recurs in the later anonymous three-part Mass for alto and two trebles, which possibly also reflects an established Scottish tradition of virtuosic alto singing.

But it is the bass and tenor voices that seem to fascinate Carver, and a distinctive trademark of many of his Mass settings are sections where the upper voices are silenced to expose the deep sonorities of the lower voices. In the *Gloria* of the Mass *L'Homme Armé* just before the concluding 'cum Sancto Spiritu' he lifts the top off the music, much as one might remove the back of a watch to reveal the ingenious, well-lubricated works beneath.

Example 2.6

It is an extraordinary effect which he invokes in other settings of the Mass. Indeed, as we shall see, word painting in general is a feature of Carver's work which sets him sharply apart from his English contemporaries.

In the fifteenth and early sixteenth centuries there was a considerable vogue for *cantus firmus* Masses: settings of the Mass using a pre-existent melody, either sacred or secular, as a unifying thread which appeared repeatedly, usually in the tenor part, often disguised in sustained notes, providing a skeleton about which the composer wove an elaborate web of polyphony. The earliest *cantus firmus* Masses in the late fourteenth century *Old Hall Manuscript* like those of John Dunstable used plainchant melodies, and as a rule set only the latter part of the Ordinary of the Mass, that part which the composer could rely upon appearing in the service, regardless of the liturgical calendar: *Gloria, Credo, Sanctus* (and *Benedictus*) and *Agnus Dei*.[6]

Carver's earliest work, the ten-part Mass *Dum sacrum mysterium* of 1506, uses as *cantus firmus* a variant on the plainchant melody of the antiphon to the *Magnificat* at Vespers on St Michael's Day,[7] which first appears in the tenor part, and later, in the *Angus Dei*, begins to pervade other voices.[8]

By the time Carver had written his Mass *Dum sacrum mysterium* in 1506, the choice of material for *cantus firmi* elsewhere in Europe had become more unorthodox. Perhaps in anticipation of the sentiment that the Devil should not have sole claim to the best tunes, religious composers began to make use of secular song melodies in their Mass settings. When this fashion finally spread to England, John Taverner (c. 1490–1545/6), Christopher Tye (c. 1500–1572/3) and John Sheppard (c. 1515-c1560) used the popular tune *The Western Wynd* as *cantus firmus* while in the late fifteenth and early sixteenth centuries composers on the Continent vied with one another in settings using the mediaeval French recruiting song, *L'Homme Armé*. One of the earliest of these was the Mass of that name by Dufay, copied into the *Carver Choirbook* around 1506. It is a tribute to the international outlook enjoyed by Scotland at this time that Carver's own Mass *L'Homme Armé*, composed around this time, is the only evidence for the use in the British Isles of this European *cantus firmus*. In the *Choirbook*, Carver marks out the Dufay Mass for special attention by crediting the composer in a manner otherwise reserved for his own compositions, 'Duffa vocatur', and he probably studied it and participated in performances of it at the Chapel Royal in Stirling.

However, it comes as no surprise that there is probably a much more subtle reason underlying Carver's choice of *cantus firmus*, which also serves to link his martial Masses in four and ten parts. Although much work remains to be done on the Burgundian *L'Homme Armé* tradition, it is becoming clear that the original *L'Homme Armé* tune and the earliest Masses built upon it were very closely associated with Charles the Bold, Duke of Burgundy, and the Order of the Golden Fleece (the *Toison d'Or*), which his father, Philip the Good, had founded in 1430. This Order, a riposte to the much vaunted English Order of the Garter, served as a focus for Philip's lifelong efforts to initiate a crusade, which were given a new impetus when the Turks captured Constantinople in 1453. As Count of Charolais, Charles actively cultivated his image as the archetypal 'armed man', and when he succeeded his father in 1467 he enthusiastically took on the mantle of his crusading ambitions.[9] The parallels with James IV's campaign of self-publicity as would-be organiser of a pan-European crusade are clear, and there can be little doubt that Carver's use of the *L'Homme Armé* tune served ostentatiously to underline this parallel.

Fascinatingly, a four-part Mass by Johannes Regis (c. 1430-c. 1485) intermeshes the text of the Mass ordinary with texts relating to St Michael, most prominently the *Magnificat* antiphon *Dum sacrum mysterium*. Significantly, he replaces the plainchant melodies normally associated with the St Michael texts with the *L'Homme Armé* tune, underlaying dramatic fanfare figures with the words 'Archangelus Michael tuba cecinit' ('the Archangel

Philip the Good, Duke of Burgundy, the young Charles, Count of Charolais, and
members of the Order of the Golden Fleece wearing their insignia
(*Bibliotheque Royale Albert 1er*)

Michael sounds the trumpet'). This remarkable work was probably written in
the Burgundian town of Soignie[10] around 1460 at the instigation of the Order
of the Golden Fleece, and seems designed to emphasise the association between
the person of the warlike Charles, Count of Charolais, and the general of the
heavenly host, the Archangel Michael. It may even have been composed
specially for Charles' visit in 1460 to Cambrai, on the Franco-Burgundian
border and Dufay's place of employment, where a copy was made in a
choirbook. We can be sure that Charles, a skilled composer of church music
himself, would have appreciated Regis' musical and propaganda coup on his
behalf.

This Burgundian attempt to appropriate the potent image of St Michael
brought retaliation from the envious French monarch Louis XI – St Michael
was the patron saint of France and in particular of the French armed forces. In
1469 he founded the Order of St Michael at the French court, closely modelled
on the earlier Burgundian Order.

St Michael was also the patron saint of the Scottish Chapel Royal, and
musical celebrations of St Michael's Day, 29 September, would have been
particularly lavish at the Scottish court. But a St Michael Mass such as
Carver's Mass *Dum sacrum mysterium* could also emphasise Scotland's links

with France and Burgundy and at the same time evoke the potent image of the vengeful Archangel with sword raised in defence of Christendom against the infidel. This assertive gesture, a coded musical counterpart of James' gigantic flagship *The Great Michael*, was undoubtedly also part of James' plans to stimulate European interest in his proposals for a crusade to free Christendom from the Turkish threat. In an age obsessed with symbols and emblems, its message would not have been lost on any of the Princes of Christendom, but James IV received no more support than had Philip the Good.

The two late Masses *Pater Creator omnium* and *Fera pessima* also make use of *cantus firmi* but in very different circumstances and with very different intentions. The Mass *Pater Creator omnium* has a near-continuous *cantus* in the form of a plainchant Ordinary, indicating that it was composed for one specific service. On the other hand, the *cantus firmus* melody *Fera pessima*, from the responsory *Videns Jacob vestimenta Joseph*, has much more subtle connotations. The twelfth century French scholar Petrus Cantor described envy as a 'fera pessima', and the *cantus firmus* was used by Guillaume de Machaut (1300–1377) in his motet *Fons tocius superbie/O livoris feritas/Fera pessima*, which condemns the sins of envy and pride.[11] In his use of the *cantus firmus* Carver is probably making reference to a motet by Loyset Compère, *Sola caret monstris*, which was written for the French Chapel Royal, either in 1505 or 1511. Pope Julius II is named in the text and, in a thinly veiled analogy, is condemned as a monster and a wild beast. This may be traced to French hostility to the Pope at the time of his accession in 1505, when against the wishes of the French he seized the assets of his predecessor. The other likely circumstance for the work's composition is the Pope's formation of the Holy League against France in 1507.[12]

It seems possible that Carver used the *cantus firmus* to denote a similar set of circumstances in the Scotland of the 1540s[13] which was a time of friction between Church and State. James V's relationship with Rome grew increasingly strained in the early part of the decade as he pursued a policy of increased state control over the Church, exemplified by his act of 1542 diverting monastic revenues to the State. Alternatively, the use of the *cantus* may have been a comment on the later Protestant unrest of the mid 1540's, which culminated in the burning of the Protestant preacher and English agent George Wishart in March 1546, in ostensible reprisal for which the Archbishop of St Andrews, Cardinal Beaton, was assassinated in May of the same year at the instigation of Henry VIII. The condemnation of pride implicit in the *cantus firmus* might even refer to Beaton's ostentatious lifestyle and extreme personal arrogance, evinced in his belligerent relationship with Gavin Dunbar the Archbishop of Glasgow.[14]

There is no shortage of figures whose pride merited criticism, but the most likely candidate is the heretic Henry VIII, whose vicious mauling of the Lowlands and attempted genocide in 1544 and 1545, the so-called 'Rough Wooing',[15] brought considerable suffering and destruction. The Earl of Hertford, the English commander, was instructed to

The burning of the Scottish Reformer, George Wishart, in 1546
(*The Hulton Deutsch Collection*)

put all to fyre and swoorde, burne Edinborough towne, so rased and defaced when you have sacked and gotten what ye can of it, as there may remayn forever a perpetuel memory of the vengeaunce of God lighted upon (them) for their faulsehood and disloyailtye. Do what ye can out of hande, and without tarrying, to beate down and over throwe the castle, sack Holyrod house, and as many townes and villaiges about Edinborough as ye may conveniently, sack Lythe and burne and subverte it and all the rest, putting man, woman and childe to fyre and swoorde without exception[16]

Church properties, unsurprisingly, were a particular target of these raids, and the catalogue of Hertford's achievements lists a number of 'Paryshe churches, abbeys, frere-houses cast down or burnt' in 1544, and seven 'monasteries and frearhouses brent, raced and cast downe'[17] in 1545. This might help to account for the elaborate setting of 'dona nobis pacem' in Carver's five-part Mass *Fera pessima* and the comment 'Deo gratias' which he appends to it. While Henry's death early in 1547 did little to moderate Anglo-Scottish enmity or alleviate the situation in southern Scotland, Carver's comment must have been on many lips when the news of Henry's demise reached Scotland.

Carver's knowledge of this rather obscure *cantus firmus* and his evident acquaintance with Compère's motet, underlines his close links with the Franco-Flemish school in the early part of the sixteenth century, making a period of study in Louvain all the more plausible,[18] and at the same time provides a bridge between the later Mass settings and the vintage works of the period before Flodden.

3

With Trible Sweit, and Tenor Just

Carver's Mass *L'Homme Armé*

From the very opening of Robert Carver's Mass *L'Homme Armé*,[1] it is clear to the listener that he is in a sound world different from anything he is likely to have heard before.

Example 3.1

The rich embellishment so typical of Carver's work is initiated by the alto voice and is taken up and extended by the treble line. Carver has stamped his identity on the opening section and the die is cast for the rest of the Mass. As the *L'Homme Armé* tune sounds again and again in the tenor line, sometimes in sustained notes, sometimes in the decorated idiom of the upper parts, a compelling impetus is built up until the bass line responds with a soaring phrase which takes it from the bottom of its range to the top and back again.

But it is in his setting, patently for the more transparent texture of a group of solo voices, of the 'qui tollis' section of the *Gloria* that, as Kenneth Elliott expresses it,[2] 'Carver's imagination takes wing in extended flights of pure musical invention and great beauty'. The vocal lines become even more encrusted with embellishment and the waves of imitation draw even more closely together as melodic fragments undergo the sea-change of Carver's boundless creative genius.

Example 3.2

The rhythm and vitality of dance is never far away in these solo sections, and on the word 'mundi' Carver sets the voices tripping away in compound rhythm to end this solo section in a whirling syncopated reel on the word 'nostram'.

The idea of introducing sections in compound time into religious music was nothing new in itself. Described in the later theoretical treatise, *The Art of Music*,[3] as 'proportionat prolation', it was used to great effect by the *Eton Choirbook* masters to elaborate on the penultimate syllable of any given section, and Carver may also have observed this device in Dufay's widely admired *Mass for St Anthony of Padua*. But in Carver's case there is something about the vigour and gusto with which these compound dance-rhythms burst through the more sober textures, which bring to mind the lively secular songs of late fifteenth and early sixteenth century England and Scotland, rather than the more rhythmically restrained church music being written in England at this time. English composers such as Cornysh and Fayrfax, who contributed both to sacred manuscripts such as the *Eton Choirbook* and secular collections such as *Ritson's Manuscript* and *Henry VIII's Manuscript*,[4] seemed to draw a line between their worldly and sacred rôles. It is possible that Carver also composed secular music which has since been lost; but perhaps he poured all of his genius, worldly and ethereal, into his church music with the kaleidoscopic results to be observed in his Mass *L'Homme Armé*.

The concluding section of this *Gloria* seems to synthesise the playfulness of secular music with the nobility of sacred music in a final emphatic reiteration of the *cantus firmus*. As if to emphasise the re-entry of the full choir on 'qui sedes', Carver brings his voices together rhythmically on 'dexteram' to provide a gathering point before the customary elaboration sets in again.

In the concluding 'cum Sancto Spiritu' section, the tenor line unexpectedly shakes off its *cantus firmus* rôle and rises to monopolise the melodic interest, the alto line dropping to the depths of its range to fill in the *L'Homme Armé* tune at a suitable register. As if a weight has been lifted from their shoulders, the tenors soar to g' and a', stimulating a final flourish of embellishment in the other three parts, and bringing the Amen to a florid and assertive conclusion.

Example 3.3

Harmonically, Carver draws very heavily on the Dufay Mass *L'Homme Armé* and indeed some sections of the Mass sound like highly decorated Dufay. It is also to Dufay that one must turn for an explanation of Carver's intentions in his setting of 'vivos et mortuos' in the *Credo*.

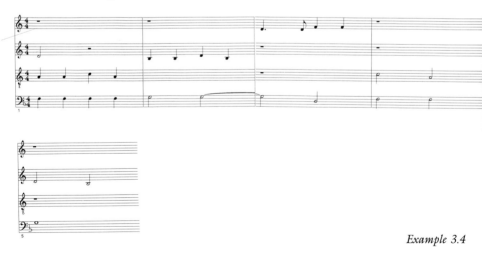

Example 3.4

Are the monotonous juxtaposition of F and G major and turgid imitation in the upper parts actually an evocation of the 'passing bell', sounded to mark the passing of the powerful from this world? Or is this phrase a representation of the Last Trumpet—the sound of trumpets would have been disturbingly familiar to the ears of sixteenth century Scottish churchmen, accustomed to accompanying their monarchs to war.[5] Dufay uses a very similar device in his Mass *L'Homme Armé* and it may simply represent music in embryonic form, stripped of melismata and elaboration that mirror the vanities of this world. What better way to portray 'the quick and the dead' undergoing judgement at the hands of their omniscient maker? Whatever the explanation, both Carver and Dufay sound an appropriately martial note in the Amen.

Carver's treatment of the *Sanctus* opens with a beautifully fluid setting of the opening words, coming to an exotic cadence on the word 'Sabaoth', perhaps in deference to a tradition of accentuating 'all nounis barbarous or Hebrew' mentioned in *The Art of Music*. Suddenly the 'pleni sunt celi' breaks in with a virtuosic burst of nervous phrases which owe much to the *Ars Nova* style of Guillaume de Machaut or to the even more ancient *Notre Dame* style of the thirteenth century anonymous Scottish composer of *Haec Dies* in *The St Andrews Music Book*. This seems a surprising example of conscious archaism on the part of the sixteenth century Carver, and one can only wonder at his eclectic assurance as he plays about with fragments of the *L'Homme Armé* tune in hectic hocketting imitation in treble and alto parts,[6] while the tenor gives a complete rendition of the same material *a tempo*. The fanfarelike 'Osanna', underpinned by an ingeniously syncopated version of this same *cantus firmus* in the tenor part also owes a debt to Dufay. After a serene 'Benedictus', the 'in nomine' is set with obvious relish, an intriguing welter of interweaving voices in which Carver contrasts the timbres of the solo voices in a rapidly alternating interchange of material—music of haunting beauty. In the concluding Osanna, the underpinning *cantus firmus* is varied in yet another way by putting it into triple time against the duple time of the other voices. His method conforms exactly to that described in *The Art of Music* as 'proporcion inequall', but it is a technique which he could frequently have seen in practice in the work of Dufay.

The *Agnus Dei*, noble and expansive and with an ornate central solo section, is crowned by a timeless concluding statement, which Carver made a memorable feature in all of his Mass settings. The *L'Homme Armé* cantus firmus is slowed down until it barely moves forward at all, and the basic crotchet unit of the original becomes a dotted minim in modern notation, giving the other voices long spells of static harmony to embellish and decorate at their leisure, which they accomplish with considerable creativity. The concluding 'dona nobis pacem' is an extraordinary feat of elaboration, with the penultimate syllable extending through well over two hundred modern crotchet pulses in the treble and alto voices to be joined some fifty pulses into this by the basses, while the tenor moves inexorably through its ultimate statement of the *L'Homme Armé* tune

The Mass *L'Homme Armé* is a work of great vitality, admirably displaying the versatility and creativity of its gifted composer at his most individual, drawing upon a broad gamut of stylistic devices and yet being restricted by none of them. The distinctive hallmarks of the 'integrated' Carver style turn up again and again in his work, and a consideration of his different settings of the Mass and his motets reveals that all these works, for all their diversity, carry the diagnostic fingerprints of a thoroughly consistent genius.

4

As Thondrand Blast of Trumpatt Bellicall

Carver's Six-part Mass

One of the earliest of Carver's settings of the Mass is that for six voices.[1] Although the piece is not dated, reasons of style and foliation suggest that it was written around the same time as the ten-part Mass and the Mass *L'Homme Armé*. Like this latter piece, the six-part setting relies for effect upon the alternation of weighty sections for full choir and virtuosic music for solo voices, but the six-part setting takes this formula a stage further than the *L'Homme Armé* setting. The sections for full choir are rhythmically very simple indeed, while the virtuosity of the solo episodes is also exaggerated.

Example 4.1

Isobel Woods accounts for this disparity by suggesting that the piece may have been written for the choir of Stirling Parish Church with soloists from the Chapel Royal.[2] It is equally possible that the setting was written in some haste to be performed at short notice by the Chapel Royal. The choir would require relatively little preparation time and the soloists, already acquainted with Carver's idiom, could carry the day with their virtuosity, again with very little specific work on this piece. The simple polyphony of the full-choir sections, in marked contrast to those of the Mass *L'Homme Armé* and the ten-part Mass, would also make its composition a fairly speedy exercise.

What makes this piece special is its iridescent sound, resulting partly from its predominantly major tonality, but mainly from its scoring for treble,[3] three altos and two basses. The luminous sound created by this unusual combination of voices is further enhanced by the extensive use of a bold musical figure which dominates the sections for full choir. This motif, consisting of a rising fifth followed by a falling third, is complemented by a figure of a rising fourth, redolent of the melodic shapes of trumpet fanfares and recalling figures in the *Missa tubae* by the fifteenth century English composer Cousin and Dufay's *Gloria ad modum tubae*. In addition to establishing the major tonality of the piece, these figures provide much of the raw material for musical development both in the sections for full choir and the solo episodes.

Example 4.2

Carver was apparently aware of the danger of harmonic stagnation presented by such a relentless use of major tonality, and he adopts the same solution as the *Eton Choirbook* masters, whose works he clearly knew well. After establishing the major tonality at the opening of each movement, he shifts the harmonies through a number of related keys (in modern terms, from C major to G major, F major, B flat major, G minor and C minor, although in Carver's mind this process would have been the logical result of the interchange of hexachords). So extensive is this process of harmonic variation that Carver feels bound to end each of the sections for full choir with an extended cadence, in which the harmony settles on the home key and then the voice parts continue to present this same chord in a number of inversions for as many as fifteen further pulses, as if to re-establish the tonality. Kenneth Elliott has observed that the use of a head-motive at the beginning of each movement gives the impression that this is a 'parody' Mass, and Muriel Brown has demonstrated that the six-part Mass is in fact a reworking of phrases from the freely composed sections of the Mass *Dum sacrum mysterium*. Although the six-part setting abandons the *cantus firmus*, it is possible that Carver had at least the words of the *Magnificat* antiphon in mind as he emphasised the fanfare elements of his original concept.

Dum sacrum mysterium cerneret Johannes, Archangelus Michael tuba cecinit. (While John beheld the sacred mystery, Michael the Archangel sounded the trumpet.)

This neatly ties in the six-part Mass with Carver's four- and ten-part settings, providing us with a trilogy of related martial Masses from the years preceding Flodden.

The cumulative effect of all these elements in the six-part setting is to create an impression of brimming confidence, an indication of the context in which it was probably written. Scotland's considerable political prestige in Europe in the early years of the sixteenth century, and the surge of enthusiasm which preceded the invasion of England in 1513, saw national self-confidence at a peak. James IV's plans for a pan-European crusade against the infidel were at their zenith, and the six-part Mass, with its bold gestures and confident tonality, was presumably another of Carver's contributions to this wave of cultural propaganda.

The association with trumpets may even tie the six-part Mass in with the celebrations accompanying the launch of James' battleship the *Great*

A model of James IV's gigantic warship, the *Great Michael*, an ostentatious affirmation of Scotland's status in Europe (© *The Trustees of the National Museums of Scotland*)

Michael at Newhaven on 12 October 1511. Jim Reid Baxter has observed that three trumpeters were employed for the event, and it is not inconceivable that when Mass was sung, the musical forces combined to give this embodiment of Scottish maritime pretensions a suitably bombastic send-off. Certainly the open intervals of a fourth and a fifth which predominate in the thematic material of the Mass would have lent themselves to performance on the valveless Renaissance trumpet, and had this mode of performance been a factor in Carver's mind at the time of composition it would provide a convincing explanation for the relative melodic simplicity of the sections for full choir compared to the solo sections, when the trumpets would have fallen silent and the virtuosi of the Chapel Royal would have held the stage.

Perhaps it was a youthful memory of this event that survives in Sir David Lindsay's *Testament of the nobill and vailzeand Squyer Williame Meldrum* transformed in the poet's imagination to a requiem at the Court of Venus:

> Solemnitlie gar thame sing my saull mes,
> With organe Timpane, Trumpet and Clarion.[4]

Whether performed with trumpets or in vocal imitation of them, cadential figures in the six-part Mass which come to dominate the 'pacem' at the end of the third petition of the *Agnus Dei* are very similar to fanfare figures already identified in the Mass *L'Homme Armé*. This interpretation of the word 'pacem' seems to have less to do with the inner peace of the individual prior to the taking of communion than with the subjection of the infidel and the ensuing *pax romana* into which Scotland hoped to draw Europe in the years preceding Flodden.

5

Decoritt with Crafty Musick
Carver's Mass *Dum sacrum mysterium*

Without doubt the most impressive work in the whole *Carver Choirbook*, and arguably the greatest single achievement of late Mediaeval/Renaissance Scottish culture, is Robert Carver's ten-part setting of the Mass, *Dum sacrum mysterium*.[1] There is some evidence that the native Scottish school of composition postulated earlier specialised in large-scale Mass settings: mention is made by Alexander Alesius[2] of a nine-voice setting in honour of the angels by Patrick Hamilton (1504–1528) performed under the composer's direction at the Cathedral in St Andrews.[3] Hamilton's ill-timed advocacy of the Reformed faith led to his being burned at the stake, which doubtless also explains the loss of his Mass. In view of the possibility that liturgical improvisation in ten parts may have been a Scottish choral speciality, Isobel Woods points to the high incidence of passing dissonance in Carver's ten-part Mass as an indication that it may spring from just such a tradition of polyphonic improvisation.[4]

Carver exploits the opulent ten-voice texture with a consistent boldness and ease which brooks comparison with the forty-part setting of *Spem in alium* by Thomas Tallis (c. 1505–1585). The most probable date of composition for the Tallis work is 1570, and the direct inspiration would appear to have been the setting by Alessandro Striggio (1535–1592), also for forty voices, of *Ecce beatam lucem*. Striggio had composed his motet in conjunction with a number of other works for large numbers of voices (which include a sixty-part *Sanctus*) in the early 1560s, and Tallis may well have seen the score when Striggio visited London in 1567.[5]

But this mid-century interest in works in a multitude of parts post-dates the Mass *Dum sacrum mysterium* by some fifty years. Carver's setting belongs not to that culmination of Renaissance polyphony which flowed so easily into the large-scale splendours of the early Baroque, but to 1506. In the early years of the sixteenth century works on such a scale were a considerable rarity. Josquin had composed a setting for twenty-four voices of *Qui habitat in adjutorio* in the late

Patrick Hamilton, composer and Reformer, burned in 1528. The inscription,
'Punished with Cruel Death, Feb. 1527', reflects the fact that until late in the sixteenth
century 25 March was treated as the turn of the year
(© *Hunterian Art Gallery, University of Glasgow*)

fifteenth or early sixteenth century, and a setting of *Deo gratias* in thirty-six parts,
ascribed to Ockeghem, probably pre-dates this. Both of these works rely for effect
on rich counterpoint, in contrast to Striggio's reliance on a largely chordal texture,
and as such they have much more in common with the ten-part Mass by Carver.

A curious anonymous twelve-part setting of *Inviolata, integra et casta es,
Maria*, once thought to be the work of Josquin, combines the smooth

polyphony of the Flemish school with the dramatic chordal effects of the *Eton* masters, but most relevant in relation to Carver's Mass is the twelve-part Mass *Et ecce terrae motus* by Antoine Brumel (c. 1460-c. 1520). This Flemish master, renowned in his own lifetime for his eccentricity of behaviour and compositional technique, probably composed his Mass for the court chapel choir of Alfonso d'Este I at Ferrara in whose employment he found himself from 1505 to 1510. Although much of the setting relies for effect on alternation between contrasted groups of singers, a technique employed most dramatically in the concluding sections of the *Gloria*, there are impressive passages, most notably in the *Kyrie*,[6] in which the twelve voice parts appear simultaneously in rich polyphony. The weighty texture, the passing dissonances and the use of rising and falling phrases make this piece a very close cousin of Carver's setting, and it is extraordinary to think of two composers at opposite ends of Europe, apparently with no contact, producing almost simultaneously works of such similarity. One cannot help but feel that some link other than their shared idiosyncrasy will emerge eventually.[7]

Brumel was in his mid forties and at the height of his powers when he composed his masterpiece. For Carver, a young man in his twenty-second year, to undertake a complete Mass setting in ten parts which makes consistent use of flowing counterpoint throughout both solo and full choir sections was indeed an immense challenge and he responds with an assurance which is breath-taking—the almost disdainful self-confidence of genius in the flower of youth.

The composition of the Mass *Dum sacrum mysterium* was linked many years ago with the coronation of the infant James V which took place on the twentieth day after the unexpected death of his father at Flodden in September 1513. As Isobel Woods points out,[8] this is an inconceivably short time for a new Mass to be composed and rehearsed, particularly one on the scale of Carver's *Dum sacrum mysterium*. It now seems that Carver had composed the Mass in 1506, in his twenty-second year, at which point it was copied into the *Choirbook* with an inscription to this effect. But in 1513 when the work again went into rehearsal, with the intention of celebrating James IV's triumphant return to Scotland, the original inscription was changed to read 1513 in an attempt to obscure the fact that an 'old' Mass was being revived for this important occasion. There must have seemed little doubt in 1513 that the Scots would prevail against the numerically inferior force of an enemy fighting on two fronts; it was under very different circumstances that the work was eventually performed at the coronation of James' infant son.

But why did Carver choose precisely ten voices? The prime reason may well have been theological rather than musical. The nine orders of angels are mentioned both in the *Kyrie*[9] and in the Sequence for St Michael's Day, and Carver may have been acquainted with the *Eton Choirbook* copy of Wylkynson's nine-part *Salve Regina* in which each of the nine voice-parts is given the name of an order of angels. We can also assume that Patrick Hamilton's nine-voice Mass in honour of the angels was drawing a similar analogy. The Michaelmas sequence *Ad celebres, rex caelice* not only names the nine angelic orders, but also refers to mankind as 'the tenth piece of silver' brought back by Christ.[10] The sequence goes on to state that as the angels rejoice above, mankind makes glad on earth below, and it may well be that Carver added the 'voice of mankind' to create a ten-voice texture, reflecting the restoration of harmony and symmetry in creation as mankind joins the angels in praising God.

The ten voices of the Mass *Dum sacrum mysterium* are weighted in the direction of deep sonority: two trebles, two altos, three tenors and three basses, one of these a wide-ranging voice which covers two octaves.[11] In the 'in nomine' of the *Benedictus* Carver demonstrates the dramatic potential of the scoring he has chosen, by snuffing out the upper voices to leave a catacomb of bass voices resonating in the resultant darkness, an unnerving effect already referred to in the Mass *L'Homme Armé*. The ten-part Mass is full of original touches such as the lilting treatment of 'Deum de Deo, lumen de lumine' in the *Credo*, but it is in the *Agnus Dei* that the full potential of the massive forces is unleashed.

The workings of overlapping hexachords are apparent from the outset, with a rapid interchange and juxtaposition of major and minor chords occurring within a miasma of occasional dissonance and decoration, a complexity of texture which is compounded rather than simplified when the full choir enters on the pleading 'miserere nobis'—almost as if the young Carver has made no provision in the density of embellishment for the fact that he is writing for ten independent voices. Almost, but not quite.

From the luminous opening bars of the *Gloria* it has been clear that this vast work is by no means the garbled rambling of an incompetent novice. Again and again throughout the Mass the sure, masterly hand of a genius makes its presence felt. A wealth of elaboration unparalleled even in Carver's work, leading to a

Example 5.1

profusion of passing dissonances, forces the listener to attend not to any individual moment, chord or voice, but to adopt an ever-expanding overview and a time-scale which spans and encompasses phrases of increasing length. In the 'qui tollis' of the central petition of the *Agnus Dei*, Carver suspends time altogether in a seamless episode of incomparable beauty, as two trebles float almost insubstantially above an alto ostinato, disembodied and serene. It is worth noting that if Carver's voice parts do correspond to the hierarchy of the angels, we are witnessing the flight of Seraphs and Cherubs above Thrones and Dominations, singularly apposite to the original intention of the Mass. (See Example 5.1)

This section owes something to Cornysh's setting of 'Commemorans praemoenia iam versa in maestitiam' in his *Stabat Mater*,[12] but Carver both extends and refines the original idea.[13] Seemingly aware of the genius of this timeless moment, he goes on to consolidate his manipulation of the listener's concept of time. In the concluding 'dona nobis pacem', he launches forth upon an ocean of sound where texture and harmony ebb and flow under a welter of melodic motifs and melismata: a sumptuous representation of his monarch's dream of Christendom triumphant and at peace. The massive ten-voice texture sweeps back and forth between the adjacent tonal centres of F major and G minor in a visionary and almost obsessive representation of duality, that basis of so many life forces. Here is a youthful Scottish monk addressing himself to the vastness of eternity—and in his Mass *Dum sacrum mysterium* he has forged a medium and musical language worthy of his momentous vision.

6

Habundance of Concordis and Semeconcordis

Carver's Motets

Perhaps predictably Robert Carver's two surviving motets, *Gaude flore virgi-nali*[1] and *O bone Jesu*[2] draw heavily upon the style of the *Eton Choirbook*. The composers who contributed to this *Choirbook*, William Cornysh, Richard Davy, Walter Lambe, John Browne and Robert Wylkynson were, after all, consum-mate masters of the occasional motet. Their impressive alternation of explora-tory solo episodes and animated full-choir chordal sections, making use of slightly quirky harmonic progressions, aroused deep admiration in the early sixteenth century, as the presence of the English settings of the *Magnificat* and *Salve Regina* in the earliest sections of the *Carver Choirbook* attests. It seems likely that these works came north with Margaret Tudor in 1503, possibly as part of a substantial collection of devotional music drawn from a number of choirbooks including *Eton*, and were subsequently copied into the *Carver Choirbook*.[3] Carver may even have come across a setting of *Gaude flore virginali* in such a collection. The poem is from the *Book of Hours* of which James IV's own copy still survives, and the *Eton Choirbook* contains two settings by Edmund Turges (fl. late fifteen century) and lists a third in five parts by John Dunstable, now lost.[4]

Carver's setting is also for a five-part choir comprising treble, alto, two tenors and bass[5] and each of the seven sections of the text beginning with the word 'Gaude' is carefully delineated with a change in vocal comple-ment. The texture is rather lightly embellished by Carver's standards although the fifth section has a higher degree of rhythmical interest, as well as a strangely archaic melisma in the treble part which sounds somewhat out of place in a piece which largely relies for its effect on smoothly flowing harmonies.[6]

The conclusion of this fifth section also finds Carver rapidly interweaving the two tenor parts over the same range. The sixth and seventh sections for full choir are rich and warm in harmony, but Carver cannot resist momentarily removing the upper three voices just into the seventh section to reveal the workings of the lower voices, before bringing the piece to a sonorous conclusion involving interplay among all five voices and distinctive rising and falling ornaments, beautifully illustrating the text's references to the abiding 'flourishing' of the Virgin's joys into all eternity. The text and the scale of Carver's setting of *Gaude flore virginali* indicate that it was intended for private rather than public devotions, in marked contrast to his other surviving motet.

The *Eton Choirbook* is probably most widely admired for its ostentatious use of full textures, featuring music in five and six parts and, most opulent of all, Wylkynson's nine-part setting of the *Salve Regina*. It seems that Carver was not content merely to match this magnificence, he aimed to overshadow it with a motet even more opulent and more magnificent.

The result of his attempt to out-Eton Wylkynson is the nineteen-part motet *O bone Jesu*, a work on a scale so unprecedented that it dominates the entire *Carver Choirbook*.[7] Its vocal complement of two trebles, three altos, eleven tenors and three basses is in itself astonishing, but the way in which the voices

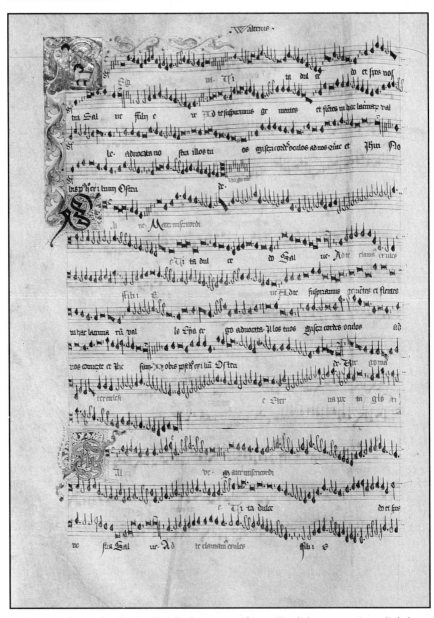

A page from the *Eton Choirbook*, a magnificent English manuscript, slightly predating the *Carver Choirbook* (*Reproduced by permission of the Provost and Fellows of Eton College*)

are exploited to produce breathtaking effects makes any performance of this piece a truly overwhelming experience. These effects are derived largely from the Eton formula of alternating full-choir and solo passages, but when even these solo episodes employ up to eight voices, and the full-choir sections display all nineteen voices in relatively animated style, any notion of an underlying formula is rendered irrelevant.

It is difficult to imagine the effect that this monumental motet would have had on its first audience as voice after voice of the Chapel Royal chimed in with the words 'O bone Jesu', gradually building up to the first of many massive F major chords, spanning three octaves and a third from a bass F to a treble a'', with every triad filled except the open fifth in the bass—such richness of sound, such complexity of texture must have astounded even those who had already heard the Mass *Dum sacrum mysterium* sung by the Chapel Royal. (See Example 6.2, pp 38–9)

But there is a closer and more surprising link between Carver's two mammoth works *O bone Jesu* and his ten-part Mass *Dum sacrum mysterium*. About three-quarters of the way through *O bone Jesu*, Carver quotes almost note for note two entire sections in four and five voices from the Mass *Dum sacrum mysterium*. The linking of a Mass and a motet had been initiated in England by Robert Fayrfax, who in fact wrote a Mass *O bone Jesu* with a related motet and *Magnificat*.[8] But it was customary for such related pieces to be consistent reworkings of material from one another, rather than for sections simply to be quoted in their entirety.

Setting this time the words 'Rogo te, piissime Jesu, ne perdas me quem fecit tua bonitas', (I ask you, most pious Jesus, do not destroy me, whom your goodness has made), Carver re-uses the distinctive 'crucifixus' of the ten-part Mass, while that moment of breathtaking beauty in the central *Agnus Dei*, where 2 trebles soar above an alto ostinato, is invoked for the words 'O dulcis Jesu, recognosce quod tuum est et absterge quod alienum est' (O sweet Jesus! Recognise what is your own and reject what is not).

It is quite possible that Carver had an imperfect understanding of the relatively recent English concept of linking Mass and motet, but it seems more likely that he simply recognised that these sections were moments of exceptional expressiveness and beauty and wished to place his finest musical offerings before the sweet Christ of the text. In the introduction to his edition of *O bone Jesu*, J A Fuller Maitland draws attention to the symbolic significance of Carver's placing of a rest (which he would have called a 'corona') above the name of Jesus, literally crowning Christ each time the choir sing his name, and there can be little doubt that these rests also served to permit the choir and listeners, including the King, to show their respect by bowing their heads before the King of Heaven.

In *O bone Jesu* the voices are skilfully manipulated to create maximum dramatic effect, appearing in exploratory combinations of wide variety (there are sections scored for four tenors and bass, for alto, three tenors and bass, and for two trebles and two altos) selected voices being held in reserve, bursting in on chordal *coups de théâtre*, and finally combining in a massive architectural monolith of sound as all the voices draw together in chordal pillars linked by a tracery of moving figures, and built upon relatively simple harmonic progressions and open fifths in the bass parts—'concordis intermixtie fluresing craftelly upone sympill and mensurall grundis' as *The Art of Music* expresses it.[9]

O bone Jesu shows Carver at his most impressive, marshalling the massive forces of his nineteen-part choir with the skill of a master strategist. Evidently by 1513, when this work was copied into the *Choirbook*, the young Carver was at the height of his powers. It would be difficult to imagine a greater contrast within the output of a single composer than that between *O bone*

Example 6.2

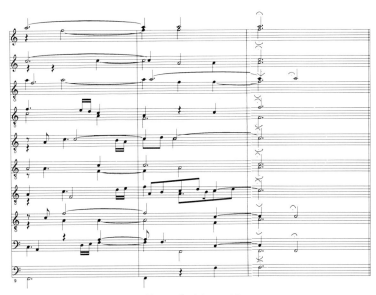

Example 6.2 cont'd

Jesu and the next work in the *Carver Choirbook* to bear his name, the intimate four-part Mass *Pater Creator omnium* of 1543, but then the era which produced the magnificence of *O bone Jesu* had passed with the passing of James IV on Flodden Field, and Scotland would never be quite the same again.

7

Curiosity Shunned

Carver's Mass *Pater Creator omnium*

Robert Carver's Mass *Pater Creator omnium* of 1543[1] is something of a curiosity: a plainsong Mass of very modest proportions for adult male voices (alto, two tenors and bass), built upon the appropriate Sarum chants, which appear throughout each movement in the form of a practically continuous *cantus firmus*. The fact that Carver uses a Scottish variant of the troped *Kyrie Deus Creator omnium*[2] and that the *Benedictus* is also troped with the words 'Mariae Filius' indicates that the Mass was written with one particular occasion in mind, a ceremonial event when these tropes would have been appropriate.[3]

On 25 August 1543 the Scottish ratification of the treaty of marriage between Mary, Queen of Scots and Prince Edward of England was celebrated in the Abbey Church of Holyrood with a High Mass 'solemnly sung with Shalms and Sackbutts'.[4] While these instruments would have found the simple lines of the Mass *Pater Creator omnium* quite conducive, neither the *Kyrie* nor the *Benedictus* tropes would have been particularly appropriate for the occasion. Later in the year, however, an event was staged for which both would be relevant.

The coronation of the infant Mary took place in Stirling Castle on 9 September 1543, thirty years to the day after Flodden. It was masterminded at ten days' notice by Cardinal Beaton, following the dramatic switch of allegiance on 31 August of the Regent Arran from the pro-English to the pro-French party, and it was overshadowed by the threat of invasion by Henry VIII. Notwithstanding the inauspicious circumstances, or perhaps precisely because of them, Beaton would have had a vested interest in ensuring that the ceremony was marked with due pomp and ceremony, and what better way to underline the overtly political choice of date than to commission a special Mass from Scotland's foremost composer, the man whose music had dignified the coronation of James V immediately after Flodden? Furthermore, 8 September was the Feast of the Nativity of the Virgin, for whose octave the *Benedictus* trope 'Mariae Filius' was appropriate, and a coronation demanded the *Kyrie* trope *Pater Creator omnium*,[5] reserved for solemnities of the highest order.

It is likely that the assembled nobility would have appreciated the coincidence of the crowning of the baby Mary and the celebration of the birth of the Virgin Mary, just as they would have been left in no doubt as to the analogy that Beaton was drawing with the circumstances preceding the crowning of another Stewart infant, Mary's father.

The relatively modest musical demands of the Mass *Pater Creator omnium* and its scoring for adult male voices only, reflecting perhaps the urgency of the commission and the shortage of rehearsal time, also suggest that the Chapel Royal was at a relatively low ebb and in no position to replicate the musical splendours that had marked the coronation in 1513. The four-part sections lack Carver's customary complexity and are marked by frequent cadential pauses, while the most challenging music appears in sections clearly intended for three soloists. Carver also makes concessions on vocal range. Only the upper tenor part approaches the extremes of range Carver normally requires of his singers, and where the basses are asked to sing low F, he offers an alternative of the octave above.

The opening page of the Mass containing the alto and second tenor parts for the *Kyrie* and *Gloria* is missing. The latter is easily reconstructed from the Sarum plainchant, which fits practically note for note, with the exception of some augmentation of note values in the third section of the *Kyrie*. Otherwise, the only complication is that the precise variant of the chant that Carver uses has not been preserved, and the standard version from the Sarum Gradual has to be adapted slightly to fit.

Later in the Mass the plainchant is treated more freely. In the *Credo*, the chant appears in the alto part, while in the *Sanctus* and *Agnus Dei*, the appropriate chant returns to the second tenor part, although it also makes isolated appearances in the first tenor part. It is omitted altogether when the second tenor part drops out in the more embellished solo sections.

While the whole Mass is very modest in scale, the *Credo* is particularly remarkable in this respect. It is written entirely in faburden, a very simple method of harmonisation springing from an improvisatory technique and described in detail in *The Art of Music*.[6] In faburden the *cantus firmus* (normally in the tenor) is set note for note according to a strict system of parallel and contrary motion. Using the terminology of *The Art of Music*, in 'the ferd (fourth) kynd of faburdoun' the 'baritonant' moves at intervals of a third, a fifth and an octave below the 'tenor', while the 'counter' and 'tribill' move at an interval of a fourth and a sixth above it respectively. Carver adapts this method slightly by exchanging the 'tenor' and 'tribill' parts, with the result that the plainchant appears in the top line. In this respect it is similar to 'the secund kynd of faburdoun' where the top line has the chant, shadowed at the sixth below by the tenor. However this 'secund kynd' requires that the other two voices be 'partis artificiall' (i.e. freely composed), and Carver's literal setting, apart from a brief flourish on the Amen, is clearly an adapted version of the 'ferd kynd'. (See Example 7.1, p 42.)

In all, Carver sets only a small fraction of the text: 'Factorem celi et terra, visibilium et invisibilium,' and 'Et expecto resurrectionem mortuorum, et vitam venturi seculi. Amen.' Isobel Woods[7] suggests that the rest of the *Credo* may well also have been sung in faburden, improvised by analogy with the existing sections. Carver omits even the plainchant for this central section, but it is obvious from his cramped writing that he was running out of space, and as the Sarum chant for the *Credo* was identical for every celebration of Mass, it is more than likely that all of the singers would know it by heart.[8]

Example 7.1

In the *Sanctus*, *Benedictus* and *Agnus Dei*, Carver returns to the more embellished idiom of his other settings, although the overall scale is still very modest with frequent full cadences and melodic development limited to the solo sections, notably the beautiful central *Agnus Dei* and the ensuing brief but dramatic final petition.

Example 7.2

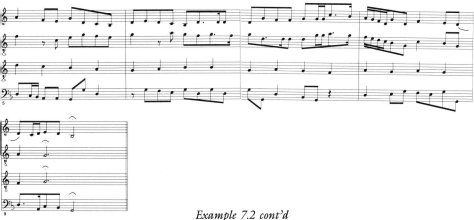

Example 7.2 cont'd

Some thirty years had elapsed since Carver's earlier works had been copied into the *Choirbook*, and the absence of the first page of the Mass *Pater Creator omnium* may indicate that a body of music from the intervening period has been lost. On the other hand, this 'gap' may be attributed to the drastic changes which the musical climate had undergone during this period.

The year 1546 saw the setting up of the Council of Trent with its wide-ranging consideration of church affairs, including the composition of church music. But Trent was in reality merely a belated official response to criticism which had been gathering momentum during the previous twenty years. The Reformation, initiated by Martin Luther in 1517, had rocked the Catholic Church, and a period of critical self-scrutiny ensued, during which the Old Church sought belatedly to set its house in order and get to grips with some of the unacceptable aspects which had crept into services. In response to the enormous popularity of direct and simple Protestant psalms, many Catholics grew critical of the lavish display which characterised Mass celebrations in the early sixteenth century.

Particularly outspoken on the subject of church music was Robert Richardson,[9] a Canon of the Scottish Augustinian Abbey of Cambuskenneth near Stirling, who in 1530 in Paris wrote a treatise which he entitled a *Commentary on the Rule of St Augustine*.[10] In striking anticipation of the conclusions of the Council of Trent, he roundly condemns display and over-decoration in church music, which he sees as a distraction rather than as an aid to devotion, and he exhorts religious composers to simplify their style in line with a process which he observed was already underway in France.

> Nowadays, skilled and worthy men are eradicating vain sophistries and tricks which were contained in their works and to which they previously dedicated their whole lives.[11]

Such was the effect of this fundamentalist clarion call from the much-admired cultural epicentre in France that music-making at the Chapel Royal seems to have been drastically curtailed and indeed may have been restricted to plainchant and faburden improvised upon it.

A fully-fledged faburden Mass, possibly dating from this period, is preserved among the musical examples in *The Art of Music collectit out of all ancient Doctouris of Music*.[12] The anonymous setting includes the *Kyrie* and *Deo Gratias* as well as the more customary parts of the Ordinary, considerably truncated, and is based on Sarum chants in a manner similar to that used by Carver in his Mass *Pater Creator omnium*. It seems likely that the anonymous Mass was written as a comprehensive musical example to illustrate the application of faburden, possibly for an earlier treatise written in Latin; as such, its survival is a testament to its technical interest rather than to its musical quality. This possibility also means that its presence in *The Art of Music* cannot be taken to mean that faburden replaced polyphony all over Scotland: this would imply a degree of organisation and homogeneity which we know the Scottish Church did not possess.

However evidence of the widespread cultivation of faburden has been recently discovered in a series of musical fragments now thought to have originated between 1525 and 1560 in the Sang Schule attached to Inverness Parish Church.[13] These include a number of settings of verses from the processional psalm for Easter Vespers, *Laudate pueri*, in three- and four-part faburden conforming to two of the types described in *The Art of Music*. In common with the faburden Mass and the other anonymous native material cited in *The Art of Music*—and this includes a faburden *Magnificat* and canonic Mass movements—this music is of great academic interest, but is vastly inferior in scale and intention to the work of Carver.

Carver's Mass *Pater Creator omnium* could be regarded then as a tentative attempt to roll back the rather draconian restrictions of the previous twenty years without ruffling too many fundamentalist feathers. It certainly bears all the hallmarks of a composer testing the waters after the long years of austerity at the Chapel Royal. The Mass may also be seen as part of an attempt by Mary of Guise and Cardinal Beaton to heal religious divisions in the government in the face of the threat of English invasion. The simplicity of Carver's setting may have been intended to draw moderate Protestants back into the pro-French camp and at the same time to reinforce the commitment of recent converts to the cause such as Regent Arran, who had spent the eve of the coronation with Cardinal Beaton doing penance for his apostasy.[14] The cleverly calculated blend of simple faburden, limited use of embellishment and modest scope may well have struck just the right note, as the Mass *Pater Creator omnium* marks a turning point in the fortunes of Chapel Royal polyphony. After 1543 the musical/devotional climate at that institution seems again to have become temporarily more favourable to polyphonic composition, the Chapel seems to have benefitted from an injection of new personnel, and after the Mass *Pater Creator omnium* a number of vastly more ambitious works were added to the *Choirbook*, among them a five-part Mass by Carver himself.

8

Grave and Scherp Soundis Sweitly
Carver's Mass *Fera pessima*

The foliation of the *Carver Choirbook* indicates that Carver's five-part Mass[1] was entered shortly after the Mass *Pater Creator omnium* of 1543, an impression confirmed both by the advanced musical style of the work and by the fact that these were the only two works by Carver which have had their underlay altered retrospectively to include repetitions of the phrase 'dona nobis pacem' in keeping with the new drive towards textual clarity.[2] In both Masses the phrasing of the music seems to suggest that textual repetitions were foreseen at the time of composition and that the retrospective alteration of the underlay may simply have been committed to paper in order to reflect something which was already established performance practice. At any rate, for all their vast difference in scale, these two Masses seem to be closely linked, and may have been the only two Carver works still in repertoire when the textual changes were executed.

The opening page of the Mass in five parts bears a damaged inscription 'Tenor -a pess-a' and Kenneth Elliott's work on this Mass[3] has uncovered the *cantus firmus* as a section from the responsory *Videns Jacob vestimenta Joseph*, which refers to the discovery by Jacob of the blood-stained clothing of his son Joseph and his cry, 'Fera pessima devoravit filium meum Joseph'. As has been observed,[4] the *cantus firmus* had acquired implications of tensions between State and Church, and this coded message and the modal colour dictated by the *cantus firmus* combine to give Carver's setting a dark brooding quality.

Example 8.1

The Phrygian mode (a scale based on the relative intervals of the white keys of the piano from E to e) was felt in the sixteenth century to have sinister connotations. In a poem in *Archbishop Parker's Psalter* published in England in 1567 it is said of the Phrygian mode that 'the Third doth rage: and roughly braythe',[5] another link with the 'fera pessima' of the *cantus firmus*. Carver may have felt that both mode and *cantus firmus* were particularly appropriate for the dark years of the mid-1540s, years which saw devastation at the hands of the English, and religious upheavals both within and outwith the established Catholic Church.

The Mass is dominated by a so-called head motive, a phrase which recurs in similar form at the opening of each movement and in which the second tenor line quotes the plainchant melody for the words 'fera pessima'. Although Carver limits his attention to this small section of the plainchant, he also makes reference to the distinctively ungainly leaps of a fourth and a fifth which permeate Loyset Compère's *Sola caret monstris*.[6] These phrases seem instrumental rather than vocal in conception and in Carver's setting are irresistibly reminiscent of the articulations of bagpipe playing and more particularly prescient of the bold intervals of pibroch, the *ceòl mór*, ('great music') or art music of the Highland pipes. This similarity is brought dramatically into focus when Carver introduces elements of this same angular phrase in the alto part of the 'pleni sunt celi' above an exceptionally protracted tonic drone in the tenor.

To say that Carver's five-part Mass is dominated by the Phrygian mode is almost an understatement. Only occasionally do the harmonies depart from the sinister world of the third mode and then usually as a result of the B flat / B natural alternation observed in the Mass *L'Homme Armé*. At each cadence the music is drawn inexorably back to the inevitable A minor chord of the Phrygian mode. The dark quality of the mode is further emphasised by Carver's choice of vocal colour. He chooses a five-part choir consisting of a treble, an alto part, two tenor parts and a bass part. The resulting sound is markedly darker than the customary English five-voice texture of high treble, mean, alto, tenor and bass, such as that of the five-part motets *Ave Dei Patris filia* and *Aeternae laudis lilium* by Robert Fayrfax which appear in the *Carver Choirbook*. One of the youngest contributors to the *Eton Choirbook*, Fayrfax had come to be regarded by the early sixteenth century as the greatest living exponent of the English tradition, a crucial bridging figure between the *Eton* style and that of the mid-century masters such as Thomas Tallis and John Sheppard. The two motets which appear in the *Carver Choirbook* were among his most widely admired and avidly copied works; and there is evidence that Fayrfax was particularly admired in sixteenth century Scotland long after his death in 1525.[7]

In his five-part Mass *Fera pessima* Carver integrates elements of Fayrfax and of the later masters, Tallis and Sheppard. The ornate solo sections contain some of the most lavishly embellished music he wrote, a triumphant affirmation of the florid muse long obsolete elsewhere but of which Carver was apparently still possessed. (See Example 8.3, p 48.)

In contrast, some of the solo sections and much of the writing for full choir display a thoroughly mid-century sense of harmonic purpose, in which embellishment plays a more modest role, subservient to the sweeping progress of the harmonies. Gone are the timeless reiterations of the earlier settings, to be replaced with an almost relentless forward momentum, an attention to speech rhythms and an impression of perpetually shifting harmonies unprecedented in Carver's work.

Example
8.3

This is evident in the *Credo*, where the introductory statement of the cyclic material by solo voices is terser and more furtive than anything encountered in the earlier settings. Similarly when the full choir is brought in on 'et in unum Dominum', the chordal blocks never quite settle into static reiteration but constantly shift harmonic perspective and change complexion and texture with a fluidity which matches Fayrfax.

Symptomatic of this new concern with organic chordal development is a sequence of rising parallel triads, passing upwards through the full choir texture on the words 'Deum de Deo, lumen de lumine'—a truly luminous sound. Equally dramatic is the conclusion to the *Credo* where the text is set syllabically, and succinct musical phrases exploiting the B flat/natural ambiguity are set against one another, building into a tight section of rising imitative figures on 'vitam venturi' before a final flourish on the word Amen.

As the Mass proceeds, the music loses some of its initial urgency and takes on a more expressive, almost rhapsodic quality. The soaring phrases for two solo tenors and bass in the 'qui tollis' of the central *Agnus Dei* petition are exceptionally lyrical and expansive.

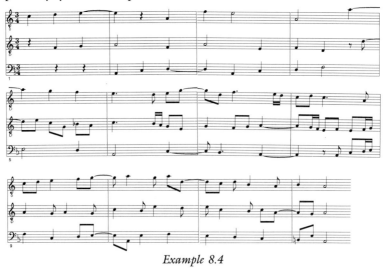

Example 8.4

This new lyricism finds its most effective expression in the final petition of the *Agnus Dei*, a section of the Mass which seems to have held considerable personal significance for Carver and for which he customarily reserved his finest moments of inspiration.[8] In the third *Agnus Dei* petition of the Mass *Fera pessima* Carver transforms material from earlier sections into a majestic reworking, conceived on an altogether grander scale than the rest of the setting. The music reaches new heights of expressiveness, spurred on by poignant semitone suspensions between alto and treble and compelling sections of imitation, most notably an episode which recalls the pealing of bells.

Example 8.5

This descending figure, a musical representation of jubilation, is fully treated in the context of Tudor music by David Wulstan,[9] who cites instances of chime imitations in the Mass *Euge bone* by Christopher Tye and John Sheppard's *Cantate* Mass. Carver's daring use of semitone suspensions in the *Agnus Dei*, again implicit in the *cantus firmus*, and the restless harmonies throughout the Mass *Fera pessima* suggest that he may well have been acquainted with the distinctive music of Sheppard. This concluding section sounds much more musically advanced than the rest of the setting, indicating that it was perhaps written at a later date. This impression supports speculation that it was added to the setting as a crowning gesture of thanksgiving, to mark the passing of the immediate threat that had prompted the composition. A further chime figure,[10] descending this time stepwise in thirds, combines with a dipping phrase which turns out to be an inverted form of the original *Fera pessima cantus*, graphically illustrating the triumph over the 'wild beast'. (See Example 8.6, p 50)

For all its jubilation, the 'dona nobis pacem' is brought to a plaintive conclusion on an A minor chord, reaffirming the dominance of the Phrygian mode.

Example 8.6

The sinister modal world that this entire setting inhabits and its relentless sense of purpose mean that there is little time for the moments of tenderness and contemplation observed in the earlier Masses. But this very relentlessness lends a certain magnificence to the sweep of the Mass *Fera pessima*. Claustrophobic it may be at moments, but then this is intentionally brooding music, expressing graphically the unease of an ageing man faced with the disturbing prospect of religious upheaval and, indeed, personal danger, and it is counterpointed with moments of hope for the future. This human dimension helps to offset the remorselessness that characterises much of this setting.

9

And Ay the Echo Repercust
Other works in the *Carver Choirbook* and the Mass *Cantate Domino*

In the same section of the *Carver Choirbook* as Carver's Mass *Fera pessima* is a Mass in three parts.[1] The style of writing strongly suggests that it may be a native Scottish work, perhaps even by Carver himself—indeed Dr Woods points out that the larger part of it is in Carver's hand.[2] Why he should have failed to identify this work as his is not clear, but it is a fine piece which combines the florid idiom of his vintage works with a new awareness of more advanced techniques of imitation and motivic development. Unlike any authenticated Carver Mass other than the Mass *Pater Creator omnium* this Mass has a polyphonic *Kyrie*, while the *Gloria* and *Credo* are both heavily truncated.

It is scored for the unusual complement of two trebles and alto,[3] a lustrous combination of voices which recalls that used by John Sheppard in his two brilliant settings of *Libera nos*, and is most closely approached by Carver in his six-part setting of the Mass.

Example 9.1

The florid embellishment of all three parts brings to mind the solo sections of the Mass *Pater Creator omnium* or even those of the Mass *L'Homme Armé*, while the turn figure, which comes to dominate the texture, is also used in the Mass *Fera pessima*. It is this same turn which in a flourish of imitation rounds off the three-part Mass.

This glittering piece most probably dates from a period between the mid-1540s and the early 1550s when polyphonic composition at the Chapel Royal seems to have flowered again after the restrictions placed upon composers in the 1520s. It was to prove a brief if fruitful period, framed on the one side by the wasted years between the 1520s and the composition of Carver's Mass *Pater Creator omnium* in 1543, and on the other by the Reformation of 1559.

The *Carver Choirbook* also contains a number of fragments which demonstrate features akin to the work of Carver, and some of which seem to represent 'rough working' in an incomplete form. These include a section of the *L'Homme Armé* tune (perhaps, as Isobel Woods points out,[4] part of Carver's working for his Mass on this tune), a three-part *Miserere*, intriguing but fragmentary settings of a Sarum Litany of Saints for Holy Saturday and *Ave gloriosa virginum regina*, the latter concluding in an exaggerated display of embellishment, as well as a post-Reformation treatment of the 1st Psalm.[5]

But ultimately the importance of the *Carver Choirbook* resides in the fact that it stands as a remarkable testament to the powers of one titanic musical genius. Always ruggedly individual, Carver stands at the confluence of different cultural styles but also at the intersection of two ages. During his lifetime the Gothic splendour into which he was born was giving way to the Humanist poise of the High Renaissance. When he was at the peak of his powers, circumstances at the Chapel Royal seem to have imposed upon him a period of musical inactivity or even enforced absence, after which he simply picked up where he had left off, making few concessions to the fact that fashions had changed during the intervening years. The realm of church music where he had once held undisputed sway had been infiltrated during this time by the warm-blooded species of the High Renaissance: sensuous motets influenced by Josquin and his contemporaries became the order of the day, and Carver was left as something of a dinosaur, magnificent but totally unsuited to the climate of this new era. His only real attempt at concession, the Mass *Pater Creator omnium*, is the product of a chameleon mediaeval mind—but adaptability has its limits, and mimicry tends to be only skin-deep. In this work it is not the 'innovative' sections but those in the conservative florid style of the vintage works which are most convincing musically. While other composers outside the restrictions imposed upon the Chapel Royal were engaged in integrating the High Renaissance style with the native Scottish tradition, Carver continued to devote himself to the florid muse which had presided over his youthful masterpieces.

But it now seems likely that the greatest triumph of Carver's later creative period is to be found not in the *Carver Choirbook* but in a set of part-books otherwise devoted to music in the High Renaissance style, the *Dowglas/Fischar Part-books*.[6] Such are the similarities in style and even in material between Carver's Mass *Fera pessima* and the anonymous Mass *Cantate Domino*[7] in the

The opening bars of the Tenor part of Carver's Mass *Cantate Domino* from the
Dowglas/Fischar Part-books (*Edinburgh University Library*)

Dowglas/Fischar Part-books, that there seems little doubt that it too is the work of Robert Carver.

The six-part Mass *Cantate Domino* seems to be a fundamental reworking of melodic material used in the Mass *Fera pessima*, but the Phrygian modality has been abandoned and another *cantus firmus*, which has so far defied attempts at identification, seems to have been adopted. It is a magnificent work, written on a grander scale than the Mass *Fera pessima* and betraying a more intimate knowledge of musical developments in the England of Taverner, Tallis and Sheppard. It is even possible that the composer knew Sheppard's *Cantate* Mass—there are certainly similarities between the two works. In the *Credo* of the Scottish Mass, the Amen features a sudden and dramatic turn-around in harmonic direction which recalls many similar headstrong moments in the music of Sheppard.

Like the Mass *Fera pessima*, *Cantate Domino* seems to develop stylistically through the course of the setting: excepting a rather advanced section of imitation around 'Rex celestis', the *Gloria* is relatively conservative, although even this movement is markedly more assured than the corresponding movement in the Mass *Fera pessima*. After the obligatory statement of the cyclic material, the *Credo* presents a number of sections of much more confident imitation, such as that at 'et ex Patre natum', and a startling new degree of attention to speech rhythms and short-term harmonic direction, as in 'qui propter nos homines et propter nostram salutem'. The Amen begins with a figure similar to the chime imitation noted in the *Credo* of the Mass *Fera pessima* and culminates with the descending chime figure which crowns the third *Agnus Dei* petition of the five-part setting. In the *Sanctus* the more elaborate embellishments have been almost entirely dispensed with, and the musical ideas are worked out in a much more consistent and thorough manner. This process of refinement is continued in the final movement. In the opening of the third *Agnus Dei* the composer succeeds in reconciling the ancient and the modern by subjecting an embellished Carveresque figure to rigorous imitation, one voice answering the other in an exchange again worthy of Sheppard. This was what the composer of the three-part Mass in the Carver Choirbook attempted to do in setting 'dona nobis pacem' but with nothing approaching the assurance demonstrated here. The Mass *Cantate Domino* ends in dramatic style as all the voices combine in a declamatory setting of the repeated plea 'dona nobis pacem'.

Whether or not the Mass *Cantate Domino* is by Carver, it certainly represents the logical outcome of a number of developments to which he began to address himself in his later creative period, in the fifteen years up to the Reformation. It is also a splendid affirmation of the ideal of Carver's later years: that the rich musical vocabulary which he had learned as a young man, and in which he excelled, was a language which transcended the vagaries of mere fashion.

10

Curious Singing in These Days
The Music of Carver in Performance

While the main part of this account of Robert Carver's music has been based upon documentary evidence, the following section must necessarily involve an increased level of speculation and subjective opinion. In view of the radically unique sound of Carver's music, what did performances of Robert Carver's music in the early part of the sixteenth century and in the 1540s sound and look like? Alesius' account of the performance of Patrick Hamilton's nine-part Mass reports that Hamilton superintended in person in his capacity as Precentor of the Cathedral in St Andrews.[1] While no illustrations or substantial accounts of such performances by the Scottish Chapel Royal survive, much can be deduced from contemporary Continental and English evidence and of course from the *Carver Choirbook* itself and its contents.

Typical of many illustrations of Renaissance church music in performance is the portrayal of Johannes Ockeghem,[2] the distinguished Franco-Flemish composer and teacher of the even more distinguished Josquin, leading the French Chapel Royal in a performance of his own music. Perhaps the most interesting aspect of this and other illustrations is that the composer leads the singers from the ranks of the choir and apparently vocally as much as by gesture. The choir stands in loose formation around a single lectern which holds the choirbook. All the singers are looking approximately in the direction of the choirbook, but it is hard to believe that those at the back can actually make out the notes and the underlay. What then was the rôle of the choirbook?

Sections of the *Carver Choirbook*, with its meticulous but occasionally cramped hand, must have been impossible to decipher at any distance and so it follows that many of the singers must have relied entirely upon memory. This feat seems incredible to modern sensibilities dulled by centuries of print, but less so to the Mediaeval mind with its labyrinthine capacity for memorising, honed by necessity. Anyone who has watched and listened to a Hindu priest unhesitatingly pick his way through the elaborate melismata of a lengthy and

The Franco-Flemish master, Johannes Ockeghem (wearing spectacles), conducts a performance by the French Chapel Royal (*Bibliotheque Nationale, Paris*)

precisely predetermined wedding service entirely from memory has witnessed something remarkable, and yet something which must have had many close counterparts in Mediaeval and early Renaissance Europe.

So perhaps the choirbook simply recorded compositions for the purpose of initial part-learning, for copying and for posterity, putting in a token appearance at performances. But there are indications in the *Carver Choir-book* that it was intended to be consulted in performance. In certain of the animated sections in compound time someone has placed small marker dots above the 'down-beats'—surely to facilitate unified performance. A possible solution to this apparent contradiction might be that a leader-cum-soloist in each voice-part was in a position to refer to the choirbook in the event of a lapse of memory, or in the more rapid and complex solo sections, while the composer/director, also with reference to the choirbook, would exercise control over the whole performance. *The Art of Music* is at some pains to differentiate between the ordinary singers and 'lectoris', surely referring to those performers who read the music during the performance and led the others. This may also account for the rather impractical placing at the top of each *Choirbook* page of the treble part. If the boy choristers were expected to read this during performances, the logical place for the part would be the bottom of each page where even the most diminutive choirboy could see it, but of all the sections in the choir, the choirboys would be those most probably expected to learn their part by heart. In this event, the only person who would have to consult the treble part would be the director of the performance.

The Art of Music[3] also gives practical instructions on how music should be conducted, and while it was probably compiled as late as 1580, the conservative nature of much of its contents would indicate that the practices it describes were also those of previous generations. It is stated that the performance should be directed by 'ane continuall mocioun or ane chop witht the hand of the preceptour, dressand the sang mensuraly that the modulatouris everrie ane till ane uther fail the(e) nocht in the perfyt mensuring of the quantaties of all noittis and pausis in equall voces devydit'.

The placing of a downbeat or 'chop' depends upon the density of diminution, the unstressed beats of which are to be 'twichit'. When the embellishment necessitates, the 'mynnym' rather than the 'semebreve' can become the basic unit of beating. In all of this the 'preceptour' is to apply 'certane jugment befoir the chop be ordarly constitut'. More specifically, the compiler recommends that when 'proporcion inequall' arises (that is, instances of two beats against three, three against four etc.) the singer of the part at odds with the others should 'chop his noit be himself secretly, sua that it offend him nocht in his mesur that (there be) singis (signs) econtrar the proporcion to the quhilk for distance of mesur sum jugment of earis discreitly is to be observit'— an ideal solution to episodes such as the conclusion to the *Sanctus* of the Mass *L'Homme Armé*, where the tenors find themselves at odds with the general pulse.

Energetic sections, such as the 'pleni sunt celi' of the same *Sanctus,* are also covered. Here the compiler proposes that the music 'be mair swiftly tuichit or twa choppis ever for ane to be colorit'—possibly accounting for the marker dots in the *Carver Choirbook*.

I have been fortunate enough to be able to put some of these ideas to the test in a series of liturgical reconstructions of Carver's music by Musick Fyne of Inverness, The Clerkes of Old Aberdeen and The Aberdeen Carver Choir. Interestingly, the most successful formation proved to be a loose semi-circle with soloists leading their respective sections, while I directed proceedings from the ranks, leading the alto section and taking the alto part in the appropriate solo sections—an arrangement which seems to balance autonomy and cohesion.

But any attempt at authentic performance must address more fundamental issues than disposition of vocal forces. What voices were involved? The written music simply represents the relative ranges of the voices, not necessarily their actual pitch in modern terms, and a number of scholars, principally David Wulstan, have claimed that the music must be transposed to restore the intended pitch.[4] The direction and extent of this transposition is indicated in the configuration of clefs used by the composer, and Wulstan has formulated a system which, notwithstanding one or two anomalies between the English and Continental practice, has proved exceptionally plausible and has been adopted by many modern performers of Renaissance music.

Isobel Woods has endeavoured to apply Wulstan's clef configurations to Carver's music,[5] but is at a loss to account for the range of *O bone Jesu*, which transposed up a minor third in accordance with Wulstan's 'English practice' would demand regular and sustained high c''' from the treble voices. Rather than being the awkward exception which she dubs it, *O bone Jesu* is surely the one piece in the *Carver Choirbook* which is the touchstone for the others. It is

The author (with hand raised) conducting the soloists of the Carver Choir of Aberdeen in a rehearsal of Carver's six-part Mass, in the Chapel of Elphinstone's University, King's College

just possible to entertain the possibility that Carver's attempt to outshine the splendour of the *Eton Choirbook*, *O bone Jesu*, also demanded a vocal range from the trebles which exceeded by a full tone that normally expected of the finest of English choirs. Yet it seems unlikely that such exceptional treble singing, unparalleled even in England where the taste for high treble singing seems to have been insatiable, should flourish for a decade in Scotland, without leaving any trace. But to conclude that *O bone Jesu* should be not be transposed in performance has considerable implications for the other works in the *Carver Choirbook*. If low F's are acceptable in the bass parts of this motet—and most bass singers would regard a low F as a reasonably sonorous note in their range rather than a weak pedal note which would demand doubling of the section— then low F's are also permissible in the Mass *Dum sacrum mysterium*. This would seem to be borne out by the Mass *L'Homme Armé*, which, when subjected to the upward transposition of a minor third suggested by Wulstan, produces the unlikely combination of treble, mean, tenor and bass. Further- more, the new tenor range seems improbably high (c' is called for on occasion) and the second highest voice seems uncharacteristically low for a mean and impossibly high for an alto. However, if this piece is performed at 'written pitch', the voice parts lie very comfortably for a moderately high upper voice, an alto range, a tenor range with an upper limit of high a' and a bass part, again with a lower limit of F.

In fact, in respect of consistency of vocal ranges the motet *Gaude flore virginali* is the only work by Carver to present problems. While the middle parts lie well for alto and two tenors, the highest and lowest voices are set curiously low. The upper voice is limited to the octave between d' and d" (with two isolated c's) and is unlikely to be an alto part as there is no attempt to use the lower part of the range or the complementary tenor range as was Carver's normal custom. It must be concluded that this line would have been sung by boys, although for some reason in this case the composer foregoes the upper register. The non-liturgical nature of the text may suggest a possible reason for this in that the piece was probably intended for domestic rather than liturgical use, where the acoustic may have rendered high treble singing inappropriate— not to say hazardous!

This may also account for the other anomaly, the fact that the bass descends regularly to E-flat, a full tone lower than is required anywhere else in Carver's work. Again it was possibly felt that a more intimate acoustic and the fact that the piece would probably have been sung by five soloists would allow a pedal note such as this to be heard clearly.

The picture that this creates of the types of voices at Carver's disposal may be summarised as follows. In the early years of the sixteenth century the trebles were expected to sing high a" in an exceptional piece such as *O bone Jesu*, although their customary upper limit seems to have been g", as in the Mass *Dum sacrum mysterium* and the Mass *L'Homme Armé*, and f" in the six-part Mass. Later, in the works of the mid-1540s, this upper boundary appears to have settled on f", reflecting perhaps a decline in high treble singing corre- sponding to that in England.

The alto range remains relatively stable throughout Carver's output, with an upper limit of c" or d" and a lower limit of g or f, presenting no problem to male altos who could drop to their tenor range for the lower notes, a facility clearly required in the six-part Mass, where the altos are frequently asked to use this lower tessitura. The tenor parts, too, demonstrate a remarkable consistency, with an extreme upper limit of high a' (but a more usual ceiling of g'), which seems to hold even for those pieces such as *Gaude flore virginali* and the Mass *Fera pessima* which have more than one tenor part. In contrast, in the Mass *Pater Creator omnium* the second tenor part is given a subservient *cantus firmus* rôle, the music is simple and sustained and tends to lie in the lower part of the range, indicating that this rather uninspiring rôle was taken by less experienced singers. The usual lower limit of the bass part seems to have been G, with F required in some works, although in the Mass *Pater Creator omnium* an f is offered as an alternative. The E-flats in *Gaude flore virginali* are exceptional. Noteworthy in Carver's treatment of all the voices is the wide range he expected from each part. The Mass *L'Homme Armé* demands a range of an octave and a fifth from each voice and is by no means exceptional in Carver's terms. In the Mass *Dum sacrum mysterium* one maverick bass voice extends over two octaves (F to f'), apparently encompassing both bass and tenor ranges.[6] Clearly Carver had individual singers of outstanding flexibility in mind when he composed this part, singers who were also available to sing in *O bone Jesu* where parts of this sort also feature.

But what did an early sixteenth century choir like the Scottish Chapel Royal sound like? Fortunately, nobody has used the contorted cartoon heads of the *Choirbook* initial letters or contemporary accounts of James V's 'rawky and harske' singing voice to deduce the style of vocal production used by the Chapel Royal! Most references to the musical detail of vocal performances in the sixteenth century are maddeningly imprecise. Robert Richardson is by no means untypical as he ranges from the simplistic in his account of the confusion and dissension caused by the use of polyphony, to the inadequate in his description of voice production. Is he referring to falsetto singing when he writes of monks singing 'cum puerili, dulci, leni et sonora voce'?

The most reliable set of indications of how the music should be performed would appear to be the music itself. Assuming that the details of Carver's ornamentation were intended to be heard, the music would seem to demand purity of tone, clarity of articulation, virtuosity and stamina from all the performers, which nowadays would suggest the use for the upper voice parts of specialist women 'trebles', such as those preferred by most leading early music choirs with their ideal combination of iron vibrato-less control and pure ease of production. Carver's treble parts demand precision in throat articulation which results in an almost instrumental production.

Carver's virtuosic alto lines also call for vocal agility over the complete range, suggesting the use of the adult male falsetto voice, although the question of the falsettist's rôle in sixteenth century British church music is a matter of heated debate. It has been pointed out that no mention is made of falsettists in English music until the early seventeenth century, and this has been taken to mean that the vocal lines in question would either have been sung by high tenor voices or low means. This seems to place inordinate weight on the lack of specific documentation describing falsetto singing. Had this been an accepted practice it would have no more required description than, for example, treble singing. The issue has been further complicated by the fact that arguments surrounding the use of falsettists have become unnecessarily enmeshed in the transposition debate mentioned above.

There may be no unequivocal documentation to decide the matter either way, but there is considerable implicit evidence that Carver's alto lines were indeed taken by adult falsettists rather than boys or high tenors. The Scottish Chapel Royal rolls indicate that the choir could call upon a maximum of only six boys, all of whom would have been needed to fill out the top line. The 'alto' line may have been taken by high tenors, and indeed this has recently been done most effectively by Andrew Parrott's Taverner Choir, but there is a price to be paid. Carver frequently contrasts the alto and tenor parts in passages of rapid interchange which cover the same notes and which were in my opinion designed to bring out the contrast between the falsetto of the alto voice and the 'true' vocal production of the tenor voice over the same range. The exclusive use of tenors sacrifices this effect. The adult male alto voice, with its complementary falsetto and tenor ranges, also permits the composer to call upon the complete head and chest registers, allowing him where necessary to use the altos as 'reserve tenors'. Carver does this most extensively in the six-part Mass where an apparent gap in the scoring is filled in this way. In the section 'qui propter nos homines' of the *Credo*, the first alto part takes on a rôle of this kind, while the third alto occupies the upper alto range. At the end of this episode, ironically as the full choir enters on 'descendit', the first alto is dramatically restored to its upper tessitura:

Example 10.1

The tenor and bass parts require consistent agility, and the incisiveness of the bass part is further enhanced if the singers cultivate a slight edge to their tone. Once again any degree of vibrato destroys the focus and clarity essential for the more embellished sections. Naturally, this clarity is also dependent upon the number of singers employed on each part, and here contemporary Scottish documents can again be of assistance.

The provision for the Scottish Chapel Royal in 1501[7] mentions sixteen canons and six boy choristers, twenty-two singers in all, but on 4 June 1504 Pope Julius II issued a mandate 'commanding the Abbots of Dunfermline,

Scone and Cambuskenneth to institute the following offices in the patronage of the King: a treasurer as the fourth dignitary, with 10 canons and a like number of prebends with similar portions to the other 16 canons'.[8] We do not know whether the number of boy choristers was increased in proportion, but even if there were still only six of them, the choir was thirty-two in number and well placed to tackle with ease works in many parts. Furthermore, it is likely that the boy choristers were more mature than their modern counterparts and could sing with much more volume[9] thereby obviating the modern phenomenon of throngs of altogether smaller and less experienced voices on the top part.

It is entirely possible that Carver's music may well have been in the repertoire of any of the excellent cathedral choirs in Scotland. Many of the larger religious establishments in central and southern Scotland, such as the cathedrals at Dunblane, Dunkeld, Glasgow and St Andrews, or the monasteries at Holyrood, Melrose, Cambuskenneth and of course Scone would have had ample provision for singers to perform the works in the *Carver Choirbook*. As we have seen, by 1506, St Machar's Cathedral in Aberdeen, under the inspired direction of Bishop William Elphinstone, boasted twenty vicars choral and six boy choristers,[10] forces which could clearly do justice to any of the works in the *Carver Choirbook*, while Elgin Cathedral, the magnificent 'Lantern of the North', may well have echoed to the sounds of Carver. Even the remote St Magnus Cathedral in Orkney was by the 1540s endowed with sufficient forces and the essential Sang Schule support to tackle the more modest works.

It is important to bear in mind that the Ordinary of the Mass (those parts which were normally set polyphonically) constituted only one element of an elaborate and cohesive celebration, which also included sections of plainchant which varied according to the particular service being celebrated. Composers of Mass settings would never have imagined their polyphonic movements in any other context, and it is imperative to try, wherever possible, to restore the polyphony to its appropriate framework of plainchant.

There are several advantages to this mode of presentation. Quite apart from any religious considerations, the aesthetic effect of the alternation of plainchant and polyphony is very pleasing, while from the point of view of the performers, the strenuous polyphony is broken up into manageable sections. But perhaps most satisfying is the restoration of the full sonorous glory of a sixteenth century celebration of the Mass, a full liturgical reconstruction which, in Jim Reid Baxter's phrase 'allows Carver's glowing polyphony to shine out from an appropriate framework of plainchant, just as the stained glass of a noble cathedral blazes with colour and light amid the solid granite blocks of its walls'.[11]

The plainchant most widely employed throughout Scotland in the early sixteenth century seems to have been that of the Sarum Rite, perhaps with the type of local variants implied by the *cantus firmus* of the Mass *Pater Creator omnium* and the fragments of plainchant preserved in other manuscripts such as the *Inverness Fragments*.[11] In 1507, in an apparent rejection of the Sarum Rite, James IV had urged that breviaries eftir our awin Scottis use and with legendis of Scottis sanctis as is now gaderit and ekit be ane reverend fader in God and our traist counsalour Wiliame bischop of Abirdene and utheris be usit generaly within al our realme als sone as the sammyn may be imprentit and providit; and that na maner of sic bukis of Salusbery use be brocht to be sauld within our realm in tyme cuming[13]

However the rest of the pronouncement makes it clear that his real intention was the protection of his 'lovittis servitouris Walter Chepman and Andro Millar', whom he had encouraged to set up a printing press in Edinburgh and whose monopoly he now wished to guarantee by the erection of trade barriers.[14] When Bishop William Elphinstone's *Aberdeen Breviary* with its Scottish saints and feast days[15] was finally printed by Chepman and Millar in 1510, it became clear that the attempt to establish a truly independent Scottish liturgy had been a largely cosmetic exercise in that the bulk of the Sarum Rite was preserved unchanged.

It remains up to the taste of the performers how much of the relevant Sarum plainchant they will choose to use in performance, but there is a particular satisfaction to be derived from using the chant appropriate for the day of the performance—a rewarding link with the original context of Carver's works.

There is considerable debate about the details of chant performance, ranging from a vigorous, regular rendition in something resembling compound time, to a more bland style with emphasis on flowing phrases and gentle word stresses. An interesting contribution to the plainchant debate was made in 1988 by a recording of Josquin's Mass *Pange Lingua* in liturgical context.[16] Working from performance practices outlined in the anonymous fourteenth century English treatise *Quatuor Principalia*, the performers 'florify' or decorate the plainchant using a variety of ornaments. The very plausible results, which sound similar to Byzantine chant, would complement beautifully the ornamented idiom of Carver's polyphony. Whichever performance style is chosen, it is worth bearing in mind just how familiar this music would have been to singers who performed plainchant every day of their lives.

Some work has also been done on the sixteenth century pronunciation of Latin,[17] and there is now a broad consensus that a rendering very similar to that of the native vernacular was probably the order of the day. At any rate the Italianate style adopted subsequently throughout Europe in the wake of the Counter-Reformation is almost certainly an anachronism in the music of sixteenth century Scotland. This vernacular pronunciation seems to be confirmed by the occasional spelling corruptions in the Latin underlay of the *Carver Choirbook* and of *The Art of Music*. These include 'potenciam' for 'potentiam' (the 'c' probably representing a sound similar to that in the modern 'potential'), and the delightfully indigenous 'michi' for 'mihi'. In conjunction with the hardening of 'g' in words such as 'magnam' and 'Agnus', close attention to pronunciation can entirely change the complexion of a performance.[18]

When the striving towards authenticity springs from a profound respect for the music and a desire to allow it to live and breathe in its accustomed framework, enthusiastic performers are frequently rewarded with startling insights into the music itself. The ultimate act of respect which can be paid to Robert Carver's exceptional music is to restore it to its original liturgical context and to allow it to speak for itself, as it did more than four centuries ago.

11

Soft Releschingis in Dulce Delivering
Motets of the High Renaissance

Fortunately, church music in Scotland possessed talents other than those of Robert Carver, talents able to respond to the dawning age of refined elegance we know as the High Renaissance. In the period from 1520 to the mid-1540s, when the Chapel Royal was devoting all its energies to plainchant and simple improvised faburden, composers elsewhere in Scotland appear to have continued to draw upon changing Continental fashions as the refined High Renaissance style came to dominate European polyphony. A number of fine Scottish motets from as early as 1520 are recorded in a set of part-books compiled by Thomas Wode between 1562 and the late 1590s, the treble, alto, tenor and bass parts copied and bound individually rather than being written out together on the same page as in the earlier choirbooks.

The *Wode Part-books* were originally conceived in the years following the Reformation as a collection of metrical psalm tunes harmonised in four parts by David Peebles, a canon at the Augustinian Priory of St Andrews, and under the personal supervision of Thomas Wode, Vicar of St Andrews. This remarkable individual, whose love of music and warm humanity shine from the pages of his manuscript memorial, was a monk at Lindores Abbey until the Reformation, when he converted to Protestantism and became a minister in the Reformed Church. It was shortly after he took up his appointment in St Andrews that he was approached by James Stewart, illegitimate son of James V (and so half-brother of Queen Mary), Commendator of St Andrews and later Earl of Moray (1563) and Regent (1567). Thomas Wode himself takes up the story:

> my lord Jamis (wha efter wes Erle of murray and regent) being at the reformation pryour of sanctandrous causis ane of his chanons to name David pables, being ane of the cheiff musitians into this land to set three pairts to the tenor, . . . or common pairt of the psalme buke . . ., and my lord comandit the said david to leave the curiosity of musike, and sa make plane and dulce.

The task given to Wode by his religious superior must have seemed both agreeable and simple—to oversee Peebles' work. He could hardly have foreseen that it would dominate the rest of his life. James Stewart had made a shrewd choice of supervisor in the tenacious Wode, who threw himself into the enterprise with evident enthusiasm:

> the said david he wes not earnest; bot I being cum to this toune to remaine, I was ever requesting and solisting till they wer all set.

After the Reformation, Peebles had rented a property within the Priory walls, married Katherine Kynneir and raised two sons, Andrew and Thomas.[1] Understandably, as 'ane of the principall musitians in all this land in his time' according to Wode, Peebles seems to have regarded the Reformed Church with a degree of antipathy, and with the obvious exception of his monastic oath of celibacy, he would appear to have clung to many aspects of his Catholic faith, continuing to live in the religious settlement where he had been a monk, setting Latin texts to High Renaissance polyphony even in his old age, long after the Reformation, and stoutly resisting Wode's attempts to wean him off 'the curiosity of musike' and on to simple harmonisations of metrical psalm tunes.

Quite apart from the challenge of coercing the reluctant Peebles, the compilation of the original psalter was a laborious task for Wode, who had to write out no fewer than one hundred and four psalm tunes into his Tenor book and then copy up in the other three books the harmonisations he winkled out of David Peebles. It was at this point, however, that the exercise seems to have taken on a momentum of its own as settings of eighteen Canticles and Religious Songs by a number of composers followed. On completion of this, the indefatigable Wode turned his attention to more ambitious polyphonic settings of the psalms and also incorporated a treasury of earlier choral works, such as the two surviving Latin motets of David Peebles[2] and other High Renaissance sacred works. It would seem that in this latter enterprise Wode was acting on his own initiative rather than following the wishes of his patron. Even as Wode's mission of cultural conservation was saving a handful of Scottish Latin motets from obscurity, James Stewart, Earl of Moray, was consigning a wealth of comparable music to the bonfire.

To accommodate the fifth part involved in some of these pieces, Wode added a fifth part-book to his original set of four, designed to contain the additional voice regardless of its pitch. Miraculously, these part-books have all survived the vagaries of time in a remarkably complete state—the Treble, Tenor and Bass books in Edinburgh University Library, and the Fifth and Alto books in Trinity College Library, Dublin, and the British Museum respectively. Undaunted by his ambitious undertaking, the redoubtable Wode then embarked upon the production of a duplicate set, of which the Treble and Bass books survive in Edinburgh University Library. A duplicate Alto book in Georgetown University Library, Washington DC, identified and described as early as 1971, has only recently been discovered to contain some original

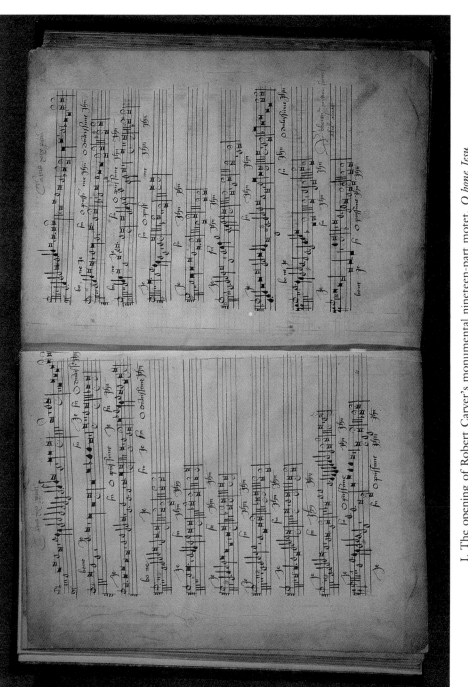

I. The opening of Robert Carver's monumental nineteen-part motet, *O bone Jesu* (by courtesy of the Trustees of the National Library of Scotland)

II and III. The opening of Robert Carver's Mass *Dum sacrum Mysterium*. On the left hand page to the right of the Tenor part Carver identifies the *cantus firmus* on which the mass is based, and proudly enters his signature 'dominus Robertus carwor, canonicus de Scona'. He declares that he composed his magnificent mass 'ad honorem dei et sancti michaelis'. A later transcription appears at the bottom of the page (*by courtesy of the Trustees of the National Library of Scotland*)

Hen as we sate ī Babilon, the

riuers round about, And in remembrance

of Sion the teares for grief brafte out: we

hangde our harpes and inftruments, the wil-

lowe trees vpon: For in that place men for

their vfe had planted manie one

IV. The Bass part of Psalm 137 from the *Wode Part-books*. Thomas Wode has used the words of the psalm, singularly pertinent to his own circumstances, as an excuse to illustrate the instruments he must have been so familiar with. Hanging in his luxuriant 'willowe trees' we see (from top right to bottom left) a pair of lutes, a clarsach, a set of three Renaissance recorders, possibly a set of bells and a tambour, a bass viol, two curved trumpets and the pipes of a portative organ (*Edinburgh University Library*)

material which has helped to complete pieces which have hitherto existed only as editorial reconstructions.[3]

In their final form, the *Part-books* divide into four broad sections: the original psalter, a set of eighteen Canticles or Spiritual Songs, and a group of twenty-six selected pieces including the Latin church music, all in Wode's own hand, and an appendix of secular songs in a later hand. Wode is touchingly aware of the immeasurable cultural importance of the task he has set himself:

> To ane great man that has bot ane resonable gripe of musike; thir five bukis wer worthy thair wayght of gould,

although his pride in his achievement is more usually modestly veiled in becoming understatement:

> Sum gud lytill sangis worthy of roume.

The pages are profusely adorned with colourful renderings of flora and fauna, fantastic beasts and armed towers bristling with cannon. More interesting to musicians are illustrations of contemporary performers and instruments. The former include a shawm player rather ambitiously endeavouring to play with one hand from a part-book held in the other, while the original Treble *Part-book* portrays a young man, perhaps a boy treble, singing from another hand-held part-book; and the latter are intricate if rather fanciful representations of wind and stringed instruments. The *Part-books* are also glossed with marginalia which include conversational accounts of the fortunes of some of his contemporaries in St Andrews, including the leading Reformer Christopher Goodman,[4] tetchy acknowledgements of errors made in copying the music and invaluable background information on the pieces and composers, as well as general prognostications about the state of music in the later sixteenth century. Of the early Latin motets which he records, Wode plaintively comments:

> god grant we use them all to his glory. Notwithstanding of this travell [travail] I have taken, I can understand not but Musike sall pereishe in this land alutterlye.

But when these fine motets were composed, such dire fears lay in the future. Probably the earliest of them, *Descendi in hortum meum*[5] dating from around 1520, is already radically different in style from the slightly earlier works of the *Carver Choirbook*. Gone are the extended melismata and the colourful, almost anarchic pageant of creative ideas which constituted the essence of Robert Carver's monumental Mass settings. Instead, this motet presents the essence of Josquin: smooth, refined vocal lines, regular and taut imitation, and a thorough working out of a limited number of musical ideas. There is a new subtlety about the harmonic progressions and the gradual building up of textures, and the softening effect of suspensions heralds a new indulgence in refined sensuousness. (See Example 11.1, p 69)

A shawm player from the *Wode Part-books*, confirming that the music within was as suitable for instruments as for voices (*Edinburgh University Library*)

Example 11.1

The choice of text from *The Song of Solomon* gives the anonymous composer ample scope for word painting and evocative phrases, antiphonal treatment of the choral forces, and a cadence made ravishing by the dictates of *musica ficta* rounds the piece off.

Example 11.2

Descendi in hortum meum sets itself modest aims but achieves them with a compelling poise. It is extraordinary to think that this music, demonstrating such eloquent mastery of advanced compositional techniques, was written in the same decade as *O bone Jesu*, but it would be pointless to seek for Scottish music charting this transition. The development took place not in Scotland but in the wealthy courts of Continental Europe where Josquin and his Franco-Flemish contemporaries had synthesised northern polyphony and Italian influences. What is witnessed in Scotland is the final overwhelming of a native insular tradition, a bubbling ferment of influences, by the cosmopolitan Franco-Flemish style. The rich Continental spring, which Robert Carver tapped, rose up to overwhelm those of a less ruggedly individual nature.

It is easy to lament the anonymity (stylistic as well as literal) of a motet which could have been written almost anywhere in post-Josquin Europe, but this sentiment must give way to a feeling of pride that a piece of such perfect narcotic beauty could be written in Scotland. None of the early Scottish motets in the *Wode Part-books* display the turbulent genius of Carver's great works, but they are breathtaking in a much more subtle and polished way—they are wonderfully crafted masterpieces of understatement.

Within ten years of the composition of *Descendi in hortum meum* however the new High Renaissance style in Scotland found perhaps its finest expression in David Peebles' *Si quis diligit me*,[6] a motet which absorbs the Continental idiom with ease and yet manages a degree of individuality into the bargain. Peebles displays an intuitive gift with the new style of pervading imitation which is unparalleled in Scotland, and which makes other Scottish music of the High Renaissance sound somewhat wooden by comparison. It is indeed regrettable that of all the music surely composed by David Peebles in his years as a monk at St Andrews Priory where, as we have seen, he established himself as one of Scotland's leading composers, only one exceptionally beautiful motet survives.

In *Si quis diligit me* the harmonies merge effortlessly with one another in a seamless process of organic development, and amid the sensuous flow, melodic phrases of striking elegance rise and fall.

Example 11.3

This music illustrates the same 'classical' restraint and streamlining as Michelangelo's David: a deceptive simplicity masking superb mastery of medium. The elaborate decorative principle of Carver (almost 'romantic' in the sense of extravagant or excessive) has been superseded by a new finely-tuned striving towards perfection. In *Si quis diligit me* this aspiration is as near to fulfilment as was possible in Renaissance Scotland. Francis Heagy, a student of Peebles, added a second alto part to the original four-part texture, but not with unqualified success. While the fifth voice does serve to enrich certain sections, the generally tight texture of the original occasionally reduces Heagy's contribution to repetitive havering. Wode at least seemed to regard it as being a worthy addition. In attributing the added voice, he admits to having forgotten which of the parts was by Heagy—'it is sa lang since I notit this that I have forgot'—although later, in the relevant part-book, he is able to identify it and pay a typically generous compliment to its composer.

francy heagy, sumtime ane noveice in the abbay of Sanctandrous maid this fyft part
. . . and wes a trim playar upon the organs and also ane dissciple to david pables

There is a curiously furtive quality about much music, sacred and secular,
written in Renaissance Scotland, a quality easier to account for than to define. It
lends a certain enigmatic impression to even the most exultant moments in
Carver, the most dogmatic utterances of the later psalm settings, the 'mirriest'
of music for consort.[7] But for the duration of *Si quis diligit me* this shadow cast
over the music of a whole era seems held at bay. Some hint as to the nature of
this fundamental peace and optimism may be contained in the inscription
which accompanies *Si quis diligit me* in the *Wode Part-books*. This states that
Peebles composed the motet around 1530 and 'presentit the sam to Kyng
Jamis the fyft' and 'being a musitian he did lyke it verray weill'. It seems likely
that Peebles, and indeed many others, viewed the eventual emergence from a
particularly troubled minority in 1528 of this gifted monarch as the advent of a
Golden Age of security and prosperity. It was a dream which within ten years
would begin to cloud over. The almost total musical eclipse which came with
the Reformation and which so perturbed Thomas Wode lay but thirty years in
the future.

The relative security of the 1530s was bought at a price. The stability of the
Catholic Church in Scotland demanded the persecution of those who
attempted to bring radical Protestant ideas from Europe and from England.
The cultural links which had allowed Scottish church music to keep up with the
latest stylistic trends now posed a threat to the very existence of the Catholic
Church. For all its decadence and corruption, the Church struck out decisively
at this threat from abroad and among the victims of the ensuing persecution
there were many clerics, including composers.

While the first generation of Lutheran Reformers was running the gauntlet
of official witch-hunts (we would recall the fate of the composer Patrick
Hamilton, burnt at the stake in St Andrews in 1528), Robert Johnson, a
skilled composer from Duns, fled with his Protestant convictions to England,
where he continued to produce religious and secular music until his death some
thirty years later. Among these compositions, both choral and instrumental, is a
setting of Psalm 67, *Deus misereatur*[8] from about 1550, preserved in the *Wode
Part-books* and in High Renaissance imitative style.

It is a work of polished craftsmanship rather than of profound inspiration
but, beside sections of rather mechanical imitation, there are moments of charm
and invention.

Example 11.4

While the music sounds very English in character this is partly the result of the influence that Johnson himself had on English music. David Wulstan[9] points out that it was probably Johnson's links with the Continent and conversion from more lavish textures to the restrained High Renaissance idiom exemplified by *Deus misereatur* which in turn influenced Tallis and Sheppard, and redirected the course of church music in England.

However, it now seems likely that a number of equally influential works by Robert Johnson recorded in English manuscripts predate *Deus misereatur* and were probably composed in Scotland before his flight. These include a sensitive two-part setting for alto and bass of *Dicant nunc judei*, the central part of the Easter processional *Christus resurgens*, which makes subtle use of imitative techniques.

More spectacular in scale are two five-part votive antiphons *Ave Dei patris filia* and *Gaude Maria virgo*. Notwithstanding superficial similarities in form and scoring, Johnson's settings have little in common with Carver's *Gaude flore virginali*, and in fact the adventurous harmonic movement and flowing melodic lines relate much more closely to the early votive antiphons of Tallis and Sheppard, illustrating a further dimension of Johnson's possible formative influence on later English church music. Quite why a recent convert to Protestantism should have preserved and promulgated music praising the Virgin Mary is hard to explain, as are many other aspects of Johnson's life and work,[10] but musicians should be grateful that this fine music did not fall victim to any rash rejection on the part of Johnson of his musical heritage.

If Johnson found himself at odds with current religious trends prior to his flight to England, his contemporary, David Peebles, suffered a very similar fate after the triumph of Protestantism in Scotland in 1560.

If his late motet *Quam multi Domine*[11] is in any way representative of the music he wrote during this period, he would seem, in circumstances somewhat akin to those of William Byrd in Elizabethan England, to have embarked on a similar course of implicit criticism of the New Order. By 1576 Queen Mary's cause was lost, and John Knox had died in the knowledge that Scotland was irrevocably Protestant. It was in these inauspicious circumstances that David Peebles was commissioned to set the text of the third Psalm. Fourteen years earlier the reluctant Peebles had set a number of psalms for the Protestant cause, but this new commission was remarkable in several respects, not least in its request for Latin words and polyphonic music—both associated with the now discredited Old Church. Furthermore, the commission came from Robart Stewart, Bishop of Caithness, and at that time the successor to Wode's patron as Commendator of St Andrews Priory, but soon to be briefly Earl of Lennox (1578) and later Earl of March (1580), James VI's nearest surviving male relative, and a prominent Reformer. Most remarkable of all was the combination of the choice of text and the naming of a composer with apparent Catholic sympathies. There can be little doubt whom Peebles regarded as the subject of the psalm.

> Lord, how are they increased that trouble me,
> Many are they that rise against me.

Many one there be that say of my soul
There is no help for him in his God.

And who can miss the relish with which the beleaguered composer responds to the words:

Up Lord and help me O my God,
For Thou smitest all mine enemies upon the cheekbone,
Thou has broken the teeth of the ungodly.

Example 11.5

This piece owes its survival to either a singular lack of perception on the part of the Protestant circle for which it was composed, or to an uncharacteristic degree of tolerance.[12] It is also a testimony to the broadmindedness of the Protestant Thomas Wode, who recorded it in his *Part-books* and magnanimously described it as 'verray grave and dulce'.

It is indeed a fine piece, embodying the very latest in compositional techniques from the Continent, and there are even suggestions of that sense of theatre which would come to saturate Baroque Catholic composition at the turn of the century. However, in keeping with the context of its composition, from the first phrase it is clear that the customary shadow of Renaissance Scotland broods once again over the music—the tautness of *Si quis diligit me* has become tension, a tension heightened by the dramatic devices Peebles employs.

Example 11.6

Frequently the tenor line instigates succinct climaxes which sound very like the mature work of Giovanni Gabrieli, and which subside as rapidly as they arise.

Once again, tacked on to the end is a brief chordal section in compound time nervously animated with syncopations, and suddenly the motet becomes an essay on transience. This striking gesture can be equated with whistling in the dark, a final attempt on the part of an eminent exponent of Scottish High Renaissance culture to convince himself that this culture had a future. As he sets the significant words 'sicut erat in principio, et nunc, et in omne evum', the feverish melody subsidies into a plangent conclusion in slow simple time.

Example 11.7

To David Peebles it must have seemed in 1576 that a night of awesome darkness had gathered over the world as he knew it.

12

In Voice Virgineall
The Mass *Felix namque*

The *Wode Part-books* illustrate how David Peebles and others steered the Scottish motet into the mainstream of the High Renaissance, but what of the Mass? It comes as no surprise that the *Part-books* contain no examples of Mass settings, and Carver's late Masses offer few concessions in the direction of modernity. To discover how the Mass fared in this new musical climate it is necessary to consult the other significant Scottish manuscript source of High Renaissance church music, the so-called *Dunkeld Antiphonary*.

This manuscript, housed in Edinburgh University Library, consists of five part-books from an original set of six, bound together probably during the nineteenth century. There is no evidence in the manuscript of connections with Dunkeld, and indeed Kenneth Elliott[1] has surmised that the ascription derives from a misreading of a Latin contraction of Lincluden. At this time Lincluden was a Collegiate Church, an establishment devoted to the performance of polyphonic music by a college of highly trained clergy whose only task was the celebration of services, and in 1508 it had been subordinated to the Chapel Royal. The close administrative links between these two establishments may well have facilitated the sharing of musical material and even the exchange of personnel. As the Collegiate Church of Lincluden probably also fell under the restrictions which dominated music-making at the Chapel Royal from 1520 until 1543, the part-books with their wealth of continental and insular material may well represent a revival in the fortunes of polyphony at Lincluden, parallel to that which took place after 1543 in the *Carver Choirbook*.

Given the misleading nature of the traditional title, Dr Elliott has proposed an alternative: the *Dowglas/Fischar Part-books*, deriving from an inscription on the manuscript which possibly refers to the owner and copyist respectively. This piece of evidence ties in neatly with the presence of one Robert Dowglas as Provost of Lincluden from 1547. Furthermore, this man is known to have visited Paris in the early 1550s around the time the manuscript was probably compiled, although the flamboyant inscription—'ROBERT DOWGLAS with my hand at the pen—William Fischar'—can only be linked definitely with one brief section of secular underlay without music which seems to have been added to the *Part-books* at a later date. At most, perhaps, the inscription simply indicates the acquisition or logging of an already complete manuscript by Fischar on behalf of Dowglas—and at worst it may simply be an example of ostentatious sixteenth century graffiti!

The *Dowglas/Fischar Part-books* contain a copy of Josquin's motet *Benedicta es* and a number of motets by Franco-Flemish composers of the post-Josquin generation. Some of them such as Claudin de Sermisy (c. 1490–1562) and Adrian Willaert (c. 1480–1562) have regained much of the fame they enjoyed in their own lifetimes, others such as Pierre Certon (d. 1572) and Johannes Lupi (d. 1539) have to date been less fortunate. Added to the manuscript are three Mass settings: a fragment by the English composer Thomas Ashewell (c 1478-after 1518), the Mass *Cantate Domino*, which has been assumed to be a late work by Robert Carver, and an anonymous six-part Mass *Felix namque*.[2] Although the *cantus firmus* on which this Mass setting is based is a Sarum offertory which enjoyed great popularity in England from the early sixteenth to the mid seventeenth century as a *cantus firmus* for organ pieces,[3] the Mass *Felix namque* contains phrases which resemble material in contemporary Scottish part-songs and which are distinctively Scottish in flavour. As it appears in conjunction with the Mass *Cantate Domino* which is undoubtedly Scottish, it seems likely that this Mass is also part of an indigenous contribution to the *Part-books*.

The choice of music in the *Dowglas/Fischar Part-books* confirms the fundamental shift in Scottish musical taste already observed in the music of the *Wode Part-books*. One indication is the selection of Josquin's motet *Benedicta es*, a highly significant choice from the vast output of this Franco-Flemish master, for it is, perhaps of all his works, the piece which most directly anticipates the church music of the late Renaissance. Indeed this very motet, with its extreme refinement of phrase and economy of means, so appealed to the young Palestrina that he based a Mass setting on it in the early 1560s. So the compiler of the *Dowglas/Fischar Part-books* had his finger on the pulse of Continental taste, and whether the Mass *Felix namque* is (as Henry Farmer assumed[4]) the work of Robert Dowglas himself, or that of some other Scottish master, such as David Peebles, it fits in very well with the prevailing musical currents on the Continent.

The new fashionable tautness of phrase, demonstrated by the High Renaissance motets of the *Wode Part-books*, is apparent from the very beginning of the Mass *Felix namque*. Here, too, is the attention to natural speech rhythms to which Carver paid lip-service in his later works, and the composer of the Mass *Felix namque* has dispensed almost entirely with embellishment in favour of simple vocal lines.

Example 12.1

In the 'et incarnatus est' section of the *Credo* there is an irresistible sense of harmonic direction, both because of a more fluid progression from chord to chord, and due to the fact that this momentum is never retarded or masked by elaborate decoration. Examples of that classic High Renaissance motif, the introverted figure which literally turns in on itself, abound in a number of variants in all of the movements of the Mass.

Example 12.2   Example 12.3

English dissonance,[5] avoided so assiduously by Robert Carver, also occurs in a variety of forms, such as the unusual cadence at the end of the penultimate statement of the *Agnus Dei*, adding piquancy to the warm harmony of the six-part texture.

Example 12.4

The Mass *Felix namque* includes a *Kyrie* as well as the customary elements of the Mass Ordinary and is set for treble, two altos, tenor and two basses. The *Gloria* and *Credo* are both truncated: the former cuts from the first 'qui tollis' to 'cum Sancto Spiritu', while the latter sacrifices textual sense in the interest of brevity by jumping abruptly from 'et resurrexit' (which appears only in the second alto part and almost as an afterthought) to 'et vitam venturi seculi. Amen'. By contrast the treatment of the *Sanctus* and *Agnus Dei* is more expansive, culminating in the final petition of the latter, where the six voices settle into a state of almost complete rapt stasis in the concluding 'dona nobis pacem'.

It is easy to picture the Mass *Felix namque* as the work of the mature David Peebles, who certainly had the necessary grasp of High Renaissance style to produce a piece of such consistently high standard. If this is the case, the Mass would fill the long gap between the two motets of 1530 and 1576 respectively, which are his only other surviving extended compositions. But this is to ignore some curious points of contact between the Mass *Felix namque* and the other six-part Mass in the *Dowglas/Fischar Part-books*, the Mass *Cantate Domino* assumed to be the work of Robert Carver. Listening to sections such as the descending chime figures in the concluding ten bars of the 'in nomine' section of the *Sanctus* and in the first ten bars of the 'miserere' section of the first petition of the *Agnus Dei* or the distinctive suspensions in the 'miserere' section of the *Gloria* and in the final section of 'Domine Deus Sabaoth' one is reminded of the *Cantate Domino* Mass, and its antecedent, Carver's Mass *Fera pessima*, while the tenor part of 'pleni sunt celi' retraces the idiosyncratic leaping figure observed in the latter Mass.

Is one of Carver's contemporaries paying passing tribute to the great master in these brief and isolated moments, or is it possible that the listener is witnessing the momentary slipping of a High Renaissance mask to reveal glimpses of a very familiar face behind it? Could Carver's chameleon talents have enabled him to assume belatedly and almost convincingly the High Renaissance guise of the mid 1550s, leaving the merest traces of his accustomed idiom? If only Robert Dowglas or William Fischar had been as assiduous as Thomas Wode in cataloguing the compositions in their manuscript, we might have had the answer to these tantalising questions.

Like Carver's Mass *Pater Creator omnium*, the text of the *Benedictus* in the Mass *Felix namque* includes the trope 'Mariae Filius'. The practice of troping religious texts involved intermeshing an explanatory commentary with the original text for special occasions, and this particular trope was appropriate for various Marian feasts, including the Vigil of the Assumption of the Blessed Virgin on 14 August. As the offertory *Felix namque*, the *cantus firmus* of the Mass, is also appropriate for this service, it is possible that, like the Mass *Pater Creator omnium*, this Mass was written with one specific occasion in mind.

This date makes the Mass *Felix namque* a candidate for the music 'solemnly sung with Shalms and Sackbutts' to mark the the ratification of the Anglo-Scottish marriage treaty of 1543.[6] Although this celebration took place on 25 August, eleven days after the Vigil for which the chants were appropriate, it may have been felt that the pertinence of the text of the Offertory allowed for some poetic licence in this respect.

> For truly, happy one, you are the Virgin Mary, and worthiest of every praise, for out of you is risen the sun of justice, Christ our God.

Perhaps the sound of the voices of the Chapel Royal blending with the sombre tones of shawms and sackbuts in celebration of High Mass played some small part in moving the Regent Arran to repentance and into the arms of the French party.

However, the advanced High Renaissance style of the Mass *Felix namque* makes it unlikely that it predates Carver's Masses *Pater Creator omnium* and *Fera pessima*. The fact that the Mass has an untroped *Kyrie* suggests another possibility. It may have been part of a body of work composed for Mary by musicians in her retinue while she was resident in France, where there was no need for a troped Sarum *Kyrie*. We have already seen how a collection of church music probably accompanied Margaret Tudor to Scotland when she came north to marry James IV, and while Mary's departure for France was a rather more urgent affair, this suggestion provides an alternative explanation for the

Mary Queen of Scots

A reflective study of the twice-widowed Mary, Queen of Scots, the Morton or Dalmahoy portrait (*Glasgow Museums: Art Gallery & Museum, Kelvingrove*)

provenance of the *Dowglas/Fischar Part-books*—a manuscript collection of French music acquired by one of the Scots musicians in Mary's company, to which was added music brought over from Scotland or specially composed in France for the young Queen, possibly in association with her wedding or coronation, or indeed any of the regular visits paid to the French court by Scottish diplomats and nobles.[7]

Whatever occasion it was actually written for, a further plausible context for a performance of the Mass *Felix Namque* would seem to be Mary's return from France on 19 August 1561. Her first Sunday on Scottish soil was marked by the singing of a Mass by the Chapel Royal at Holyrood, which so outraged the worshippers at the Protestant service being held next door in the Canongate Parish Church, formerly the Abbey Church, that a riot ensued.[8]

The celebratory tone of the setting as well as the calendar and textual relevance of the *cantus* make the Mass a strong candidate for this Royal occasion.[9] And if *Felix namque* was the music performed against the backdrop of a mounting cacophony of riot, as the Queen's half-brother, James Stewart, held back the baying mob, we are presented with a telling symbol for the future of the Mass in Scotland. At the very moment when it attained a state of High Renaissance perfection, it also faced obsolescence. Presently there would be neither the will to commission Mass settings nor the religious context in which to perform them.

13

To the Merciment of Fire
The Reformation

The Reformation eventually broke upon Scotland in 1559. To understand the nature of this Reformation and the circumstances which brought it to fruition, it is necessary to trace its protracted period of gestation both in Scotland and abroad.

Scottish intellectuals studying on the Continent came into contact with Lutheran writings in the early 1520s, although attempts to introduce these ideas into Scotland were met with intransigent opposition. In 1525 the earliest Protestant writings to reach Scotland provoked a decisive response from Parliament, under the control of the French-born Catholic Regent Albany, in the form of an Act 'anent heresy':

> Forasmekle as the dampnable opunyeounis of heresy are spred in diverse cuntries be the heretik Luther and his discipillis and this realm and liegis has fermelie persistit in the halifaith sen the samin was first ressavit be thaim and never as yit admittit ony opunyeounis contrare the cristin faith bot ever has bene clene of all sic filth and vice, therefore that na maner of persoun strangeare that hapnis to arrife with thair schippis within ony part of this ream bring with thaim ony bukis or werkis of the said Lutheris, his discipillis or servandis, desputt or reherse his heresyis or opunyeounis bot geif it be to the confusioun thairof under the pane of escheting of thair schippis and gudis and putting of thair persounis in presoun[1]

This hard line was maintained by James V until his death in 1542. During the minority of Mary, the Earl of Arran as Regent underpinned his policy of *détente* with Protestant England by permitting some relaxation of restrictions on the reading of Reformed literature in Scotland. But when the still powerful pro-French party under the doughty leadership of Mary of Guise and Cardinal Beaton intervened to prevent the proposed marriage between Mary and Edward, the son of Henry VIII, Henry's violent reprisals on southern Scotland in the mid 1540s (the so-called 'Rough Wooing') discredited at one stroke the pro-English stance of Arran and his tolerant attitude to Protestantism.

The call for reformation from within the Old Church, resulting incidentally in the spartan measures advocated by Robert Richardson in his *Commentary on the Rule of St Augustine* and the more restrained use of music in services, temporarily took the wind from the sails of the Lutheran Reformers, whose moderate ideas went little beyond those advocated by reformers within the ranks of the Old Church.

In 1554 the pro-French party gained ascendancy, Mary of Guise was appointed Regent, and Mary's marriage to the Dauphin in 1558 cemented the bond with France. By this time the choice for Scotland was between alliance with Catholic France under Henry II and the now Catholic England under Mary Tudor. The selection of France meant ironically that Mary of Guise could practise a degree of tolerance in her relations with the Scottish Reformers, who were no longer synonymous with the English threat.

But while a hard core of Protestant feeling persisted, particularly among the lower echelons of 'Temporalitie', the Reformed movement had reached a trough from which in the late 1550s there seemed no immediate escape. Catholicism reigned supreme in Scotland, England and France, and popular support for Protestantism seemed on the decline, as the early efforts of the Old Church to combat some of the more glaring abuses within its ranks began to bear fruit. With much of Northern Europe closed to them, the more radical Scottish dissidents sought refuge in Geneva where they came into contact with extremist strains of Protestantism. While the uncompromising nature of Calvinism undoubtedly had a personal appeal for individuals like John Knox, embittered by years of persecution and suffering as a galley slave, it was also undoubtedly more viable as a clear alternative to the revitalised Scottish Catholic Church of the 1550s. A radical Protestant creed such as Calvinism could side-step the mires of moderation which had all but claimed Lutheranism, and press home a decisive attack on Catholicism.

In 1558 the first chink in the Catholic armour presented itself in England with the unexpected demise of Mary Tudor and the accession of the Protestant Elizabeth I. Then in 1560 came the fortuitous confluence of events which gave the second-generation Reformers a toe-hold in Scotland. Amid growing unrest provoked by Protestant lairds and focused upon John Knox, whom they had invited to return to Scotland in 1559, the reins of state passed abruptly and unexpectedly from the sure, steady hands of Mary of Guise to the impulsive grasp of Mary, Queen of Scots. The interregnum between the death of Mary of Guise and the return to Scotland of her daughter in August 1561 provided the Reformers with the opening they had been waiting for.

The ensuing struggle, superficially a duel between Mary, as the champion of Catholicism, and John Knox as defender of the Reformed Faith, was in fact a deal more complex than appearances suggested. But even taking into account the further factor of armed intervention by both France and England, few of those who witnessed the events of 1559 would have predicted their startling outcome. In 1560, when the dust settled after sporadic outbreaks of mob violence, a Reforming Parliament was instituted to sever links with Rome and to abolish the Mass. Mary returned a year later to a country already committed to radical Reformation, and her determined rearguard action did little more than delay the rise of Protestantism and the demise of the Old Church.

But in 1560 the eclipse of the Old Church was far from inevitable. Popular support for the Reformation was strident but patchy, 'Temporalitie' was divided, and 'Spiritualitie' was still a considerable force to be reckoned with. The odds seemed stacked against Knox and the Calvinists.

Explanations of the ultimate triumph of Protestantism which rely solely on the relative effectiveness of individuals such as Knox and Mary, or even the relative theological integrity of practitioners of the two creeds, overlook the fact that the whole of Scottish culture had reached a watershed. When Sir David Lyndsay in *Ane Satyre of the Thrie Estaitis* had called for 'reformation' he was simply advocating change. The Renaissance was no respecter of the *status quo*, calling all in question, and in Scotland this questioning mentality came of age in the Reformation. Change (in itself anathema to the Old Church and to the Crown with their vested interest in perpetuity) was in the air, and the Reformers who seemed to be the only people in a position to offer an alternative to *status quo*, attracted a motley following of factions prepared to follow anything that moved. The striking feature about the period of Reformation in Scotland is that once the Reformers had seized the initiative they succeeded in holding on to it against all the odds.

The Catholic Church in Scotland had conspicuously failed to reform itself and had done much to alienate the populace. This had been compounded by the excesses of the Catholic faction in the government and their reliance upon foreign aid in the form of French troops. When Elizabeth I acceded to Protestant pleas and sent English troops to engage the French, the Catholics

John Knox and Christopher Goodman direct a 'Blast of the Trumpet' at women rulers, probably representing the Catholics Mary Tudor and Mary of Guise. With the accession of the Protestant Elizabeth to the throne of England, Knox tried to forget his fulminations against the 'monstrous Regiment of Women' – Elizabeth never did
(*By permission of the British Library*)

in Scotland were deprived of their main prop, and Catholic support quickly crumbled in the face of a genuinely popular Protestant uprising. When the 'Thrie Estaites' met in August 1560 parliament was crowded out by over a hundred Protestant landowners, who ensured the ratification of a number of Protestant measures including the denial of the authority of the Pope, the banning of the Mass and the official endorsement by Parliament of the Protestant doctrine in the form of a Confession of Faith. Mary's refusal to ratify the decisions of this Reforming Parliament had little effect. While the religious question remained technically undecided, there was little doubt where popular support now lay.

For music the implications of this victory of fundamentalist Protestantism were immense. In those parts of Europe where Lutheranism had taken root in the first half of the sixteenth century, by 1560 composers felt sufficiently secure to begin a tentative rediscovery of the potential of polyphony, while the Catholic nations were responding to the cultural challenge of the Counter-Reformation. But the Geneva of Calvin, which had provided sanctuary for John Knox, was musically silent except for the strains of unison psalms, and it was this purely functional concept of church music, coupled with a venomous hatred of the organ, which was viewed as a symbol of papist ostentation, that Knox and the Calvinist pioneers brought to Scotland. Knox's venomous outpourings on the subject of ornate choral music still send a chill down the spine:

> But as there is no gift of God so precious or excellent, that Sathan hath not after a sort drawen to himself and corrupt, so hath he most impudentlye confused the notable gift of singing, chieflye by the Papists his ministeris, in disfiguring it, partly by strange language, that can not edifie, and partly by a curious wanton sort, hyringe men to tickle the eares and flatter the phantassies[2]

Rather than working to establish Protestantism, the Reforming Parliament of 1560 was obsessively bent upon the destruction of the Old Church. The abolition of the Mass was simply the official seal upon a campaign of physical destruction, which involved violent attacks upon friaries, the wanton destruction of church buildings and property, including vestments, choirbooks and organs, and the often violent coercion of reluctant churchmen.

A particularly poignant example of this occurred on 14 December 1561 as the Chapel Royal, preparing to celebrate High Mass at the Queen's request, were set upon by the Earl of Argyle and his followers who 'so disturbed the quire, that some both priests and clerks, left their places, with broken heads, and bloody ears'. It is possible that they were about to perform music by the aged Robert Carver, who may, as John Purser observes, have been present to witness the end of all he had worked for. This adds further pathos to a sickening episode which the account observes 'was a sport alone, for some that were there to behold it'. Small wonder that others who witnessed it 'shed a tear or two, and made no more of the matter'.[3]

The initial spate of mob vandalism was followed up by a systematic dismantling of the religious superstructure of the Old Church and all its physical manifestations. Whether a cathedral or an abbey was razed to the ground by the mob in 1559 or was allowed to fall more sedately into ruin after the smashing of its stained glass and the stripping of the lead from its roof, the end result was the same. Similarly, a choirbook which escaped the initial holocaust which consumed cathedral and abbey libraries was unlikely to survive the ensuing neglect by a religious regime to which the music on its pages was obsolete and, ultimately, incomprehensible.

It was clear that the Calvinists meant to destroy utterly every aspect of the Old Church before providing any viable alternative. And this realisation prompted the Lutheran Thomas Wode to begin his squirrel-like hoarding of High Renaissance motets and to give individual expression to a general panic which must have animated many Catholic and moderate Protestant minds at this time.[4]

What did the Calvinists have to offer in place of the ethereal Latin motets and magnificent Mass settings they were so anxious to sweep away? It is a comment on how unexpected the Protestant breakthrough in 1559/60 was to the Reformers themselves that they had so little on hand to replace the edifices of the Old Church. By way of a stop-gap, they turned to the *Gude and Godlie Ballatis*, a volume probably compiled by one of three Wedderburn brothers from Dundee and published on the eve of the Reformation.[5] These *Ballatis* were *ad hoc* adaptations of vernacular folksong texts interspersed with original material and designed to be sung to traditional melodies. Their intended contribution to the Protestant cause is clear, but their place in Scottish Renaissance culture is more questionable. They are impassioned expressions of the basic tenets of a radically new faith, revolutionary songs full of sound and fury. Poetically they seldom rise above the level of hackwork and frequently plummet to vulgarity. The mechanical adaptation of the secular song *John cum kis me now*, where the arranger feels bound to spell out his implausible analogies, is representative of the crudity of method employed in several of the *Ballatis*.

> John, cum kis me now, John cum kis me now;
> John, cum kis me by and by and mak no moir adow.
> The Lord thy God I am, That John dois the call;
> John representit man, be grace celestiall.[6]

The original texts deal in rather earthy terms with some of the more contentious issues facing the Reformed movement. *God send everie Priest ane wyfe* proposes an eminently practical solution to the promiscuity of churchmen, an abuse which was undoubtedly widely practised[7] and equally roundly condemned by internal reformers within the Old Church.

> God send everie priest ane wyfe, and everie Nunne ane man,
> That thay micht leve that haly lyfe, as first the Kirk began.
>
> For than suld nocht sa mony hure be up and downe this land;
> Nor yit sa mony beggeris pure in kirk and mercat stand.

> And nocht sa mekill bastard seid throw out this cuntrie sawin;
> Nor gude men uncouth fry suld feid, and all the suith war knawin.[8]

Other texts attempt to encapsulate Protestant policies in pithy couplets, but the courtly alliterative style and red-faced Reformed ranting prove uneasy bedfellows:

> The Paip, that pagane full of pryde, he hes us blindit lang;
> For quhair the blind the blind dois gyde, na wonder baith ga wrang.[9]

There are some texts in the *Gude and Godlie Ballatis* which attain a certain puritanical nobility, such as the masterly vernacular rendition of the Creed, *We trow in God allanerlie*,[10] but the bulk of the collection falls far short of this standard. On reflection, it is scarcely surprising that there is little in the *Gude and Godlie Ballatis* to stir the finer feelings. They were produced as easily digested propaganda, hard-hitting texts set to simple melodies which would have an immediate impact, and were used to promulgate the Protestant message in the years of consolidation of the early 1560s. To compare them with High Renaissance motets, which sprang from a complex, refined musical establishment with few axes to grind and all the time in the world to grind them, is a meaningless exercise. More constructive would be a comparison between the *Ballatis* and modern protest songs: committed, catchy and sometimes kitschy, written to be sung by idealistic amateurs with a minimum of resources and preparation.

As the *Ballatis* began to achieve their intended aim of consolidation, they were gradually replaced by more permanent manifestations of the Calvinist ethos. In 1564 the first *Scottish Psalter* appeared, incorporating text (significantly in English not Scots) and tune, and much influenced by the 1562 *Genevan Psalter*, while the church service endorsed by Knox and the Reformers revolved around the unison performance of these psalm tunes by the entire congregation.

The theological reasoning behind this functional view of music was central to Protestantism. If the common people were to have direct access to the scriptures, they had also to participate in the sung psalms; for these to be kept within lay grasp it was essential that they should be in the vernacular and set as simply as possible. This rather literal interpretation of the concept of participation in the service replaced the earlier assumption that participation was essentially a spiritual act, responding to the complex cluster of stimuli offered by the celebration of the Mass. In the Old Church these celebrations were intended primarily for God, a fact which demanded the most ornate and refined offering possible from a group of true specialists, a gifted and highly-trained composer using all the skills at his disposal, a Chapel Royal or a cathedral choir trained to a peak of perfection, and a magnificent and highly decorated building, the result of further skilled efforts, in which the resulting music could resonate. Rather than appreciating what could be achieved by compounding human skills, Protestant theology encouraged the Reformers to look at the lowest common denominator, that which every person shared, the capacity of the common man. At a stroke they had done away with the requirement for any embellishment of the relationship between man and God, and the great musical institutions of the Old Church—the Sang Schules, the cathedral and collegiate choirs with their libraries of music, and even the church organs—were rendered redundant. As the Reformed Church established itself throughout Scotland, the old musical foundations were either systematically rooted out, or were left to rot in neglect. Music-making, both sacred and secular, entered a period of alarming stagnation which lasted for almost fifteen years.

But what the Reformers had failed to recognise was the fact that harmony and polyphony, fundamental to all part-music, have a very immediate popular appeal. The aesthetic element of worship, which can be a most eloquent vehicle for any religious message, was purged from the Reformed service on the grounds that it interfered with the direct communication between man and God. It is indeed a neat irony that after some four centuries of Presbyterianism, the psalm-singing congregations of the Western Isles have perfected their own distinctive, almost Carveresque, polyphony of performance. In Lewis, the precentor introduces the Psalm tune by singing the opening phrase, much as must have happened in the earliest days of the Reformed Church in Scotland, and then in a startling filigree of imitation and embellishment the congregation spontaneously decorates the original tune.

From the early 1560s composers had experimented with settings of the psalm tunes in an attempt to reconcile the musical traditions of the Old Church with the strictures of the New, and among the earliest results were the settings recorded between 1562 and 1566 by Thomas Wode of tunes from the *Scottish Psalter* harmonised in four parts by David Peebles.[11] It may have been Wode's original intention to publish these harmonisations, but as the persisting Calvinist climate rendered this aim fruitless, the collection remained in manuscript form to enjoy a limited circulation in sympathetic aristocratic and court circles. Meanwhile, in those Sang Schules which had not had their resources redirected by the Reformers, the appreciation of polyphony was still preserved and nurtured. The result was that when in 1579 James VI found himself in a position to take decisive steps to revitalise the musical establishment, in particular the Sang Schules and the Chapel Royal, musicians were able to pick up strands of pre-Reformation culture which had survived the initial conflagrations of 1559/60 and the ensuing lean years of neglect.

The underground network in which manuscripts such as Wode's circulated was in the main Protestant, but its members had come to the realisation that the more sophisticated musical structures were not in themselves incompatible with Protestantism, a view which was lent considerable authority by Luther's praise of the polyphonic mastery of Josquin Desprez.[12] It was only the more radical strains of Protestantism, such as that cultivated by Calvin, that branded polyphony as irrevocably papist in nature. Like Thomas Wode, more moderate Protestants must have watched with horror as the Calvinists struck at the very heart of Scottish Renaissance culture.[13]

For a man like David Peebles who did not even share Knox's religious beliefs and seems to have remained a Catholic at heart, the situation must have been all the more galling. How extraordinary then that he agreed to accept the commission from James Stewart, Commendator of St Andrews, to set the psalm tunes in four parts, even if, as Wode records, 'he wes not earnest'. Perhaps he felt that in harmonising the psalm tunes he was salvaging something from the ruins of the Old Church, or perhaps in such religious climate as this, 'ane of the principall musitians in all this land in his time' realised that he had survived beyond his time and into a bleaker age, where his intimate knowledge of the complexities of the art of music were no longer valued. He must have recognised too that in these straitened circumstances he was in no position to pick and choose.

The resulting settings are competent and pleasing, but recalling the fact that the same mind had produced *Si quis diligit me* a mere thirty years before, the restrictions under which he must have been toiling become apparent. The commission stipulated that the settings should be in a plain style, and treating a pre-existent melody in this manner leaves precious little scope for creativity.

Example 13.1

Peebles' mastery of harmony saves the results from mundanity, but his lack of commitment to this enterprise is as clear from the music as from Wode's comments. Here is a true artist reluctantly doing justice to an interior decorating job.

Again we turn to Thomas Wode for an incisive encapsulation of the dilemma faced by all the Scottish composers, trained in institutions now in terminal decay, to decorate, with magnificent music, services which would never again be celebrated. Referring to the English master, Robert Fayrfax, Wode attached the following comments to his draft of Peebles' *Si quis diligit me*: 'if doctor farfax were alyve in this cuntry he would be contemnit & pereise for layk of mentinance'.

14

All Together in a Plain Tune
Part-music in the Reformed Church

More promising evidence of the 'closet' cultivation of part-music comes later in Wode's manuscript, where he records a four-voice homophonic setting of the *Te Deum* by Andro Kemp,[1] canticles by John Angus, and polyphonic five-voice settings of psalm texts by Andro Blakhall. Kemp was master of the St Andrews Sang Schule and composed his syllabic chordal setting of a vernacular prose version of the *Te Deum* text in 1566. While the composition demonstrates that the Sang Schule masters were tackling texts from a wider liturgical context than the *Book of Psalms*, the part-writing is extremely mechanical, see-sawing up and down in monotonous parallel motion, with the occasional attempt at contrary motion applied equally mechanically. There is something about this piece and the other music by Kemp recorded by Wode which suggests that he is another composer labouring under impossible restrictions. As an example of creativity, the *Te Deum* shows little more than an occasional glimmer of promise, but it is enough to indicate that the products of Sang Schule training were beginning to champ at the rigid Calvinist bit.

This is certainly the case with John Angus, whose Canticles range from the simple note-for-note setting used by Kemp to a more adventurous and creative style of composition, although always with that hint of reserve which earned him the epithet recorded by Wode, 'meike Angus'. On the other hand, the court of the youthful James VI made little secret of its preference for more elaborate part-writing than that offered by homophonic settings, and indeed, dominated by the pro-Anglican Morton, the adoption of vernacular religious texts was practically the only concession it made to the Calvinists. Andro Blakhall had been a Canon at the Abbey of Holyrood before the Reformation. After 1560, he became Protestant minister to a succession of parishes in the vicinity, but seems to have maintained contact with court circles, using several of his compositions in attempts to gain favour with Morton and with the young King himself, in whom he perhaps recognised a potential patron of considerable discernment. The earliest of these compositions which Wode records is Psalm 101 *Of mercy and of judgement both*,[2] which he dates 1569 and mentions was 'giffin in propyne to the king', who was three at the time and despite his extraordinary intellect, unlikely to have appreciated its finer contrapuntal features! However, when he heard this beautiful five-part piece for two trebles, two tenors and bass, the King, young as he was, may have perceived something of Blakhall's mastery in his treatment of the two interweaving treble parts—and the sudden and unprepared harmonic twist of the knife at the conclusion of the phrase 'that man will I distroy' must have made the serious-minded infant cringe. Blakhall's close acquaintance with aspects of the High Renaissance style is further demonstrated in the five-voice settings for treble, alto, two tenors and bass of Psalm 128, *Blessed art thou*,[3] written in 1573 for a dynastic wedding linking the Mar and Angus families, (and closely involving the then Regent, James Douglas, Earl of Morton) and Psalm 43 *Judge and revenge my cause*,[4] personally commissioned by Morton in 1579. Clearly Blakhall's style enjoyed considerable popularity at court.

Blessed art thou demonstrates true facility in the application of imitation, and discounting the rather pedestrian impression occasionally created by the syllabic setting of the text, it is an impressive achievement. Blakhall alternates homophony with polyphony to emphasise sections in the text, and his charmingly wayward tenor lines are used to maximum dramatic effect, most memorably in their illustration of 'fruitful vines'. The wedding graced by Blakhall's music had been engineered by the Regent Morton to consolidate his control over the young King James, who was at this time in the safe keeping of Alexander Erskine in Stirling Castle. Erskine's neice, sister of the Earl of Mar, was selected to marry Morton's heir, his nephew, the Earl of Angus and head of the House of Douglas, in whom Morton had invested his hopes for the future, as his own wife had been mad for many years and he had no legitimate children of his own[5]. The commission was clearly intended as much to ease Morton's access to the young monarch as to mark the linking of these two powerful dynasties. This was not the only occasion on which Andro Blakhall's beautiful music would serve the Regent Morton's clandestine political purposes.

Judge and revenge my cause also has a fascinating and somewhat squalid background.[6] As early as 1567 the opening words had been associated with the young King, being 'put into his mouth' retrospectively by Robert Sempill in his ballad *The Kingis Complaint* (1570) in the form of a plea for divine justice and retribution against James Hepburn, Earl of Bothwell, who became James' step-father by marrying Mary on 15 May 1567.

> Quhen I was not yit ane yeir auld
> Bothwell that bludy bouchour bauld
> My Father cruelly devorde,
> He him betrayit and his blude sauld
> Judge and revenge my cause O Lord[7]

While any number of the Scottish aristocracy, including Morton himself, may have been privy to the plot to kill Darnley, it served the Protestant camp to

Mary, Queen of Scots, and her son, in a fanciful representation of the happy childhood
James never had. In early infancy he became a pawn to be used against his mother
(*The Hulton Deutsch Collection*)

point the finger of accusation at Mary's new consort. When Bothwell and Mary were defeated by Protestant forces at Carberry Hill on 15 June 1567, a banner depicting the murdered Darnley and bearing the legend *Judge and revenge my cause* issuing from the mouth of the infant James was flaunted in Mary's face as she was led captive through Edinburgh.[8]

After the assassination of Regent Moray by James Hamilton of Bothwell-haugh on 23 January 1570, Morton saw to it that the Carberry banner, now further embellished with a depiction of the murdered Moray, was put on public display a fortnight after the Regent's funeral, and Sempill produced *The Kingis Complaint* with its savage denunciation of 'ane tyke tratour Hammiltoun'. The brief Regencies of Lennox and Mar, the former also killed by the Hamiltons, ensued and Morton himself became Regent on 24 November 1572, coincidentally the very day John Knox had finally given up the ghost and gone to his just reward.

In March 1578, however, Morton's power base collapsed, and it was only by machiavellian manoeuverings that he was able to regain real power while acknowledging James VI as a nominal king in his own right. In February 1579 Blakhall's *Judge and revenge my cause* was presented to the King, perhaps as a way of deflecting attention from long-standing rumours of Morton's own involvement in Darnley's murder and, above all, enlisting the monarch's support for the destruction of the House of Hamilton. Morton's decision to use the art of music to ingratiate himself with James indicates that the boy's love of music was already well developed. Whether it was finally as a result of Blakhall's sugar coating or the bitter pill of Morton's power over him, James acceded, and in the spring of 1579, fired by a heady mixture of avarice, anti-Catholic zeal and sense of personal grievance at the murder of his ally Moray, Morton rained death and destruction upon the House of Hamilton. It was the long-anticipated dénouement of a drama which had begun in May 1570, when

> It was concluded that Hammiltons sould be punished in their substance, and by demolishing of their castells and houses . . . the castell [of Hamilton] was spoiled, and thereafter blowne up with powder.[9]

Blakhall's setting of *Judge and revenge my cause*, appropriately built upon a *cantus firmus* in the second tenor part consisting of a Sarum *miserere*, establishes a suitable tone of supplication by the frequent use of suspensions, and as the psalm proceeds, Blakhall demonstrates that he is a worthy heir of the tradition of High Renaissance polyphony. The vocal lines are beautifully crafted and evocatively reflect the sentiments of the text in ways which are at the same time subtle and unexpected.

Example 14.1

A variety of vocal textures alleviates the monotony which threatens less skilled syllabic settings.

Example
14.2

He makes masterly use of an inspired motif (in its High Renaissance introversion a close kinsman of phrases in the Mass *Felix namque*) which germinates in the first tenor part and surfaces first in the treble part only to pervade gradually the whole conclusion. This section is worthy of the great Thomas Tallis, and indeed there is more than a passing similarity between the final phrases of Blakhall's setting and and those of Tallis' *If ye love me*.

Example
14.3

This obvious English influence on Blakhall's music is a reflection of its provenance and also suggests the means by which Wode came by the three psalms mentioned above and the other music by Blakhall that he records. The head of St Mary's College and Rector of St Andrews University in the 1550s was John Douglas, a relative of the Regent Morton, whom the latter promoted to the Protestant Archbishopric of St Andrews following the execution of the last Catholic incumbent, John Hamilton—one of the principal engineers of the assassination of the Regent Moray, Wode's patron. The Douglases enjoyed close links with England at this time, and undoubtedly expected this to be reflected in the music they commissioned, an expectation that the aspiring Blakhall seems to have been only too pleased to satisfy.

The ascendancy of the pro-English faction, which seemed so complete with the triumph of Morton over the Hamiltons, was to be short-lived. In September 1579 there arrived at the Scottish court a man who would have an immense political and cultural impact, Esmé Stewart, Seigneur d'Aubigny, a first cousin of Darnley and a nephew of Robart Stewart, Earl of Lennox. The impressionable thirteen year old James, orphaned and starved of affection, was instantly star-struck with his sophisticated French cousin, showering him with titles and favours. In return Esmé Stuart, now Earl of Lennox, and soon to be created Duke, undertook to free him from the domineering Morton, an end finally accomplished, after much intrigue, with the beheading of the latter on 2 June 1581—for the murder of Darnley. It can hardly have been the outcome Morton had expected as he repeated his litany calling on the Lord for judgement and revenge.

Lennox's influence on James' policies had been evident before this though, and it is likely that it was he who persuaded the boy, a less than committed Calvinist, to exercise his royal prerogative to institute a 'tymous remeid' to the musical establishment.

Also round this time, and possibly in association with James' measures, there appeared *The Art of Music collectit out of all Ancient Doctouris of Music*. Besides the faburden Mass and *Magnificat* mentioned earlier[10] it contains a number of Protestant pieces including four harmonisations of psalms and an interesting variation on this, a *Psalm in Reports*, probably the work of Andrew Blakhall.[11] This piece takes the form of a canonic treatment in five parts of the original tune of Psalm 18, in the manner of a primitive fugue, with the voice parts answering one another in modified forms.

The Art of Music may have been compiled for the musical education of his pupils by a Sang Schule master[12] such as Andrew Buchan, Master of the Edinburgh Sang Schule in 1579. There are references to children in the text and the Sang Schules were enjoying a new lease of life at this time following James VI's 'tymous remeid'. If the treatise was a Sang Schule textbook, the education offered at these establishments was clearly of a very advanced order. This would seem to be borne out by the *Inverness Fragments'* inclusion of multiple settings of texts, which Stephen Allenson argues would have been used to train the boys in the performance and composition of the various kinds of faburden.[13]

Tracing their origins back to the twelfth century, the Sang Schules were

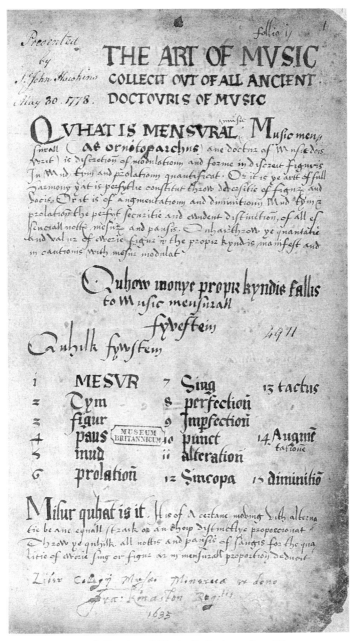

The title page of *The Art of Music* displaying a list of its contents
(*By permission of the British Library*)

intended to teach the basics of literacy and numeracy to choristers, who were also expected to be very well versed in all aspects of music. The contract of employment drawn up by the City of Aberdeen for Andro Kemp in 1570 gives us a good idea of what was expected of masters:

> To teiche and instruct thair youthheid and childreine in the said facultay of myseik, meaners and wertew, for payment of sic lesum dewtie as wse hes beine, and as in apparentis with the parentis and freindis of the bairns.[14]

In the sixteenth century many of the Sang Schule masters were respected mentors, performers and composers, and those whose music has been identified well deserve this respect. While standards obviously varied considerably, the best of these masters provided their students with a firm theoretical and practical grounding, thereby disseminating an appreciation and understanding of part-music.

During the disruptions of 1559/60, the Sang Schules suffered both materially and through the dismissal and intimidation of reluctant masters. But more fundamentally damaging was the advent of the Protestant service which removed the demand for skilled singers and polyphonic composers, and instead required personnel with only the most rudimentary knowledge of music. The mutually beneficial relationship built up over centuries between the Church and the most advanced forms of music-making began to break down. As the Reformed Church stifled part-music, the Sang Schules stagnated, and by 1579 the vicious circle had closed. The art of music was dying.

It was at this crucial point that the thirteen year old James VI stepped in with a statute which alerted the nation to the imminent demise of part-music, and which threw his regal weight soundly behind a reversal of this process of decay.[15] Issued on 11 November 1579, the statute contained specific and practical recommendations for the revival of the Sang Schules.

> For instruction of the youth in the art of musik and singing, quilk is almost decayit, and sall schortly decay, without tymous remeid be providit, our Soverane Lord with avise of his thrie estatis of this present parliament, requeistis the provest, baillies, counsale, and communitie of the maist speciall burrowis of this realm, and of the patronis and provestis of the collegis, quhair sang sculis are foundat, to erect and set up ane sang scuill, with ane maister sufficient and able for instructioun of the yowth in the said science of musik, as they will answer to his hienes upon the perrel of their fundationis, and in performing of his hienes reqheist do unto his Majestie acceptable and gude plesure.[16]

The 'Third Estaite', the Burgesses and Merchants, were being chided for their lack of commitment and forced to come up with adequate finance to provide for a whole network of Sang Schules. The plan was a notable success, and the Sang Schules took on a new lease of life, producing instrumental and vocal performers and, largely from the pens of such masters as Andro Kemp and John Blak, part-music to grace the less stringent Reformed services. The Edinburgh School re-opened in 1579 under its new master, Andrew Buchan, and by the turn of the century, with the ample support of the Burghs, many other Sang Schules were again thriving, albeit within the limited and limiting context of the Reformed Church.

Clearly, given a less astringent climate, talents such as those of Andro Blakhall might have flourished into the kind of post-Reformation flowering enjoyed in Elizabethan England. In Andro Blakhall and David Peebles, Scotland possessed composers with the creative potential of those giants of post-Reformation English music, the Protestant Thomas Tallis and the Catholic William Byrd, but while these latter were afforded the vital freedom and patronage to fulfil their potential, both Blakhall and David Peebles fell victim to the fundamentalism of radical Calvinism. While the Scotsman Robert Johnson produced a steady stream of accomplished instrumental and choral works in the conducive environment of Tudor England, back in Scotland his compatriots Peebles and Blakhall were frequently reduced to tinkering with psalm tunes. Such were the constraints under which it was composed that the bulk of the music in this section of the *Wode Part-books* does little more than bridge the gap between the Reformation of 1559/60 and James' 'tymous remeid' of 1579.

But thanks to the efforts of enlightened individuals such as Thomas Wode and the compiler of *The Art of Music*, the art of polyphony had survived the twenty-year war of attrition waged on it by the Calvinist Reformers. James VI also revived the flagging Chapel Royal by restoring its financial lifeblood and appointing as master Thomas Hudson.[17] When James called upon the singers of his Chapel to celebrate the baptism of his son Prince Henry in 1594, during the baptismal service, 'the provost and prebends of the Chapel Royal did sing the 21 psalme of David according to the art of musique to the great delectation of the noble auditorie'.[18] In respect of resources and aspirations, something of the old glory of this noble institution had evidently been restored.

15

The Amyable Organis
Music for the Organ

Of all the Calvinist obsessions which Knox absorbed during his stay in Geneva the most all-consuming was his hatred of the organ. It is an indication of the ubiquitous and conspicuous rôle played by this instrument in Old Church services that it became for Knox and the Calvinists a potent symbol of all that was most detestable about Catholicism. But any attempt to define the precise role of the organ in pre-Reformation services is confounded by the lack of Scottish music of this period written specifically for the organ. Since organists (then as now) would have been expected to improvise spontaneously, this absence of written music is scarcely surprising, but it makes any attempt to identify possible uses for the organ largely speculative in nature.

The history of the instrument in Scotland from the time of its reported introduction by James I in the fifteenth century to the early sixteenth century is relatively well documented.[1] A continuing royal interest in the instrument is increasingly complemented in the surviving records by the mention of instruments and players associated with cathedrals, collegiate and parish churches, and abbeys. By 1500 organs were established in the Parish Church of St Nicholas in Aberdeen, St Andrews Cathedral, the Collegiate Church of the Holy Trinity and St Giles Cathedral in Edinburgh, St Mary's in Dundee and in Dunglass, and in Kinloss and Fearn Abbeys. In 1496 mention is made of instruments being transported at James IV's request to Stirling and back to Edinburgh the following year, while shortly afterwards payments were made to John Goldsmith of Inverness for various services associated with the transportation of the royal instrument accompanying James on a pilgrimage to St Duthac's shrine at Tain in the Highlands, taking in Aberdeen on the way.[2]

Chapel Royal inventories noted in 1505 that that establishment owned no fewer than three organs, two pipe organs and a reed organ, while, as we have seen, James' extensive improvements to his palace at Linlithgow in 1512–3 included the installation of an organ there by a member of the Carver family.[3]

Payments are also made in 1511–2 by James IV's treasurer to 'Gilzeame, Francheman, that makis the organis' who later went on to be paid for playing them. Although the inference is that these organs were used in conjunction with the performance of choral music, the highly embellished polyphony in the repertoire of the Chapel Royal around this time (such as the earlier works in the *Carver Choirbook*) is, because of its melismatic elaboration, quite unsuited for keyboard rendition. Even the *cantus firmi* of Carver's earliest works are frequently embellished to a degree and in a manner which makes them fundamentally unidiomatic for keyboard performance.

Yet if organs played no part in the performance of polyphonic choral music, the puzzling fact remains that by the turn of the century many of the major establishments which performed choral polyphony in the early sixteenth century apparently boasted at least one organ and an organist. The fact that the organists were frequently attached to the Sang Schules gives a hint of the type of playing required of them. Is it possible that they served to help the singers to learn lines in much the same way as a rehearsal pianist functions today? Almost certainly they played some part in services, too, perhaps filling awkward gaps in the elaborate pageant which made up the celebration of the Mass, by providing extemporised treatments of motifs from the chant or the polyphonic setting of the Ordinary of the Mass.

Although not set out specifically as keyboard pieces, a number of treatments of plainchant *cantus firmi* recorded in *The Art of Music* in the section on 'Countering' lend themselves to performance on the organ and may well represent a written record of the sort of improvisations expected of organists. Typical of this body of music is a counter on the plainchant *Kyrie, Pater Creator omnium*,[4] which bears the inscription 'The plane sang brokin' but no underlay, and consists of the plainchant in stained regular notes framed above by a decorated version of the *cantus* and below by a freely composed line in a rhythmically animated style. (As the upper line is itself an embellished version of the plainchant, the *cantus* should be omitted in performance.)

Example 15.1

Elsewhere in *The Art of Music* a wealth of techniques for improvisation and elaboration on church tunes present themselves to the organist. Faburden provides a simple harmonisation of a plainchant line, while the more adventurous performer may have tried his hand at some 'countering'. The intrepid may even have investigated the obscurities of canon.

> Quhat is ane canone? It is ane institutione of noittis or wordis direckit be the arbitar of the compositor schawand be diverss signis the augmentation and diminucion of figuris and be exemplis of resolutione opynnand the enigmateis of abscuir tenoris and sangis, quhilkis be diapenthe, diatessaron, and diapason sangis or tenoris up or down for thair propir placis harmonicall dois deduce and remov. Of the quhilkis canones na certan rewill may be gevin bot that the formes of the sentence institut and observit.[5]

Whatever the rôle of the organist in the service, it is probably significant that at this time organ-playing is always mentioned as a decoration of the service quite distinct from the choral polyphony.[6]

As less ornate polyphonic music began to appear from about 1520 onwards, it is easier to conceive of a rôle for the organ in conjunction with the choir. Furthermore, in 1531 John Fethy returned from a protracted study visit on the Continent to become first a canon and then 'Chantour' (precentor) of the Chapel Royal in the mid 1540s, as well as being master of the Sang Schule in Aberdeen before handing over to his deputy John Blak in 1546, and taking up a post in 1551 as master in the choir school in Edinburgh, which he held until 1568.[7] According to Thomas Wode, this important and influential musician 'brought in Scotland the curious new fingering and playing on organs'—surely a reference to the introduction of a style of playing which involved all of the digits including the 'pinkies', allowing the practitioner to tackle 'curious' music, that is, polyphonic music.[8] A player with this facility would have little difficulty in accompanying performances of works such as the Mass *Felix namque*. This breakthrough in organ technique coincided fortuitously with the increased application of the principle of pervading imitation in polyphonic composition in Scotland, and as a result, the bulk of choral polyphony began to lie under the fingers (and, indeed, pinkies) of the next generation of organists who had encountered Fethy's new method at one of the Sang Schules at which he was active. A brief passage in the romance *Clariodus* of about this time may reflect the new situation.

> The mes was song with note full curious,
> With organ sound and thimpand melodious.[9]

It was at this promising point in the development of organ-playing that the fury of the Reformation was unleashed on the instrument. The mobs of 1559/60 undoubtedly destroyed a number of instruments, and as Calvinism became established throughout Scotland, the organ was systematically barred from church use. The court, in many respects insulated from the extremes of the religious climate in the world outside, managed to preserve the Chapel Royal instruments through the initial turmoil, but when the Earl of Mar took custody of Stirling Castle in 1567, he had all three of them destroyed, for which he was heartily congratulated by the Reformed Parliament. Elsewhere, organ-playing became an increasingly hazardous exception rather than the rule, an activity frowned upon by the Calvinists and condoned only where the New Faith was insecure. While some music which has survived from the later sixteenth century, such as the anonymous *Ground* preserved in *Duncan Burnett's Music-book*,[10] or John Blak's *Lytill Blak*[11] would be eminently suitable for performance on the organ, it is doubtful whether many people outside privileged court circles would either dare to play organ music, or indeed find an instrument in suitable playing condition on which to perform it. Increasingly deprived of their traditional rôle in church music, organs were regarded as redundant curiosities.

In the first half of the sixteenth century the royal accounts had attested to the great effort and expense lavished on the transportation, setting up and maintainance of a prized possession. From 1560 to the beginning of the seventeenth century, the most frequent mention made of organs is a sad catalogue of the sale of isolated instruments either into private hands or for scrap value. One of the more poignant stages in this inexorable decline is marked by the account of the dismantling of the fabric of Bishop Elphinstone's Parish Church of St Nicholas in Aberdeen in 1574. The Privy Council requires 'That the organis with all expeditioun be removed out of the kirk, and made proffite of to the use and support of the pure'.[12] Organs continued to make irregular appearances at court-promoted celebrations, such as the ceremonial entry into Edinburgh on 19 May 1590 of James VI and his Queen when 'Organs and Regals thair did carpe' and 'a brave youth played upon the organs, which accorded excellentlie with the singing of thair psalms'.[13] However, with the departure of the court in 1603, while the James' access to the English coffers after the Union of the Crowns in 1603 permitted more lavish celebration, the visits to Scotland became increasingly infrequent. In preparation for one such sojourn 'a fair, large, and very serviceable double organ'[14] was commissioned from a London organ maker, transported to Leith and set up in the Chapel Royal at Holyroodhouse, where on Saturday 17 May 1617 there was 'singing of quiristours, surplices, and playing on organes' and on 19 August 'the organes and musitians, four on everie part, men and boyes, agreit in pleasant harmonie'. On this occasion 'the ministers of Edinburgh were silent, neither disswading the King in private, nor opening their mouth in publick.'[15]

For the Scottish coronation of Charles I in 1633 another organ was brought north and installed at Holyroodhouse and used in conjunction with twenty singers, also specially imported for the occasion. Again the ministers of the Reformed Kirk bided their time. Then in 1638 the Chapel Royal was attacked in riots following the signing of the National Covenant[16] and 'The glorious organes of the cheppell royall brokin doune . . . and the costlie organes altogidder destroyit'.[17]

When the Chapel Royal instrument fell silent for the last time, the fate of the organ in Scotland was sealed. The Stewarts had been dedicated in their promotion of the organ, and the withdrawal of their patronage proved decisive. Organs would play practically no part in music-making in Scotland for over two centuries.

16

Viols with Voices in Plain Counterpoint

Instruments in Church Music

Ye rychteous rejoyis and love the Lord,
Just men to thank thair God dois weil accord.
Play on your lute, & sweitly sing,
Tak harpe in hand with monie lustie string,
Tyrle on the ten stringit instrument,
And pryse your God with hart and haill intent.
Sing na auld thing the quhilk is abrogate,
Bot sing sum new pleasand perfite ballat:
Blaw up organis, with glaid & hevinlie sound
Joyfull in hart, quhill all the skyis resound.

While the Scots translation of the thirty-third Psalm in *The Gude and Godlie Ballatis*[1] seems to advocate the use of a rich and varied array of instruments in praise of the Lord, such literary accounts of performance practices are rightly viewed with some scepticism. We have seen that Scots musicians outwith court circles were hardly being encouraged to 'blaw up organis' in the years after the Reformation (or at least not in the sense intended by the psalmist!), and it seems likely that while the presence of the other instruments was tolerated in a psalm text, their participation in a Reformed service would have been inconceivable.

But earlier in the century the situation seems have been rather different. Ironically it is criticism by an early reformer that suggests that instruments may have played an active part in performances of Scottish church music. In his *Commentary on the Rule of St Augustine* of 1530, Robert Richardson had made a point of condemning their use in a religious context. 'The custom of singing

and playing [instruments] in church was introduced for carnal [minds] therefore, not for spiritual [minds].'[2]

While he adds the proviso that this custom is practised 'in almost the whole
world', indicating perhaps that he was commenting only on the situation which
he observed around him in France and attempting to pre-empt the introduction of this practice into Scotland, it is equally possible that he was also
criticising the current state of affairs in Scotland, which already conformed
with what was happening in France.[3] For special occasions at the Scottish court,
the singers of the Chapel Royal seem to have been supported by organs and
other instruments. I have already speculated regarding the participation of
trumpets in a performance of Carver's six-part Mass marking the launch of the
Great Michael in 1512.[4] In February 1513 'Gilzeame, organar, Francheman,
and his comlicis, Franche menstralis' were paid for performances which may
well have involved the Chapel Royal, and later in 1513 James' treasurer settled
an account for 'Italiane menstralis for thame and the Franch tabernis, fidlaris,
organeris, trumpetteris',[5] while the ratification of the marriage treaty between
Mary, Queen of Scots and Edward of England in 1543 was celebrated with a
High Mass 'solemnly sung with Shalms and Sackbutts'.[6] Probably many of the
other instrumentalists engaged at court in the first half of the sixteenth century
also participated in the performance of church music.

Instruments such as viols may also have made a further contribution to pre-
Reformation services by providing instrumental interludes based on plainchant

Sixteenth century English boy choristers and adult male singers perform church music
from a choirbook to the accompaniment of two crumhorns and a trumpet. The
'preceptour', standing beside the lectern, directs the choir with a motion of his hand,
while behind him we can just make out a cornettist and a sackbutter
(*The Hulton Deutsch Collection*)

cantus firmi. While the anonymous two-part counter on *Pater Creator omnium* works well on the organ, more elaborate pieces recorded in the 'Countering' section of *The Art of Music*, such as the four-part counter on the same *cantus*[7] and the three-part counter on the 'gratias agimus tibi' section of the *Gloria*[8] chant defy keyboard performance and are clearly consort music.

After the Reformation, the use of instruments in conjunction with voices in church music seems to have been restricted to special celebrations at court. An account of Mary's celebration of Easter 1565 is probably intended rather to outrage the Protestant English court than accurately to reflect reality.

> Greater triumphe ther was never in anye tyme of moste Poperie, then was thys Easter, at the Resurrection and at her Hye Masse, Organyes was wonte to be the common musycke; she wanted nowe neither trompet, drumme nor fyffe, bagge pype nor tabor.[9]

Much more reliable as a piece of documentary evidence is the description of the court celebrations marking the baptism of James VI's first-born son, Henry, at which 'there was sung with most delicate dulce voices, and sweet harmonie, in seven parts, the 128th psalm, with fourteen voyces, and musical instruments playing'.[10]

Andro Blakhall had set the same celebratory text, *Blessed art thou*, in five parts some twenty years earlier, and this seven-part setting may well also have been his work. It is significant that the performance was not part of the baptismal service itself, at which the Chapel Royal sang (probably unaccompanied) the twenty-first Psalm, but rather a contribution to the secular rejoicing afterwards, organised by William Fowler, a member of the Castalian Band and personal secretary to the Queen. Sadly the music has not survived, but the sound of the voices of the Chapel Royal, singing in seven parts (two to a part) combined with the harps, viols, oboes, recorders and flutes, which are mentioned elsewhere in the report, must have been very impressive indeed.

Outwith court circles, any participation by instruments in church services would have ceased shortly after 1560. However the Reformed Church seems to have been less dogmatic about the composition of religious instrumental music for domestic use, presumably on the assumption that people would not suddenly reject instruments they had played and enjoyed all their lives, and if they were to play them, they may as well serve the glory of God and the consolidation of the Reformed Faith. To this end Protestant composers simply adopted the *cantus firmus* principle, exchanging the discredited plainchant melodies for psalm tunes.

An isolated example of this occurs in the *Carver Choirbook* in the form of what appears to be a two-part counter on the first Psalm.[11] This rudimentary piece, probably the last music to be copied into the great *Choirbook* in the mid 1560s, sets a bass line to a decorated version of the original psalm tune in the manner of the two-part counter on *Pater Creator omnium*. It was most likely the work of one of the Chapel Royal singers, and as it appears in association with pieces with underlay in Carver's own handwriting, it is just conceivable that Carver himself was trying his hand at the sort of simple composition which he realised was already replacing the great masterpieces which filled the *Choirbook*. The image of the ageing Carver, nearing the end of his long life, toying with a psalm tune, is indeed a haunting one. We can only hope that rather than seeing in it the agent of his own obsolescence, he somehow recognised the means by which the art of music would survive the darkness that clouded his final years. Perhaps before his death he had the consolation of witnessing the emergence of the first green shoots of Protestant part-music from the ashes of the Reformation. He might even have managed a wry smile as he recognised the *cantus firmus* principle now serving the New Church just as effectively as it once served the Old.

Probably the most successful of these *cantus firmus* treatments of psalm tunes are those by the Protestant composer John Blak. In addition to providing original psalm tunes and harmonisations for the Reformed cause, he also clothed these in the form of *Lessones on Psalmes*, which appear anonymously in *The Art of Music*. While Blak does seem to have embraced the New Faith, his Reformed credentials seem to have been less than watertight: he lost his job as Sang Schule master at Aberdeen in the upheavals of 1559/60, regaining it only after a sojourn of some fifteen years abroad. While the influence of Calvinism was still far from all-pervading (in Scotland some Sang Schule masters who did not abandon Catholicism managed to retain their posts), it seems more likely that the context for pieces such as Blak's *Lessones* had already shrunk to performance as part of an evening of private secular music-making—or perhaps their inclusion in *The Art of Music* indicates a further reduction in status, namely to that of abstract examples illustrating theoretical points for his Sang Schule pupils and never intended for performance.[12]

Blak's *Lessones* take the form of elaborate polyphonic fantasias in three voices built upon a fourth voice, the psalm tune, which appears in sustained notes in the tenor. Blak demonstrates that he is well acquainted with the finer points of the application of High Renaissance suspensions and English dissonances, and in his elegant *Lessone upon the first Psalme*[13], the fluidity and range of the accompanying voices is impressive.

Example 16.1

In his more assertive *Lessone upon the secund Psalme*,[14] cross-rhythms, suggested by the original psalm tune, permeate the texture, and Blak displays considerable facility with these rhythmical devices too.

Example 16.2

It is unfortunate that so little of Blak's music has survived, and it is again to be lamented that talents such as Blak undoubtedly possessed had such a restricted field in which to exercise.

Within these boundaries the composers of the early Reformed Church show a dogged inventiveness in their treatment of psalm tunes. Settings of Psalms 1, 6, 7 and 58, which appear earlier in *The Art of Music* in the section entitled 'setting of sangis',[15] consist of lively four-part instrumental consorts built around the psalm tune in the tenor, and it is perhaps significant that the composer presupposes that the tunes move rather more briskly than we might have expected. A further way of treating psalm tunes was the 'Psalm in Reports', and we have an excellent example of this in Andro Blakhall's setting of Psalm 18 in reports.[16] The writing is more adventurously contrapuntal than in the anonymous four-part settings, and the psalm tune appears in the top line. While the application of underlay to permit vocal performance poses few problems, the fact that all these works appear without text in *The Art of Music* suggests that they were intended as consort pieces, possibly with voices singing the familiar psalm tune.

More ambitious still from the point of view of its compositional technique is John Blak's *Lessoune upone the Fyfty Psalme*, a combined treatment of the tune for Psalm 50 and the secular song *When sall my sorrowful sichings slack* by Thomas Tallis.[17] This four-part consort builds upon the *cantus firmus* principle of Blak's earlier settings by placing the psalm tune in the tenor in the customary way, but then going on to interweave fragments of the Tallis piece with freely composed material in the other three parts. Blak does not quite achieve the complete mastery of his material necessary to allow him to play around with allusion in the carelessly brilliant manner of Carver in his Mass *L'Homme Armé*, but the overall intention is similar.

A fact that emerges from this consideration of music in the early Reformed Church is that all the composers of merit whose works have survived were trained under the Sang Schule regimes or in the abbeys of the Old Church, and that in producing their finest music, they were applying the same compositional devices as the previous generation and were in the main working above and beyond the strictures of the Reformed Church. The official Reformed Church, hemmed in on all sides by the musical strait-jacket of Calvinism, produced little of value, while actively smothering the creative gifts of a whole generation of composers. Again it is Wode who puts his finger on the central problem faced by the composers of music for the Reformed Church.

> I have said in one of thir bukis that musik will pereishe and this buke will shaw you sum resons quhy. We se be experience that craft nor syence is na learnit bot to the end he may leive be it quhen he hes the craft or science.

The Reformed Church denied composers their very *raison d'être*, and the complete neglect of all branches of music which ensued as Calvinism tightened its stranglehold on Scottish culture, also sealed the fate of those choirbooks containing the music of previous generations which had escaped the mobs in 1559/60. No longer comprehensible in an age which prized simple melodies and basic homophonic settings, and denied their place in church services, the surviving choirbooks were doomed.

Musicians have little to thank the Scottish Reformers for. Such is the contrast with the splendour of post-Reformation England in the later sixteenth century that it is difficult for the musician to view the influence of Knox and the Calvinists as anything but entirely negative. But musicians rarely shape history. Robert Carver and John Knox were both products of the same nation—but it is as yet upon the latter alone that Scotland has conferred immortality.

17

A New Kind of Chaunting and Musick

The Music of the High Renaissance and of the Reformed Church in Performance

The refinement of line and breadth of phrase in High Renaissance polyphony puts a new emphasis on stamina and the ability to sustain an even line rather than on vocal virtuosity. There is more time to blend the tuning and balance of each individual chord and to shape each individual phrase to an extent which is rarely possible with Carver. Yet if High Renaissance polyphony might seem 'easier' than the earlier ornate style, this is not the case.

Its very simplicity brings its own pitfalls. The vocal quality of each part must be flawless—vibrato deprives refined lines of focus, and protruding voices ruin the polished veneer of a performance. Entries must be precise but subtle, individual notes defined but linked by an uninterrupted legato, diction clear but unobtrusive, tuning impeccable.

Within these bounds there is considerable scope for the expressive singing the texts frequently cry out for. Often it is the telling detail, the single note emphasised, the almost imperceptible swell, the weighting of a significant motif which makes a memorable performance. In order to decide what is significant and what is not, the director ought to have some grasp of the structural principles underlying the construction of the piece.

There can have been few substantial differences between the choral forces which Carver had at his disposal and those which would have performed the High Renaissance works, and their vocal production must have been very similar, bearing in mind that the singers in question will have been of the same generation—possibly even the same individuals. Perhaps in the new climate of High Renaissance refinement the slight edge essential for the virtuosic articulation of Carver was mellowed somewhat.

In performing Scottish music in High Renaissance style, singers should bear in mind the acoustic properties when selecting performance venues. The sustained lines of High Renaissance polyphony are much helped by a resonant acoustic, which makes the upper parts in particular much easier to support. Important too are the ideas concerning context which were aired in the section on Carver in performance.[1] The listener can have his receptivity dulled by too much refined polyphony pouring over him without a break—and what better way to punctuate the likes of the Mass *Felix namque* than with relevant plainchant?

Finally, what of the notes the performers will choose to sing? The colouring of various crucial points in a motet will be dictated, not by the notes which the composer wrote, but by how the editor applies the controversial and negotiable rules of *musica ficta*. Performers will notice, for example, that the ravishing *tierces de picardie* at the end of Kenneth Elliott's editions of *Descendi in hortum meum* and *Si quis diligit me*, while undoubtedly justified, are both editorial. A director who feels sufficiently well versed in the vagaries of *musica ficta* may care to enter this minefield under his own colours, particularly when using older editions.

Scottish High Renaissance music is extremely rewarding to sing. As performers, we have found that of all the early Scottish repertoire, it evokes the readiest response from audiences, seduced by its sheer beauty—and it is a cold man who is not moved by the nobility of *Si quis diligit me*.

It will be clear from the account of the fortunes of part-music in Scotland during the Reformation period that the music composed differs from that of the High Renaissance in quality rather than in kind. Composers were still using essentially the same compositional techniques as previous generations, such as *cantus firmus*, imitation and the other devices outlined in *The Art of Music*. The only real difference was in the scale of the pieces they were producing in the increasingly restrictive context of post-Reformation Scotland. Of all the Protestant music which has survived from the later sixteenth century, Andro Blakhall's polyphonic psalm settings, composed under the protective wing of the Court, are the least touched by Reformed restrictions. They inhabit the same musical world as Peebles' Latin motets, and performers will probably find that a similar style of performance will be appropriate.

Homophonic settings, such as Kemp's *Te Deum* and the harmonised psalms with their short emphatic phrases and uncomplicated harmonies, rich in decisive modulation and practically devoid of suspensions, call for a more assertive delivery. They are, after all, evangelising battle songs, radically different in intention from any of the church music composed before the Reformation, and any attempt to recapture their original spirit must take this distinction into account. It should also be noted that the pronunciation of the English texts cannot by any stretch of the imagination have been other than extremely Scots; observation of this fact will assist forthrightness.[2] But as many singers will probably judge the choral music of this period inferior in conception to the earlier splendours of Carver and the High Renaissance, it seems more fruitful to move on to the rôle of the instrumentalist in church music, which was being consolidated in the second half of the sixteenth century.

If the organist is to be excluded from performances of ornate music such as that of Robert Carver,[3] and perhaps even from performances of High Renaissance music, which may be judged more effective in an entirely vocal rendition, what is left for a player interested in sixteenth century Scottish music? I have suggested that organists may care to attempt improvisatory movements on plainchant and, by analogy, on psalm tunes using the techniques described in *The Act of Music*, but a more reliable source of material is to be found in the religious consort pieces, some of which adapt readily to organ performance. Careful selection of contrasting registrations can result in a very pleasing rendition of Blak's *Lessones*, while the scalic patterns of his *Lytill Black* and the anonymous *Ground* feel very much at home on the organ.

There is also, as we have seen, no shortage of music based on church tunes suitable for a consort of instruments, and the baptismal celebrations of 1594 suggest that a consort of viols was only one of several performance options. The 'musick in greene hoylne howboyes, in fine parts' and the 'still noise of recorders and flutes' may well have been presentations of consort pieces built on psalm tunes such as John Blak's *Lessones* or Blakhall's *Reports*. Certainly much of this substantial body of Protestant consort music sounds very effective on a variety of period instruments.

As the century progressed, instruments seem to have assumed an increasingly important rôle in church music in combination with voices. Protestant part-music such as Andro Blakhall's polyphonic psalms certainly seems to invite the participation of instruments, although it should be borne in mind that, while the circle for whom he was writing seem to have tolerated polyphonic composition, their attitude to the involvement of instruments may have been less enlightened. It was, after all, the same Earl of Mar for whose daughter's wedding in 1573 Blakhall set *Blessed art thou*, who less than ten years earlier had destroyed the Chapel Royal organs!

The patchy survival of material from this period is a drawback. Where documentary evidence survives of modes of performance, as in the baptism of 1594, none of the music mentioned has survived. Conversely none of the surviving music of the period can be definitively associated with events which mention performance details–thwarting indeed for performers aiming at authentic performances of large-scale Scottish church music combining voices and period instruments! It is a state of affairs that would seem to demand some degree of pragmatism, and a presentation of a Blakhall's five-part setting of *Blessed art thou* using voices and instruments is probably as near as we can ever hope to get to the splendours of Prince Henry's baptism.

In any case, performances of church music on this scale must have been completely unrepresentative of the situation in the rest of Scotland. Since 1560, the performance of part-music had increasingly become the embattled prerogative of the Court, and as we have seen, in the first half of the seventeenth century the scale of court-promoted music-making, which marked occasional royal visits to Scotland, and the general status of music in the country between these visits, contrasted more and more dramatically.

In 1615 a Psalter was published in Aberdeen, the first since the *Scottish Psalter* of 1564. It was quickly followed in 1625 and 1633 by two further printed Psalters containing part-music, including psalms in reports by Scottish composers. In 1634 a similar Psalter appeared in Edinburgh, and in 1635 Edward Millar, Master of the Chapel Royal, brought out a lavish Psalter with part-music by John Angus, Andro Blakhall, David Peebles, John Blak and others. Two years later in 1637 the increasing dislocation between the British court and the Scots reached crisis point when an ill-judged attempt by Charles I to bring the religious practices of the northern reaches of his realm into line with the Anglican Church provoked violent resistance. At the end of February 1638 the National Covenant, detailing opposition to the 'corruptions of the public government of the Kirk' was signed in Edinburgh, and the pattern was set for the rest of the century.

Part-music, still identified in the Calvinist mind with the decadent and religiously suspect court, bore the full brunt of the backlash against Charles I. The Chapel Royal at Holyrood was ransacked, and collections of music acquired during Charles' reign were destroyed.[4] In 1650 Edward Millar's 1635 Psalter was replaced by a Psalter devoid of music. Part-music became a thing of the past, and in ensuing Psalters which did have music even the irregular rhythms of some of the psalm tunes were standardised,[5] the final stifling of compositional individuality.

Within thirty-five years of the grand exodus in 1603, the long, musically barren shadow of Presbyterianism had fallen across the whole of religious life in Scotland. At a time when cathedrals all over the Continent were resounding to the magnificent musical clarion-call of the High Baroque, Scotland was caught in the grip of a musical ice-age, the effects of which are still felt today. Attention turned from the study and composition of music to areas of knowledge better suited to the Presbyterian mentality, the sciences and philosophy. The foundation was being laid for the Scottish Enlightenment, but it was a foundation built upon the ruins of Scotland's pre-Reformation culture.

Works on the apparently irrational scale of Robert Carver's Mass settings or of the cathedrals in which they were performed have no place in a world dominated by reason. Perhaps even to attempt to understand such infinite aspiration would have threatened the new secure sense of perspective, the new metrical scale in which man was the measure of all. But then even in our own century the fundamental changes in perspective demanded by the 'rediscovery' of the sacred music of sixteenth century Scotland have proved difficult to realise.

Part Two

SECULAR MUSIC

(Previous page) This informal portrait, assumed to represent James IV, shows a man
of considerable aesthetic refinement
(*National Galleries of Scotland*)

18

A General Consort of the Best Instruments

Music at Court

It is scarcely surprising that the Stewart Kings of Scots demanded of their secular music at court standards that were every bit as high as those they required of their church music. They must have listened with rapt attention to accounts by Scottish diplomats and students returning from England and the Continent waxing eloquent about the lavish scale of court celebrations. While a limited purse, a spectre which haunted all Scottish monarchs, prevented the Stewarts from indulging in similarly boundless extravagance, they seemed determined to match their wealthy European counterparts in quality at least. The secular music which has survived from the sixteenth century represents probably only the tiniest fragment of the music composed for court, but it does at least provide a fair cross-section of vocal music, both ensemble and solo, consort music and solo instrumental music, and much of it is both distinctively Scottish and of high quality.

With the exception of James VI, whose musical gifts seem to have been restricted to appreciation, the Stewarts were accomplished practical musicians, and they seem to have made it a priority to surround themselves with music at court, in royal progression, at ceremonies, on military campaign and even in captivity. Music would seem to have satisfied a personal desire rather than representing mere regal ostentation.

While Gawain Douglas' account of music-making in the *Palice of Honour* of around 1500 clearly embodies a degree of poetic licence, the knowledge of specialist musical vocabulary that he demonstrates here and elsewhere in his poetry suggests that his idealised vision was at least based on reality.

> In modulation hard I sing
> Faburdoun, pricksong, discant, countering,
> Cant organe, figuratioun, and gemmell;
> On croud, lute, harp, and mony gudlie spring
> Schalmes, clariounis, portatives, hard I ring,
> Monycord, organe, tympane, and cymbill,
> Sytholl, psalterie, and voices sweet as bell
> Soft releschingis in dulce delivering,
> Fractionis divide, at rest, or clois compel.[1]

The methods of composition and improvisation mentioned in the first three lines all have concordances in *The Art of Music*, and we must assume that the catalogue of instruments in the ensuing four lines also had real counterparts in the Scottish court.

The range of musical instruments available to enhance the court of a Renaissance ruler was considerable—a sound to grace every occasion. For the spectacular outdoor ceremony there were fanfare trumpets (clariounis), often accompanied by sackbuts and drums (tympane), and Douglas would suggest that cymbals were also used in this context. The trumpets could be augmented or replaced by the more nimble cornett, or by a variety of loud double-reed instruments, such as shawms (schalmes), rauschpfeifen, or any of a host of other outdoor reed instruments which in Scottish documents hid their light under the all-embracing term of 'pypes'.

For more intimate indoor gatherings there were the gentle tones of flutes and recorders (at this time wide-bore instruments with a broad, breathy tone and clarity of articulation). Stringed instruments included the popular rebec and the viol, both instruments available in a variety of sizes, but which were gradually replaced during the course of the sixteenth century by the violin family. To these bowed strings may be added a number of plucked instruments such as the smaller harps and the lutes and their relatives, which seem to have been present in particular diversity in sixteenth century Scotland.

Gawain Douglas indicates that a number of more unusual stringed instruments with ancient ancestry were also in courtly use. The croud was a type of bowed lyre which can be traced back to the eleventh century and has been more recently revived as the Welsh crwth, while the sytholl or citole is thought to be an early ancestor of the gittern, a mediaeval guitar with four strings and a flat back. The psalterie consisted of metal strings stretched across a triangular sound box, and it was played by strumming or plucking with the fingers or a quill. It came to Europe from the Middle East during the Crusades and enjoyed considerable popularity. It is less clear what Gawain Douglas meant by the monycord. An instrument called the monochord which made use of movable bridges to alter the pitch of the strings did exist in the Middle Ages, but it is more likely that he is refering to the later clavichord, a more practical keyboard instrument relying on the same principle.

All of these instruments could be used on their own or in small homogeneous consorts made up of members of the same family, such as the recorders or the viols, or mixed consorts comprising both wind and strings, accompanied perhaps by a keyboard instrument of the plucked string variety or by a small regal or a pipe organ—either the small portative instrument or the full sized organe. These indoor instruments could in turn be combined with singing 'voices sweet as bell' to provide further variety.

Throughout the 1500s records of payments made to a host of musicians attest to the regular appearance at court of shawmers, sackbutters, violers, recorder players and lutenists to mention but a selection. But for the latter part of the century a more graphic record exists. In addition to providing a high proportion of the Scottish music which has survived from the sixteenth century, the *Wode Part-books* helpfully supply spectacular illustrations of many of the instruments in use at the time. In addition to the expected wide-bore recorders, shawms, harps, viols and organs there are also extravagantly convoluted trumpets and an inordinate variety of plucked instruments of the lute family, as well as illustrations offering some more curious insights into Scottish music-making such as a three-holed bladder-pipe played by a piglet! Wode's illustrations are complemented by a number of other pictorial representations of secular music-making, including most spectacularly the Muses' ceiling in Crathes Castle, which depicts women playing treble and bass viols, harp, cittern, lute, portative organ and a curious flute with a pronounced conical bell.

Sadly, few practical details have survived of instrumentation or of performance practice at the Scottish court, but by using the limited information supplied by accounts and records and by making analogies with England and the Continent, it is possible to piece together something of a picture of music-making at the Stewart courts of the sixteenth century.

19

Menstralis and Musicians
The Court of James IV

In the late fifteenth century James IV, himself an accomplished player of the clarsach, attracted a steady stream of Gaelic harper-minstrels from the north and west of his Kingdom. At this time Scottish culture was not yet entirely dominated by the Scots-speaking central belt, and James was the last Scottish monarch to speak Gaelic and to possess a genuine understanding of all areas of his Kingdom. These minstrels and their Scots-speaking counterparts combined the talents of setting their own words to music and accompanying themselves as they sang or declaimed their work—both words and music may frequently have been improvised. While its ephemeral nature has precluded the survival of this music, some idea of the high quality of the poetry can be obtained from the Scots romances that survive from the fourteenth, fifteenth and sixteenth centuries, most notably the epic *Bruce* (1375–77) by John Barbour (c 1320–1395) and Hary's *Wallace* (1476–78).[1] These poems combine historical material with anecdotal accretions in an explicitly patriotic statement couched in verse of the highest quality.

John Purser[2] has demonstrated that another of the great Scottish epic poems, *Greysteil*, fits the tune of that name in *Robert Gordon of Straloch's Lute Book*[3] and the convincing results probably come very close to the performance of the piece which is known to have been given in the presence of James IV in 1497 by two fiddlers, possibly from the Highlands.

In addition to the visiting 'Heland bardis', James' court gave casual employment to 'fydlaris' (probably at this date, players of the rebec) and to 'pyparis' (playing, probably, a variety of reed instruments, including perhaps some uniquely native varieties) as well as to 'singaris', soloists and small groups alike. More in keeping with what was expected of a Renaissance prince, James also played keyboards of the virginal type and employed a corps of trumpeters for ceremonial use.[4] But significantly, if the random survival of music from this period is anything to go by, it is the more subtle and intimate indoor music which seems to have been his chief delight.

With James' marriage to Margaret Tudor in 1503, the English influence at court began to be felt more strongly. The lute began to oust the harp as the main solo and accompanying instrument, and among the group of four English musicians maintained by the Queen for her own entertainment were two lutenists. A piece such as the anonymous song *Alas that same sueit face*[5] (which has survived in a manuscript of the mid-seventeenth century but which seems stylistically to date from the early sixteenth century) could have been given a charming and varied performance by this small group.

The other substantial piece of secular music to survive from the reign of James IV is more of a curiosity, posing more questions than it answers. Preserved in the *Wode Part-books*, *My heartly service*,[6] also known as *The Pleugh Sang*, is an extended song for two voices and accompanying bass line. The curious text, full of double meanings and topical allusions, and the episodic medley construction recall the French *fricassée*[7] or the more protracted compositions of the *Fayrfax Book* (c. 1505), such as *Joan is sick*, or *Hey trolly lolly lo* from *Henry VIII's Manuscript*; but the range of musical styles, from chordal syllabic setting to complex Carveresque counterpoint, employed in *The Pleugh Sang*, together with the rapid exchange of dialogue between the lines, set the piece outside any category one would care to name.

It begins with an appeal to the ploughmen's Lord, their employer, which is set canonically in the two vocal lines and is followed by discussion of the demerits of a certain ox, which to judge by the frequent interpolations and interruptions, would seem to have outlived his usefulness as a draught animal. The solution is proposed that the ploughmen stay on hand to replace the ox should he drop in his tracks. The musical imitation subsides as the two voices alternately call out the names of the ploughmen: 'Ginken and Wilken, Higgin and Habken, Hankin and Rankin, Robert and Colin, Nicol and Colin, Hector

Example 19.1

and Aikin, Michael and Morice, False-lips Fergus . . .' A competition among the ploughmen is announced followed by the anticipated death of 'the old ox Tripfree', and presently the upper voice embarks on an inventory of the parts of the plough, while the lower voice takes up the bass drone in canon. The final section culminates in a chaotic series of shouted instructions and encouragements, as the ploughmen urge on the competing teams, crowned rather unexpectedly with a contrapuntal appeal to the Trinity and an elaborate Amen.

Taken literally, the piece could be seen to represent ploughmen advertising their services to potential employers at a 'feeing market', much as they did in many parts of Scotland well into the present century. Just as these 'feeing markets' doubled as romantic trysting places (they were frequently referred to as 'the feeing and fairing') so there is an implicit sexual undercurrent in *The Pleugh Sang*, linking it perhaps with still more ancient fertility rites. But while the music is reminiscent throughout of folk music and may even preserve strands of popular melodies in its voice parts, the more involved part-writing would seem to set it outwith the realm of genuine folk music. Much more probably it is a parody, designed for performance by professional musicians, possibly even at court. It is possible to take this idea a stage further and picture the piece acted out in costume by enthusiastic aristocratic amateurs—a temporary rôle-reversal which has many courtly parallels. The Stewart Kings had always prided themselves on their ability to identify with their common subjects, even to the extent of passing among them in disguise to gather a genuine popular critique of their own persons, and it is perhaps significant that *The Pleugh Sang* never stoops to condescension.

But there is one further interpretation—based on the flimsiest of evidence—which has considerable appeal. In naming the parts of the plough, 'all that belangs tae the pleugh', the upper voice mentions 'mowdie bread', the mould board which turned the soil, but surely also in its idiosyncratic spelling intended as a punning reference to the mouldy bread which is the miserable diet of the ploughman. It is tempting to interpret the word 'pleugh' in more general terms as a person who works the plough, or even simply a tenant of an area defined in terms of furrow length, a 'pleuchgate'[8] and therefore by analogy 'all that belangs tae the pleugh' as those things pertaining to such a person. This is certainly the sense in which the identical phrase is used in Sir David Lyndsay's *Ane Satyre of the Thrie Estaitis*,[9] a text which illustrates that it was customary to use art as a means of social criticism at court, and here in *The Pleugh Sang* some forty years before Lyndsay's Johne the common-weill, the spokesman for the common man, stood up to highlight the exploitation of the rustic poor, there is just possibly a similar objective. The 'mowdie bread' also brings to mind the ancient custom of 'streeking the plough', where the plough blade was rubbed with old bread prior to its use in the spring sowing—giving the hound a sight of the hare, as it were!

Whatever its message, *The Pleugh Sang* is an unusual and effective piece of music which anticipates in a remarkable way and by more than a hundred years the English rustic and urban medleys of the early seventeenth century, such as Richard Dering's *Country Cries* and *The Cryes of London* by Thomas Weelkes and Orlando Gibbons.

When considering *The Pleugh Sang*, it is perhaps interesting to bear in mind that the Franco-Flemish masters of sacred polyphony also composed secular songs in the vernacular, as did the *Eton* masters, and while there is no evidence that Robert Carver and his contemporaries at the Chapel Royal ever turned their hand to secular composition, the Carveresque moments in *The Pleugh Sang* betray on the part of its composer at least an acquaintance with contemporary sacred polyphony.

This spill-over of the religious world into the secular is the direct counter-part of the use of secular *cantus firmi* for Mass settings observed in earlier chapters, and a further indication of the fact that the secular/sacred line was rather indistinct is provided by a three-part setting of the *L'Homme Armé* tune preserved in *The Art of Music*.[10] Taken at face value this short piece is a charming Scottish contribution to the body of instrumental settings of this ubiquitous melody, which appears as a sustained *cantus* in the tenor part. As such it is entirely in keeping with late fifteenth and early sixteenth century settings by Robert Morton (c. 1440—after 1476) (possibly also the composer of the original tune), Johannes Japart (fl. 1500) and Josquin, and like these masters the Scottish composer takes great delight in rhythmical complexity. He starts by setting the *cantus* in a slow 3 across common time in the other parts before introducing compound triple time in the upper part and then in the bass.

*Example
19.2*

But of course these are the very devices that make Robert Carver's treatment of that same *cantus* so memorable and indeed, suitably underlayed and performed vocally, it would not be out of place as one of the virtuosic solo sections in Carver's Mass *L'Homme Armé*. In fact several of these solo passages open with the same falling phrase as the present piece. Clearly James IV's court was one at which the sacred and secular, the earthy and the sublime mingled with ease.

This close relationship between the court and popular culture was already changing in the first decade of the sixteenth century under the influence of Margaret Tudor and of James's cultivation of his image as a European Renaissance prince. After Flodden, the English influence waned dramati-cally, while, after a short period in the political wilderness, the flood-gates to the Continent, and particularly to the Auld Ally, France, were opened wide.

20

Ring Sangs, Dancis, Ledis and Roundis

The Court of James V

When the gifted young James V eventually emerged from his minority in 1528, there was an air of vitality and expectancy in Scotland which is almost tangible. This was to be the beginning of a new age and here was the young Phoenix, risen from the ashes of Flodden. Scotland was ready at last for the full challenge of the Renaissance.

An example of this new awareness is the song *Trip and go, hey,*[1] written around 1530 and probably the earliest piece to survive from the reign of James V. It is a medley of the same type as *The Pleugh Sang*, but while the latter is essentially a naive piece of rustic merry-making laced with elements of social comment, the former makes a sophisticated contribution to the European tradition of courtly pastoral love. At the very outset of the song, in a series of exchanges among the voices, it is established that the dance which the song will go on to describe is in 'the guise of France', in those days a by-word for High Renaissance refinement. The copies of the bass and tenor parts recorded in the appendix to the *Wode Part-books* break off simultaneously as the text becomes increasingly *risqué*, suggesting that this secular appendix must have fallen into rather prudish hands at some point in its career. A complete copy of the treble part in the *Forbes Cantus* (c.1662) shows that the song was originally half as long again—and frankly explicit.

> Ever alace for shame alone;
> A joly young frier hes raised my womb
> That ever I did it, ever I did it,
> Ever I did it, did it, did it,
> Ever I did it, ever I did it,
> Ever alace for earthly shame.

The music of the medley undoubtedly preserves folk melodies, but unlike those in *The Pleugh Sang* which dictate the idiom of most of the piece, these tunes are made to conform to the High Renaissance idiom, while the text juxtaposes stylised landscapes, characters and conventional nonsense phrases with more indigenous tableaux and broader *doubles entendres*. The result is a pleasantly lilting piece, tinged with melancholy, which sets the scene for the next step in the development of music at the Scottish court when 'the guise of France', in the person of Mary of Guise, would be calling the tune.

James played the lute, an instrument which he took very seriously indeed if his frequent payments for replacement strings is any indication.[2] According to Thomas Wode, from whom the bulk of the intimate biographical details for this and later periods are gleaned, he was also a singer with a particular aptitude for sight-reading, although his voice was 'rawky and harske'. Early in his reign he employed 'fydlaris' (again probably players of the rebec) and recorder players, while the four ceremonial trumpeters were augmented by three 'quhislaris' and four 'tabernaris' (players respectively of the fife and drum).[3] But it was with his marriage in 1537 to Madeleine, daughter of Francis I of France, and, after her untimely death later that year, to the more robust Mary of Guise, that the effects of the Continental Renaissance began to make themselves fully felt on music at the Scottish court. James spent some time at the French court finalising the wedding arrangements and he was clearly impressed with what he saw and heard there.

A formal portrait of James V and his spouse Mary of Guise
(*By courtesy of the Duke of Atholl, Blair Castle*)

At this time the court of France was one of the foremost European centres of High Renaissance culture. It was here that the chanson, a simple four-part song with the melody in the tenor line, was developed to a fine art to be disseminated throughout Europe by the French and Franco-Flemish composers Claudin de Sermisy, Paul Certon, (both of whom are represented in the *Dowglas/Fischar Part-books*), Clément Janequin (c. 1485–1558), Orlande de Lassus (1532–1594) and Jacob Arcadelt (c. 1500–1568). In instrumental arrangements, they achieved still wider currency in the printed editions of Pierre Attaignant (c. 1494–1552), which appeared between 1528 and 1552. Many chansons underwent further arrangement for solo voice with lute accompaniment.

Shortly after James' return to Scotland in 1537, mention is made for the first time in court accounts of four 'violaris' (players of the viol who presumably employed a variety of sizes in consort) who soon became a staple part of court musical life.[4] With the French wives and the French 'violaris' came French music, and in particular the chanson. The earliest Scottish part-songs in the manner of the chanson were single settings of translations from the French.

One such is the part-song *Support your servand* (a Scots translation of the text of Claudin's *Secourez moy, ma dame*)[5] set to original music, possibly composed by one of the 'violaris', or at any rate by someone with an intimate knowledge of the French tradition. After a section of pervading imitation introduced by the upper voices, the melodic initiative passes to the tenor in the manner of the French chanson, and it is the tenor which prepares the ground for the concluding climax. *Support your servand* is unusual in the extent to which it relies on a contrapuntal rather than a chordal texture—in France by the late 1530s Claudin had already perfected the fully chordal chanson, a form much admired for its High Renaissance simplicity and much emulated in later Scottish part-songs.

Presided over by the youthful and dynamic King James, it is not surprising that the court promoted part-songs in celebration of youth and spring, such as *Into a mirthful May Morning* and the most popular of them all, *O Lusty May*.[6] This latter setting is in a more advanced chordal style, a jubilant affirmation of the qualities of spring. The earliest surviving copies of *O Lusty May*, preserved in manuscripts of the early seventeenth century, indicate the lasting popularity of this song, while details of the surviving chordal setting, such as the chains of parallel fourths and sixths and the final cadence betray a debt to earlier treatments, dating back perhaps to the late fifteenth century. The music is assertive and animated by cross rhythms, the harmonies are direct and uncomplicated, and the whole effect is of a spontaneous response to that headiest of seasons. (See Example 20.1)

The part-song took on a more individually Scottish character with the injection of that trace of melancholy which had coloured *Trip and go, hey*. *Richt soir opprest*[7] displays a further sophistication in its refrain, which is invested with a peculiarly native slant. The text ends with the words 'Bot to the death bound cairfull creatour', and the anonymous composer responds with music which is both subtle and moving in its harmony. Refrains charged in this way with expressive harmonies and invested with a curious melancholy would soon become a distinctive hallmark of the Scottish part-song.

A man who played a major part in drawing together these different strands was John Fethy, who had revolutionised organ playing in Scotland with his

Example 20.1

introduction of the new fingering system. In an extended part-song *O God abufe*[8] also referred to by Wode as *Shir Jhone futheis sang of repentance*, he alternates chordal and contrapuntal sections in an effective way. The song's concluding appeal 'Ask grace of him wha giffis grace to all and he will help in thy necessity' appears all the more affecting when Wode informs us that Fethy composed 'baith letter and note'.

A more vigorous contribution to this body of secular music with a religious context is the anonymous song *All sons of Adam*,[9] a lively medley of around 1540, which intriguingly embodies a number of styles from earlier periods, an indication perhaps that this piece, too, preserves traditional melodies. In addition to rapid alternation of contrasting sections in simple and compound time, *All sons of Adam* juxtaposes contrapuntal sections in close imitation with chordal sections, reflecting once again a new awareness of High Renaissance style. The text exhorts mankind to 'go love the blissed Trinitie' and tells the whole of the Christmas story from the Annunciation to the birth of Christ, weaving in a distinctly Scottish version of the apocryphal legend of the ship bearing Mary and Jesus to Bethlehem.

> Ther cam a ship fair sailland then,
> Sanct Michael was the stieresman
> Sanct John sat in the horn.
> Our Lord harpit, our Lady sang
> And all the bells of heavn they rang
> On Christson day at morn.

In the concluding stages of the song, as the angels celebrate the birth of Christ, the anonymous composer makes reference in a declamatory fanfare to the already archaic style of the earlier works in the *Carver Choirbook*, which is answered by a brief section in the unadorned parallel intervals of true faburden.

Example 20.2

The central 'plane sang' is matched by a 'counter', moving in parallel fourths above it, and a 'baritonant' in alternating thirds and fifths underneath, according to the rules governing three-part faburden detailed in *The Art of Music*.[10] While in the context of church music faburden may well have enjoyed a temporary revival around the middle of the century, the compiler of *The Art of Music*, writing no later than 1580, refers to this particular species of faburden as 'the way of auld musicians', and it may be assumed that the sudden intrusion of pure unadorned three-part faburden in *All sons of Adam* would have created a strange archaic impression. Clearly, then as now, the angels were afforded the luxury of standing aloof from the strictures of modernity. This attractive piece is brought to a jubilant conclusion by the clamorous response of mankind praising God, a hubbub of celebration captured by the anonymous composer of *All sons of Adam* with an assurance which recalls Robert Carver at his zenith.[11]

Also from around 1540 is a curious set of variations on a ground which Kenneth Elliott has christened *Boece's basse-danse* in honour of the Aberdeen University student who noted it down on the flyleaf of one of his textbooks. The repeated bass may well be a folk melody, and Dr Elliott has observed that it shares with early Scottish polyphony and present day folk music an element of 'double tonic', a sense of two adjacent tonal centres.[12] Perhaps like master Boece, James' French 'violaris' whiled away spare minutes in devising divisions to a ground in this way, but we must be grateful to the young student that he took the time to note his down. John Purser's speculation[13] that Tobias Hume, famed in the seventeenth century for his composition and performance of virtuoso divisions for viola da gamba, may well have been of Scots extraction is a fascinating postscript to this unique insight into the widely practised but rarely recorded realm of instrumental improvisation.

One of the most beautiful of all the part-songs of this period was written after the death of James V in 1542, and sets verses by the rising literary star, Alexander Scott. *Departe, departe*[14] is traditionally regarded as a poetic exchange between the Master of Erskine and the widowed Queen, Mary of Guise,[15] and with the simplest of means, it achieves an emotional impact which eludes many more ambitious pieces. Chordal throughout and direct in its harmony, *Departe, departe* somehow attains breathtaking serenity tinged with melancholy.

Example 20.3

Such perfect fusion of words and music has led to the speculation that Scott also composed the music, and indeed one Alexander Scott is listed as a member of the Chapel Royal in 1539 and again ten years later,[16] while in 1548 an Alexander Scott 'musician and organist' was appointed canon of the Augustinian Priory of Inchmahome.[17] If these Alexander Scotts are one and the same man, his brief stay at Inchmahome takes on an added significance. His transfer from the Chapel Royal coincides with the arrival at the Priory of Mary of Guise and the infant Mary, Queen of Scots, seeking a safe refuge after the Scots defeat at Pinkie Cleugh. His appointment is confirmed by the Master of Erskine, younger brother and successor of the man for whom he wrote *Departe, departe* and who had been killed in the Battle of Pinkie. In July 1547 Scott was granted leave to travel to France with the Master of Erskine, perhaps to make arrangements for the young Queen's own journey there on 7 August 1548 as the prospective bride of the Dauphin. In 1549 his name re-appears on the Chapel Royal lists in Stirling, where Mary of Guise had returned after her daughter's departure.[18]

Another chordal setting of verses by Alexander Scott *How suld my febill body fure?* seems to be later in style and probably belongs to the late 1550s, when Mary of Guise's regency encouraged French influence in all the arts. In view of what would appear to be close ties with the court, it is likely that Scott's poetry continued to attract the attention of composers, possibly including himself, during the reign of Mary, Queen of Scots and even into that of her son, James VI. The survival of tunes for his lyrics *Hence hairt with hir that most departe* and *Only to yow in Erd that I lufe best* in *Robert Edwards' Commonplace-book*, which dates from the mid seventeenth century, suggests that his verses enjoyed an enduring popularity as texts for part-songs and possibly lute songs. But by the time of his death in 1583 the mantle of Scotland's foremost poet had been usurped by Alexander Montgomerie, whose poetry would eclipse his illustrious predecessor's as a rich source of part-songs.

21

Hé! Quelle Musique!
The Court of Mary

During her formative years at the French court, Mary had become both an accomplished poetess and an able performer on the lute and on that other seemly instrument of feminine recreation, the virginals. She is also reputed to have played the harp, but that instrument was already in sharp decline in Lowland Scotland, where people now looked to the south for the latest cultural trends, and where things Gaelic were regarded with growing contempt. Mary also had a fine singing voice (a French contemporary had described it as 'très douce et très bonne'[1]) and it is entirely possible that she sang to her own accompaniment on the lute or even took a line in the ensemble singing that is described for the first time during her reign. She maintained expressly for this purpose a group of 'sangsteris' who doubled as *valets de chambre*.

The Queen also kept a group of 'violaris' (as many as seven at one stage, but settling down to four) and apparently all Scotsmen, to judge by their names.[2] These may have been joined on occasion by any of the three lutenists in her employment, while recorders and reed instruments (increasingly the more refined 'hautbois', probably already very similar to the two-keyed Baroque oboe) played an active rôle. The obligatory trumpeters were occasionally replaced by cornettists, probably guests from England or the Continent, while Italian musicians also frequented the court.[3]

Against this lively musical backdrop, one or two individuals stand out, and not always by reason of their musical prowess. David Rizzio (Riccio) came to Mary's court in the entourage of the visiting ambassador of Savoy, and seems at once to have caught the eye of the young Queen. He was invited to sing bass with her three valets, 'to be ther fourt marrow, in sort that he was drawen in to sing somtymes with the rest', and presently received a permanent post as her secretary. In addition to singing, he seems also to have played stringed instruments including the fiddle, and he possibly also composed, although

A youthful Mary, Queen of Scots, in marked contrast to the sombre subject of the later portraits (*The Royal Collection © 1993 Her Majesty the Queen*)

no music which can be attributed to him has survived. Although undoubtedly 'a merry fallow, and a good mucitien', he almost certainly did not play the seminal role subsequently credited to him in later accounts of Scottish musical history, and his main claim to fame remains his gory death at the hands of a group of Scottish nobles, led by Mary's estranged husband Darnley, in Holyrood Palace. Darnley, a neurotic and sickly young man, undoubtedly suspected that Riccio had taken advantage of his privileged position as Mary's secretary, but there is no evidence to back up the claim made in Francis Osborne's *Traditionall Memoyres* that James VI, the child whom Mary almost miscarried as a result of Rizzio's murder, was 'David the Fiddler's son'. There was surely enough of the impetuous and devious Darnley in James to scotch that libel!

Less colourful than the ill-fated Rizzio were father and son James and John Lauder. James Lauder (c. 1535-c. 1595), composer, singer and performer on the organ and the virginals, studied music both in England and in France, and took up a position at the Scottish court early in the 1560 as one of Mary's *valets de chambre*, composing consort music and part-songs. Both he and his son John accompanied Mary on her flight to England in 1568, and the latter, a player of the 'base violin',[4] stayed with Mary until her execution in 1578. By this time his father was back in Scotland, composing and playing, and a number of pavens from this period which are recorded by the eclectic Thomas Wode may well be his work.[5]

The paven is a sedate processional dance in four, or occasionally three beats in the bar, which (usually coupled with the more vigorous galliard) was in considerable vogue in the sixteenth century, both at the English court and on the Continent. *Prince Edward's Paven*,[6] recorded by Wode, appeared in a five-part setting in a collection of dances printed in Paris in 1555 by Claude Gervaise, and a number of related pieces were copied and set elsewhere in Europe. It is possible that the *Prince Edward's Paven* is a Scottish contribution to this body of music.

If the original paven melody is Scottish (although there is no evidence that it is), it possibly belongs to the period when Prince Edward, the son of Henry VIII, was being considered as a spouse for Mary Stuart, before the ascendancy of the French party at the Scottish court ensured that the two-year-old Mary 'jilted' the infant Prince in 1543, in favour of the Dauphin and the bonds of the Auld Alliance. The four-part setting recorded by Wode is almost certainly later in date than this, but its static harmony suggests that it is one of the earliest of the pavens recorded by Wode, in a style which directly anticipates that of James Lauder.

Another of the pavens, described by Wode as 'Ane uther paven verray gude',[7] also demonstrates features similar to Lauder's later work and is perhaps one of his early compositions. It displays a solid rather than inspired approach to counterpoint, but the composer does take scrupulous care that rhythmic initiative is shared among the four voices and that a constant forward momentum is maintained. There are even traces of motivic development in the final section, which explores the potential of a rising figure comprising two quavers and a crotchet, itself a development of the initial figure of the paven.

Example 21.1

In the *Dublin Virginal Book* (c 1570) this paven is coupled with a pleasant galliard which seems closely related in material and style. While Wode records only pavens, it is possible that many of them were originally composed in tandem with galliards, in accordance with English and Continental practice.

In 1584 James Lauder was commissioned to write a paven to celebrate the assumption in 1580 of the title of Earl of March by Robart Stewart, son of the third Earl of Lennox. This was the same Robart Stewart who as Commendator of St Andrews Priory had commissioned David Peebles' motet *Quam multi Domine* some eight years earlier. The resulting *My Lorde of Marche Paven*,[8] the only piece which can definitely be attributed to James Lauder, is the finest consort work of this whole period, a masterpiece of precision and invention written by a mature composer in complete control of his medium. Thomas Wode records the melody and the alto part,[9] while *David Melvill's Bassus Part-book* (1604) provides the bass, and other sources indicate that the piece was originally in four parts.

The first three bars establish a dotted crotchet-plus-quaver rhythm, while bar four covers the same ground in diminution and extends the phrase. The ensuing section is dominated by a syncopated figure, proposed by the upper voice, imitated immediately by the bass and which gradually pervades the texture with the help of the alto part. This quaver-plus-crotchet-plus-quaver figure is passed from voice to voice and is juxtaposed with a dotted quaver-plus-

Example 21.2

semi-quaver figure, which springs directly from the diminution of bar four. The syncopated figure is further explored in the concluding section, where in the penultimate phrase it undergoes diminution, simultaneously recalling bar four and leading through a tightening of the syncopation to a satisfactory cadence— a crowning stroke of inspiration.

This rhythmic sophistication is complemented by a new eloquence of phrase, making *My Lord of Marche Paven* a joy to play and to listen to, performed either by a mixed or a full consort, especially of viols.

By 1584, when Lauder composed *My Lord of Marche Paven*, much water had passed under the bridge. On 10 February 1567 Mary's second husband, Henry Stewart, Lord Darnley, estranged from her since the murder of Rizzio, had himself been brutally murdered at the age of twenty-one by a band of conspirators, who almost certainly included James Hepburn, Earl of Bothwell, whom Mary married three months later on 15 May. Bloody civil was only averted by Mary's surrender to a group of Protestant Lords at Carberry Hill on June 15. Bothwell fled and on 24 July Mary was forced to abdicate in favour of her thirteen-month-old son, James VI.

Such were James Lauder's musical skills that his reputation survived Mary's fall (and his son's continuing association with her), and by the time he had fulfilled Robart Stewart's commission in 1584, the turmoil of the 1560s was a distant memory. James VI, now a precocious adolescent of eighteen, had assumed personal control over court and nation and had established his cultural circle, the Castalian Band, a group of talented practitioners of all the arts, whose influence would bring secular music at the Scottish court to new pinnacles of excellence.

22

With Most Delicate Dulce Voices
The Court of James VI

In the period from 1567 to 1578 when the child James was little more than the political pawn of his Protestant nobility, he was assigned the great scholar George Buchanan as tutor and four English 'violaris' for his entertainment. Buchanan was one of the most consummate intellectuals that Scotland has ever produced, a poet (in the opinion of his contemporaries 'poetarum sui saeculi facile princeps') an unrivalled master of Renaissance Latin, a political thinker far in advance of his time and a formidable linguist, who spoke Gaelic and whose analysis of the Celtic languages modern research has done little more than confirm. He had once been Queen Mary's Latin tutor, and portraits of him bear the legend:

> Sic Buchananus ora, sic vultum tulit: Pete scripta et astra, nosse si mentem cupis
> (Thus Buchanan wore his features, thus his face: if you would know his mind, ask for his writings and the stars.)

The 'violaris' were Thomas, Robert, James and William, the brothers Hudson, 'sangsteris, Inglismen, violleris' and much more besides, who had reached the Scottish court in the entourage of Lord Darnley and weathered the ensuing chaos and bloodshed to emerge with the young King into a new flowering of the arts.[1]

Two consort pieces by John Blak,[2] preserved in seventeenth century sources but probably written in the 1560s, give some idea of the sort of music the king's 'violaris' might have played. *Black called fyne musick* displays an inventive approach to melody with an assertive chordal section midway through suggesting a verse and chorus structure, while *Blak major* presents a more restive and insistent aspect with deft handling of motivic development within a consistently contrapuntal texture.

By March 1578 James had achieved some degree of autonomy, and a part-song probably written to celebrate his triumphal entry into Edinburgh in October 1579, *Nou let us sing*,[3] reflects the optimism which greeted yet another emergence from minority. Chordal throughout, and not unlike *O Lusty May* in its robust simplicity, this drinking song is probably connected with the revels of this carefree time, praising the young King, calling upon Bacchus to grace the company with his blessing through the ministrations of the 'Deame' or hostess, and amusingly introducing in turn each of the voices, the 'Treble', the 'Counter', the 'Tenor' and the 'Basse', who list their own distinctive qualities and extol their own virtues, each in his own verse. The thirst of the performers is regularly reaffirmed, and in the final verse they unite forces in a mock-desperate plea to the hostess:

> Deame, ye are sweir that lets us cry
> Once fill the stoop and let us rest.

Also from this period is a delightful piece of consort music, *Ane Exempill of Tripla*,[4] probably composed as an academic exercise especially for *The Art of Music*. It consists of a vigorous *cantus firmus* in compound time, perhaps a popular melody, to which a complementary bass and two lively upper parts have been added. The piece exploits delightfully a continuous ambiguity between compound 6/8 time (two groups of three quavers) and simple 3/4 time (three groups of two quavers) with catchy syncopations and dancing dotted rhythms—in short, it is a charming little gem which belies its rather prosaic title.

Example 22.1

It is perhaps frank frivolity and pleasure-taking of this kind, as much as the King's renewed cultivation of the Catholic French connection in the person of the dashing Esmé Stuart, Lord d'Aubigny, whom James created Duke of Lennox in 1581, which stampeded his Protestant nobility into seizing him and controlling his policies until 1583. Only after this was James able to determine fully the direction he wished to follow, and there ensued the culturally prosperous years of the Castalian Band, which derived its name from the spring in Mount Pamassus frequented by the muses and by Apollo himself. The rather pretentious analogy is obvious.

This exceptional circle, grouped around the gifted young James and comprising the greatest artists of the age, produced a lively ferment of creativity and interaction, which led to the production of some of the finest of all Scottish Renaissance works. The most accomplished of these artists was the poet Alexander Montgomerie, a militant Catholic who had accompanied the charismatic Esmé Stuart to Scotland in 1579, and who survived his expulsion to lead a precarious artistic existence at court, only ever as secure as the volatile religious politics and the whim of the young King would permit—his poetry occasionally rails at the King's inconstancy with the sort of petulance normally associated with a Romantic poet crossed in love.

Although Montgomerie's poetry displays some knowledge of music and he seems to have chosen musicians for his personal friends, no music by him has been identified, and it is entirely possible that his musical gifts lay rather in the direction of performance and in producing song texts either to fit pre-existent melodies, or so well crafted as to be a joy to set to original music—and there was no shortage of capable composers in the Castalian Band on hand to do just that.

Kenneth Elliott[5] recognises features of the style of James Lauder in the settings of Montgomerie's *Evin dead behold I breathe*[6] and *What mightie motion*,[7] and the settings of his lyrics *No wonder is suppose*,[8] and *In throu the windoes of myn ees*[9] may also be Lauder's work. Thomas Wode credits Andro Blakhall with setting Montgomerie's *Adieu, O desie of delyt*[10] to a new harmonisation of a pre-existent melody, and the harmonisation of Nicholas de la Grotte's quirky melody which matches Montgomerie's equally quirky lyric, *Lyk as the dum Solsequium*,[11] could also be by Blakhall, or perhaps by another of the prominent composers of the Castalian Band, such as Thomas Hudson, his brother Robert (a particular friend of Montgomerie), or William Kinloch.

The beautifully measured setting of Montgomerie's *Evin dead behold I breathe* is among the finest part-songs of this period, almost thoroughly chordal, except for the occasional detail of rhythmical variance in one of the parts. But it is in the subtleties of harmony that one detects the advance from earlier part-songs and which calls to mind the name of James Lauder. The opening phrase displays the type of High Renaissance suspension which religious composers had been employing for a generation by this time, and some of their facility with harmonic shading is apparent in the juxtaposition of e′ natural and e′ flat in the second phrase. All of this marks a radical departure in the art of part-song composition.

What mightie motion carries this a stage further with the sophistication of its striking refrain, 'alace, alace, that ev'r I leirnd to love', where again the gentle shading of an e′ flat is juxtaposed with the expected e′ natural, this time in a way which is nothing short of masterly.

Example 22.2

Particularly in vogue at the Scottish court at this time, thanks to the admonitions of James VI, was alliterative verse, where the poet attempted to string together in each line of his poem a series of words beginning with the same sound. To the uninitiated this at first sounds rather peculiar, particularly when viewed from an age which has been more inclined to concentrate on end-rhymes and to relegate alliteration to the rôle of a special effect. But alliterative poetry has a long history in the oral traditions of most of the Germanic languages, and before Chaucer, English poetry was alliterative too.

Montgomerie carries the alliterative style of writing, already fundamental to the very earliest Scottish part-song texts such as *O lusty May*, to extremes in such lines as:

> A frentick fevir through my flesh I feill;
> I feill a passion can not be expresst;
> I feill a byll within my bosum beill;
> No cataplasme can weill impesh that pest.

The composer again intelligently responds with a rhythmically simple setting, chordal with occasional syncopation, allowing the poetry to speak for itself. The effect is all the more impressive when the seemingly inexorable flow of words and music is brought to a standstill on the first syllable of the refrain.

More contrapuntal in texture is the part-song *In throu the windoes of myn ees*, where Montgomerie's imaginative text is conducted through a rich forest of musical invention, led by the tenor part in the manner of the finest French chansons. Syncopated and harmonically varied, it complements the text pleasingly as it relates the melodramatic tale of a lover who has taunted Cupid and now reaps the whirlwind. Montgomerie's use of alliteration and his uncanny ability to breathe life into the most improbable scenarios through dialogue and description make this a most rewarding part-song text—and the anonymous composer fulfils his role discerningly and unobtrusively.

Adieu, O desie of delyt demonstrates a more elaborate interplay of music and words. Montgomerie's text uses the elaborate Helicon stanza,[12] while Blakhall's setting, part of a general striving on the part of the Castalian Band towards the perfect synthesis of words and music, is the ultimate in High Renaissance simplicity, largely chordal in texture, with the tenor and treble parts moving in parallel thirds against a backdrop of contrary motion in the other parts. And yet from its first to its last perfect open fifth, this part-song is perfection indeed, exemplifying in its calm restraint and moderation that Golden Mean so highly prized in the Renaissance.

Also written in Helicon stanzas, Montgomerie's *Lyk as the dum Solsequium* draws an analogy between the sunflower drooping its head when the sun goes behind a cloud and the lover hanging his head when his mistress is absent. The revitalisation of the flower when the sunlight returns is given erotic undertones when applied to the lover. The poem is matched with a setting of a melody by Nicholas de la Grotte, which alternates simple and compound time, even and dotted rhythms and major and minor chords in a dazzling showpiece of flair and sweeping confidence. The survival of even one galliard by James Lauder or of consort music by Andro Blakhall might have helped us to attribute this piece of exquisite craftsmanship—or perhaps, after all, Alexander Montgomerie's skills extended further than has been supposed.

A short dance tune, *Hutchesoun's Galyiard*, preserved in *William Mure of Rowallan's Cantus Part-book* (c. 1615) probably dates from the end of sixteenth century and provides us with evidence that dancing continued to be enjoyed among the Scottish aristocracy.

From the pen of another of the Castalians, William Kinloch (fl. 1582), comes the earliest surviving Scottish music for keyboard, recorded in *Duncan Burnett's Music-book* of around 1610, but probably composed in the latter decades of the sixteenth century. Ranging from simple dances (with ornamented versions or divisions written out in full) to more elaborate programme pieces, such as the *Batell of pavie*,[13] this body of music is fascinatingly informative as well as being fine original music.

Although Kinloch's is the first Scottish music for the instrument to survive, we know that there was a strong tradition of virginal playing at the Scottish court and that Mary, Queen of Scots was an enthusiast. It is entirely possible that the the leading composer of her reign and a player of the virginals himself, James Lauder, composed for the instrument, and his survival to 1595 would have allowed him to influence the style of William Kinloch

Of particular interest in Kinloch's work are the divisions, which largely follow the tenets of the English virginal masters as exemplified by the *Fitzwilliam Virginal Book*, with cascades of running scales, often with flattened sevenths at their peaks, and recurring sequential figures. While these examples of ornamentation are clearly in a keyboard idiom, they provide some picture of how Scottish musicians in general might have been ornamenting consort music in performance—clearly the florid muse of Carver was still alive and flourishing at the end of the century.

Fine examples of this rich decoration occur in *Kinloch his Lang pavane*[14] and the *Galliard of the Lang paven*[15] which, in addition to displaying a fine disdain for spelling conventions, demonstrate a particularly high degree of invention. As the magisterial *Lang pavane*, with its major/minor ambiguity, unfolds section by section, the interposed divisions each seize upon and elaborate one particular aspect with a Carveresque thoroughness and

Example 22.3

inventiveness. Related material is given still more varied treatment in the *Galliard*, with sections in triplets, double diminutions and syncopation enhancing the virtuosic impression as detailed in the section on 'prolation' in *The Art of Music*.[16] (See Example 22.3, p 137)

Duncan Burnett (fl. c. 1615–1652), who recorded Kinloch's works in his music books, continued the tradition of Scottish keyboard composition into the seventeenth century, but by that time the magic of the Castalian Band had been broken. Alexander Montgomerie drifted further and further from his

Mary, Queen of Scots, and her husband Henry, Lord Darnley, perhaps about to dance a stately paven (*Mansell Collection*)

royal patron and into the arms of Catholic conspiracy. He died in 1598 in his
late forties, having spent the last year of his life as an impoverished outlaw.[17]
The first-generation Castalians were growing older, and James' attention was
increasingly taken up with the tantalising prospect of a United Kingdom of
Great Britain and the seemingly inexhaustible coffers of England. By the time
he eventually secured his prestigious prize, the output of the Band had become
fitful. The withdrawal of patronage in 1603 left the second generation of
Castalians with an interrupted tradition and a flagging impetus. These youthful
talents dispersed themselves around the castles of the aristocracy, where they
prepared to write an epilogue to Scottish Renaissance culture.

23

Synging, Fydling and Piping
Music of the Stewart Courts in Performance

The very nature of the music which has survived from the early years of the sixteenth century suggests that there are many possible modes of performance. *Alas that same sueit face* could be performed by a small unaccompanied vocal ensemble in three parts or by three soloists, but equally effective would be two solo voices with the accompaniment of a bass instrument with a part for lute improvised upon the bass line, or one solo voice with tenor and bass recorders and optional lute or keyboard—the permutations are practically endless. This range of possibilities may seem bewildering at first to musicians accustomed to performing the music of later periods, where composers invariably dictate not only the precise instrumentation but also frequently the articulation and dynamic to be used, but in such cases this sense of disorientation will soon be replaced with a realisation of the freedom which early music offers to performers—a freedom which is actually compounded by a number of other factors. It is probable that performers at the time regarded the notes on the page merely as a starting point and felt free to embellish and decorate their lines according to conventions which had become second nature to them.

By consulting a number of relevant instruction manuals,[1] performers can approach an understanding of the range of decoration processes which were employed in different periods and places. The dangers of applying the content of an Italian or an English manual indiscriminately to a whole century of Scottish music will be apparent. This may be overcome in part by reference to a native source roughly contemporary with the music under consideration. In the absence of native ornamentation manuals as such, the performer can fall back upon sources containing examples of applied ornamentation. The embellished music of Robert Carver, for example, is a rich source of ornaments which may be used discerningly to decorate Scottish secular music of the early part of the sixteenth century. Later in the century as tastes changed, performers must look from Carver to sources such as *The Art of Music*, or the keyboard music of

William Kinloch, to formulate and digest the idiom of embellishment appropriate to the music under scrutiny.

A brief but fascinating example of applied ornamentation occurs in the *Wode Part-books* appendix in the form of two versions of the popular tune *John come kiss me now*, the second an ornamented division of the first called *The Running of John come kiss me now*.

Example 23.1

It can be seen from this comparison that the division departs quite daringly from the original, assuming considerable scope for creative self-expression on the part of the performer.

Crudely stated, ornamentation consists largely in 'playing around' the written line: filling leaps with running notes, weaving a tasteful phrase around a sustained note, moving elegantly within acceptable bounds of range and dissonance where the music on the page stands still. At what point and in what way to move and what the acceptable bounds are constitute the crucial considerations which produce effective decoration. It is easy to recognise a decoration which works to the enhancement of the music, and soon a mixture of impulse and intuition will lead to free improvisation. Much of the pleasure of Renaissance music resides in this creative interplay of ornamentation, a musical exchange of ideas among a small group of friends, and the revitalising effect on the music can be startling.

The rather pedestrian tenor line of *Alas that same suiet face* comes vividly to life:

Example 23.2

And as instrumentation will change from verse to verse of a song, so will the density of ornamentation. It is a good idea not only to commence with a 'straight' verse, thereby allowing the listener to hear, prior to embellishment, the actual lines as written, but also to insert one now and again during the performance to 'clear the air'. In other instances, ornamentation will be judged wholly inappropriate. That the composer of *The Pleugh Sang* applied ornamentation to selected parts of the piece indicates that he probably intended the rest of it to be performed as written, an impression confirmed by the declamatory nature of much of the music. This also restricts the options as regards instrumentation, and two solo tenor voices accompanied by a bass instrument with improvised lute or keyboard part seem to present the ideal performance medium.

Given the probable context of *The Pleugh Sang*, singers may also wish to experiment with a more naive, rustic vocal quality with a view to a more forceful performance. This would help to confirm links with the folk tradition and to underline the strands of popular music that are present in it.

The customary mode of performance for the part-songs from the reign of James V is either a small choir in four parts or four solo voices, but there is no reason why recorders or viols should not take some of the vocal lines, supported perhaps by a lute or a keyboard instrument. For that matter, many of these part-songs work well as consort songs, a solo voice taking the top line and instruments replacing the lower voices.[2]

As with church music, appropriate pronunciation of texts is vital if the original concept of the composer is to be recaptured. Many of these sixteenth century texts would appear to be heavily anglicised, and the performer may be lulled into thinking that some sort of modern 'received pronunciation' with a token nod in the direction of a rolled 'r' will suffice. Nothing could be further from the truth. Until 1603 the Scottish court championed the cause of Scots, and even as late as the eighteenth century, an apparent English orthography concealed an actual broad Scots pronunciation. Just as performers of Elizabethan madrigals are increasingly rejecting the rather twee 'home counties' quack that passed until recently for authenticity and are availing themselves of research into Tudor English, so singers of Scots part-songs should adopt an equally respectful approach.[3]

In view of the shortage of original consort music from this period, it is possible to go a stage further and give some of these part-songs a completely instrumental performance. A part-song like *O lusty May* is essentially dance music with words, and a precedent exists in the frequent appearance of Continental part-songs in instrumental versions in the printed collections issued in Paris from the late 1520s by Pierre Attaignant and in Antwerp from about 1540 onwards by Tielman Susato. None of these editions stipulates instrumentation, but certain of the Scottish part-songs would seem suited to specific combinations of instruments. *O lusty May* works well on small recorders or even on the louder reed instruments, while a part-song such as *Departe, departe* deserves the warmth and subtlety of deep recorders with lute, or ideally a consort of sonorous viols. Performed instrumentally, this music provides a valuable foretaste of the approaching blossoming of consort music.

The consort music which survives from the court of Mary was undoubtedly intended for performance on a consort of viols, but the presence at court of players of the lute, the recorder and other woodwind instruments and the informality of private performances suggest that the instrumentation may have been quite flexible. The *Wode Part-book* pavens sound effective on a consort of recorders, or perhaps a broken consort combining 'the still noise of recorders and flutes',[4] and a lute or clarsach enhances the focus of any consort. Particularly with the later pieces, it becomes clear that the music is for listening to rather than dancing to, and it is probable that percussion will be considered inappropriate.

In contrast, *Lyk as the dum Solsequium* works well as a brash and lively galliard on loud reed instruments, with percussion to emphasise the rhythmic subtleties. Perhaps the 'musick in grene holyne howboyes, in fine parts' which was part of the celebrations of Prince Henry's baptism in 1594 was a performance of this sort on oboes or shawms of holly wood.[5] In fact many of the Castalian part-songs make fine vehicles for consort performance, but an important element is sacrificed with the loss of Montgomerie's witty and artful texts, and performers may prefer to present them as consort songs, with a solo voice singing the tenor or treble lines. It may even be felt necessary to retain both of these vocal lines in order to preserve the element of textual interplay so vital to Castalian part-songs.

In view of the dearth of Scottish lute songs from this period, performers might also care to experiment with versions of part-songs for solo voice with lute accompaniment, by analogy with the French chanson arrangements for this medium. This sort of open-minded and flexible treatment of music fits in well with what is known of the spontaneity of the original performances in the Stewart courts, and in any case the finest of Musick Fyne can take a good deal of arranging without losing its magic.

Thomas Wode helps to recreate some of the long-lost ambiance in sharing with us his vision of the main function of music. In 1569 he observed that the 'sangis' he was recording were

> meit and apt for musitians to recreat thair spirittis, when as thay shal be overcom with heviness or any kind of sadnes, not only musitians but evin the ignorant of a gentle nature, hearing, shalbe confertid and be mirry with uss.

Performers could hardly hope for a better philosophy when approaching Scottish secular music of the sixteenth century.

24

On My Jolie Lute, by Night
An Epilogue

As the euphoria that surrounded the departure of James VI in April 1603 began to dissipate, it became apparent to the artists of the Castalian Band that they faced a crisis of daunting proportions. While some of the Castalian poets, such as Sir Robert Aytoun (1570–1638), accompanied James to London, the majority of the younger Castalians chose to stay in Scotland. Almost at once the vacuum created by the wholesale emigration of King and nobility began to have an effect.

Instead of congregating at court to exchange creative ideas and co-operate on joint artistic ventures in the manner of the old Castalian Band, the new generation of aristocratic amateurs were forced to remain in castles up and down the country, isolated and thrown back on their own resources. Deprived of much of that ferment of ideas, both indigenous and Continental, which had become the staple fare of the Scottish court, the young Castalians were forced to take stock and to consolidate their position, and in common with artists of later ages faced with insecurity and crisis, they turned to the past for renewed impetus.[1] Quite exceptionally for this age where artistic trends were radical and as a rule irrevocable, they turned their attention to collecting and preserving the Musick Fyne of previous generations and to examining and recording for the first time the traditional folk music which flourished in the Highlands of Scotland.

Since the time of James IV, when Celtic minstrels from the North and West had been welcomed at court, Gaelic culture had been increasingly rejected and vilified by the Lowland Scots courtiers who dictated fashion at the Stewart courts. By 1587 this trend had crystallised in a policy of active suppression by James VI, in an attempt to improve the compatibility of the elements of his planned Great Britain. This drive towards uniformity is already apparent in *The Art of Music*:[2]

> In the iyll of Britane tua regionis ar contenit, that is to say, Ingland and Scotland. The quhilk tua regionis tua nobill nationis dois inhabeit callit Britanis.

By 1599 James' contempt for the Highlands and Islands manifested itself openly in his *Basilikon Doron*, a textbook on kingship for the instruction of his son, Henry.

> As for the Highlands, I shortly comprehend them all in two sorts of people; the one that dwelleth in our mainland, that are barbarous for the most part, and yet mixed with some show of civility; the other, that dwelleth in the Isles and are utterly barbarians, without any sort or show of civility.[3]

After his departure for London in 1603 he continued his efforts to address what he saw as the 'grite ignorance . . . the haill commonalitie inhabitantis of the Illandis, hes bene and are subject to' by strengthening the force of law and even setting up colonies of Lowlanders in the north.

In spite of this growing pressure, Gaelic culture had continued to thrive in the Highlands as an unrecorded oral tradition, until now, once again, in the early seventeenth century, the amateur musicians of the Lowland Scots aristocracy and professional Highland Celtic harper-minstrels came into fruitful contact. In a process of recording and imitation, the age-old Celtic folk tradition became integrated into the essentially Scots realm of secular art music. Equipped with the lutes, fiddles, citterns and mandoras of their aristocratic inheritance, the sons and daughters of 'Temporalitie' set about translating bardic performances into terms they understood.

The lute manuscripts and music books which resulted from these efforts, *Sir William Mure of Rowallen's Lute Book* and Sir William Skene of Hallyard's

The coronation of James I of Great Britain. Nine silver trumpets herald his entrance into Westminster Abbey, while further trumpets, drums, muskets and cannon sound throughout the city of London (*Copyright British Museum*)

collection for that diminutive lute, the mandora (both c. 1620), *Robert Gordon of Straloch's Lute Book* (1627–29) and *Panmure 5* (c 1632), are the musical wonders of early seventeenth century Scotland. A number of later collections, such as *Lady Margaret Wemyss' Book* (1644), *Robert Edwards' Musical Commonplace-book* (c. 1680) and the *Balcarres Lute Book* (c. 1700), carried the tradition into the next century. In these collections traditional Celtic airs are presented under titles such as *Gypsies Lilt*, *I long for thy virginitie*, *Whip my towdie*, *Come Yairds* and *Port Robart*,[4] faithfully and sympathetically rendered into versions for solo lutes or their relatives. This latter piece, *Port Robart*, is a fine example of the techniques used.

The port is a uniquely Scottish form of music for clarsach, dating from the mid sixteenth to the mid seventeenth century, and examples of the genre feature in most of the lute manuscripts. Alison Kinnaird[5] has identified a number of features that these ports have in common, such as the irregular phrasing, asymmetrical structure, the introductory ascending scale, the frequent use of octave leaps, a standard repeated note figure and a curiously inconclusive tailing off at the end. She speculates that they may be a stylised survival of the standard prelude used by harpers to check their tuning at the beginning of a performance.

Example 24.1

Port Robart which appears in *Lady Margaret Wemyss' Book* is one of the earliest surviving ports and Alison Kinnaird has demonstrated that it was probably written for Robart Stewart, who was Commendator of St Andrews Priory from 1570[6] and for whom Peebles' *Quam multi Domine* and Lauder's *My Lorde of Marche Paven* were also written. Although the piece's alternative title in *Robert Gordon of Straloch's Lute Book*, *Port Preist*, does not restrict its date of composition to the period before the Reformation (the term 'priest' was applied to Reformed churchmen too), the commission probably resulted from Robart Stewart's period of employment as administrator of the pre-Reformation Bishopric of Caithness. Alison Kinnaird also speculates that the vast majority of the other ports were composed for the Atholl family and for the Gordons of Huntly, both of whom employed clarsach players, and who were related to Robart Stewart. It is interesting to think that through him Celtic harper-minstrels had contact with the influential musical group which was focused on St Andrews in the second half of the sixteenth century. We should perhaps also recall that among the instruments which adorn Thomas Wode's *Part-books*, compiled in St Andrews at the instigation of Robart's predecessor as Commendator, James Stewart, is a selection of clarsachs.

In recording this haunting air, the compilers of *Robert Gordon of Straloch's Lute Book* and *Lady Margaret Wemyss' Book* retain the melodic flavour and idiosyncratic harmonies, enhancing rather than meddling with features which may seem 'wayward' and 'primitive' to us. Clearly, it was a style of music which they knew at first hand and were intimately acquainted with. *Port Robart* is an eloquent testimony to the musical invention of the harper-minstrels, and it is easy to understand the evident popularity of the genre among the aristocracy. This careful regard for the essence of the Celtic tunes they recorded informs all of the lute books compiled in the early part of the seventeenth century.

But this belated Lowland interest in the music of the Celtic harper-minstrels failed to save a dying tradition. In decline throughout the seventeenth century, this unique Highland culture received a mortal blow in the mid eighteenth century as the failure of the Jacobite risings precipitated the ruin of many of the important Highland families who had employed harpers. A symbiotic relationship stretching back over many generations was destroyed.

Among the Lowland aristocrats an initially genuine and respectful interest in the distinctive qualities of Highland folk music was increasingly tinged with contempt and gradually degenerated into a more or less patronising and cheap attempt at imitation, usually limited to crass invocations of the pentatonic scale, coupled with a suitably ethnic title, such as *The New Highland Laddie* from the *Balcarres Lute Book*. The mists were gathering. The stage was set for the sentimental myth of Romantic Scotland.

The Stewart courts had traditionally set the standards for the composition and performance of secular art music throughout the sixteenth century, and inevitably the absence of this focal point proved fatal to original composition. The collection *Songs and Fancies*,[7] compiled and published around 1660 by John Forbes in Aberdeen, contains a number of vocal melodies which aspire to a Celtic pentatonic flavour, but to varying degrees they fall into the trap of patronising their material. The situation was to degenerate further into outright offensive ridicule in the 'Scotch songs' of publications such as *Wit and Mirth: or Pills to Purge Melancholy* which appeared in London in 1719. Representative of this very English genre is *Jocky loves his Moggie dearly*, which presents its Scottish protagonists as oafish yokels obsessed with sex and money, set to suitably 'scotch' music—sad parodies of the tunes in the lute manuscripts. The ridicule is all the more significant when it is realised that in Scots 'jocky', a contraction of 'joculator', was the term used for itinerant Celtic harper-minstrels.

The brave attempts of the seventeenth century to rejuvenate an indigenous national style of composition—a counterpart to the efforts of Thomas Wode in the previous century, but this time drawing on the legacy of folk music—consistently lacked the one crucial element which had made Musick Fyne so dynamic: its internationality. The secular music of seventeenth century Scotland is truly an epilogue in the sense that it leads original composition into an incestuous *cul-de-sac* of imitation, rich in pentatonic pretentions and little else.

In the previous century, Scotland had drawn heavily on Continental and English musical influences in both liturgical and secular spheres to create a wealth of Musick Fyne—it is scarcely to the credit of English and Continental composers, that when the time came for them to draw upon Scottish music, they left the neglected art music of Renaissance Scotland untouched, and concentrated on the folk music which was immediately available. Scotland became characterised as a land of massed bagpipes and drums and couthie ceilidhs, and when that myth, like a self-fulfilling prophecy, became reality, there was no place for art music written by native Scots. Reality faced a convenient and powerful mythology and was overwhelmed.

This protracted musical epilogue was set in motion in all innocence by the well-intentioned amateurs of the early seventeenth century, only to be distorted by ensuing generations of amateurs with varying intentions into a grotesque Celtic twilight. Perhaps now, for the first time in over three hundred years, this twilight may be viewed in its true perspective, as the feeble and artificial afterglow of a real Golden Age of music of national and international significance—a treasury of Musick Fyne, ripe for rediscovery.

Notes to the Text

FOREWORD

1 From 'Gairmscoile', *The Complete Poems of Hugh MacDiarmid* (ed. M Grieve & W R Aitken), p 74.
2 From *Gavin Douglas, A Selection from his Poetry* (ed. S G Smith), The Saltire Classics, Oliver & Boyd, Edinburgh, 1959, p 94.

INTRODUCTION

1 One of the most powerful expressions of Scottish patriotism ever penned is the anonymous Gaelic battle incitement to the Chief of the Clan Campbell, the Earl of Argyll, *Ar Sliocht Gaodhal*, written on the eve of James IV's 1513 campaign. For the complete poem and translation see *Scottish Verse from the Book of the Dean of Lismore*, (ed. W J Watson), Scottish Gaelic Texts Society, Edinburgh, 1937 (reprinted 1978), pp 158–164. For a superior poetic translation, see Derick Thomson, *An Introduction to Gaelic Poetry*, (2nd edition), Edinburgh University Press, Edinburgh, 1989, pp 31–33.
2 James IV's campaigns of 1496–7 had so cowed Henry VII that he readily agreed to the Treaty of Perpetual Peace and his daughter's marriage to James. He delivered something of a poisoned chalice, though, with his prescient observation that even if the marriage might one day lead to a Union of the Crowns with a Scot on the English throne, it would not matter, for 'in that caise Ingland wald not access unto Scotland, bot Scotland wald access unto Ingland, as to the most noble heid of the hole yle' (i.e. England would naturally predominate). See Norman Macdougal, *James IV*, John Donald, Edinburgh, 1989, pp 249–50.
3 There are many parallels between the Burgundian and Scottish situations—both states had everything to fear from their very large neighbours, England and France respectively. The Burgundian commitment to a great crusade had specific dynastic origins, but it also provided a means of accusing Burgundy's enemies of betraying Christ Himself by seeking Burgundy's ill; and indeed James IV made a very similar point to Henry VIII in May 1513 (see Macdougal, op.cit., p 264). In the case of both Scotland and Burgundy, the temporary weakness of their great neighbours allowed an extraordinary burgeoning of culture to take place under the protection of powerful, internationally respected rulers.
4 None of the European potentates could afford to offend James by openly ignoring his suggestions because of the political volatility of the situation that had arisen. In his efforts to provide himself with a secular power-base in the shape of a unified Italy, Pope Julius II had formed the League of Cambrai in 1508, which committed France and the Holy Roman Empire to the destruction of his main rival, Venice. At

this stage the Pope was anxious that James be ready to invade England should England take the opportunity to invade France, and he assiduously cultivated James' loyalty with gifts and verbal support for his planned crusade. Meanwhile, reasons of national security ensured that both the English and the French lent James a sympathetic ear. However when England joined the League of Cambrai in 1509, and the victorious French forces threatened to become a permanent presence in Italy, the Pope deftly switched allegiances, denounced the French King Louis XII as schismatic, and made France the target of the Holy League of 1511. Both sides still valued Scotland as a potentially useful ally and were prepared to pay the price of dissembling interest in James' crusade, in the knowledge that they could safely ignore him once the present crisis was past. The Papacy's ultimate *volte face* in excommunicating James for the very act it had promoted three years before, sealed the triumph of realism over idealism.

5 Quoted in Jenny Wormald, *Court, Kirk, and Community*, Edward Arnold, London, 1981, p 14.

6 A recent edition is in John and Winifred MacQueen (ed.), *Scottish Verse 1470–1570*, Faber, London, 1972, pp 118–122. For Dunbar's complete poems the edition by James Kinsley (Oxford 1979) is far superior to any other.

7 See the Mercat Press's own reprint (1978) of *The Poems and Fables of Robert Henryson*, (ed. H. Harvey Wood). The dated introduction needs to be supplemented by John MacQueen's *Robert Henryson—A Study of the Major Narrative Poems*, (Oxford 1967) and Matthew McDiarmid's study of Robert Henryson in the Scottish Writers Series.

8 Archdeacon of Aberdeen, Barbour was the professional propagandist for the new Stewart dynasty. (Selections from *The Bruce*, ed. A. M. Kinghorn, The Saltire Classics, Oliver & Boyd, Edinburgh, 1960).

9 Sir David Lyndsay, *Ane Satyre of the Thrie Estaitis*, (ed. R. Lyall) Canongate, Edinburgh, 1989.

10 As I have elsewhere endeavoured to show the people I mention the basic courtesy of using the version of their names they themselves seem to have preferred, I have used the 'French' spelling of Stuart for Mary, Queen of Scots and her son. I also restore latinised names to their probable vernacular original—John Major becomes John Mair, and Robertus Carwor, Robert Carver.

11 Selections of Alexander Scott's poems are available in The Saltire Society's *Poems by Alexander Scott*, (ed. A Scott), Oliver & Boyd, Edinburgh, 1952 and in John MacQueen's collection of courtly love lyrics, *Ballatis of Luve*, Edinburgh University Press, Edinburgh, 1970.

12 A selection of Montgomerie's verse is available in Helena Shire (ed.) *Alexander Montgomerie, A Selection from his Songs and Poems*, The Saltire Classics, Oliver & Boyd, Edinburgh, 1960. The definitive book on the poet and his work is R D S Jack, *Alexander Montgomerie*, Scottish Writers Series, Scottish Academic Press, Edinburgh, 1985.

13 In the *Scotichronicon*, Walter Bower makes lavish claims for James' prowess as a musician and composer, and although none of his music has survived, according to Alessandro Tassoni, quoted in John Purser, *Scotland's Music*, Mainstream Publishing, Edinburgh, 1992, it was as idiosyncratic as that of Gesualdo—a remarkable claim indeed! However, if James' abilities in the art of music matched the poetic skill he displays in *The Kingis Quair* ('The King's Book', of which his authorship is not seriously disputed) neither commentator may be far wide of the mark. See Matthew McDiarmid's edition of the work, Heinemann, London, 1973.

14 Quoted in C. Rogers, *History of the Scottish Chapel Royal*, Edinburgh, 1882, p xxxii.
15 The inventory of 4 November 1505, quoted in Rogers, op.cit., lists the following items:

4 printed and 1 manuscript Missal
Manuscript Epistle & Gospel books
2 old manuscript Psalters
4 large music books written on parchment, having diverse gilt capital letters
2 large printed Breviaries
1 printed Breviary—badly torn
2 volumes on parchment, having notes of counterpoint
2 Legends on parchment, one concerning temporal things the other relating to the saints
10 Processionals written on parchment & annotated
3 manuscript Gradualia and the large Gradual manuscript given to the king by the deceased abbot of St Colme.
1 large printed Breviary
1 small printed Breviary manuscript 'Ordinary in Usum Sarum'
1 small printed Missal.

16 The six-part Mass *Cantate Domino* in the *Dowglas/Fischar Part-books* (see pp 52–4) is probably also by Carver but is unsigned. I also make a case for the six-part Mass *Felix namque* in the same source being his work (see pp 76–80).
17 The whole issue of the Church in Stewart Scotland is lucidly discussed in Jenny Wormald, *Court, Kirk and Community*, Edward Arnold, London, 1981, pp 75–141. See also Michael Lynch's excellent account in *Scotland, a new History*, Pimlico, 1992, Chapter 7, 'The Medieval Church', and Chapter 12, 'Roads to Reformation', for a slightly different focus.
18 The surprising paucity of music, sacred and secular, to survive from James V's reign probably reflects the ravages of time and of the Reformation rather than any poverty of compositional activity at the court. We have seen that James was an able singer and assiduous lutenist, and we can assume that the music at his court was as magnificent as those other artistic ventures, the lavish building projects undertaken by his Master of Works, James Hamilton of Fynnart, which have survived by virtue of their more substantial nature. In James Hamilton, we would seem to be dealing with an architectural genius equivalent to the musical genius of Robert Carver. Like the latter, he has been denied the recognition he deserves and has only recently begun to emerge as one of Scotland's greatest architects, by whose remarkable skills 'it had been the intention of Scotland to earn itself its place upon the European stage as much by architecture as it had by arms.' (Charles McKean, 'James Hamilton of Finnart', *History Today*, January 1993, pp 42–7.) He also stands as a testament to the fickleness and avarice of the Stewart dynasty, brought to a fine art in James V. After a lifetime of outstanding service to his monarch, he was executed in 1540, ostensibly for discharging firearms in the King's direction, but more plausibly because of his considerable wealth, which the King promptly appropriated.
19 Several of James' predecessors on the Scottish throne had after all paid enforced and extended visits to England, and his daughter would learn the error of trusting in the Tudors' better nature.
20 See William Lamb, *Ane Resonyng of ane Scottis and Inglis Merchand betuix Rowand and Lionis*, (ed. R Lyall) Aberdeen, 1985. This is a hitherto unknown companion piece to the famous *Complaynt of Scotland*, (ed. A M Stewart), Scottish Text Society,

1979. See also the Early English Text Society's 1882 edition by J A H Murray of the *Complaynt* for the texts of several of the English proclamations concerned.

21 Genetically, since they were cousins, and Edward was a sickly individual, it is probably a blessing that the marriage never took place. The idea that this was a God-given opportunity to unite the kingdoms seems more than usually repellent in this particular case. It has to be said that in the French Dauphin, Mary found a spouse of little more physical merit.

22 From a Catholic viewpoint Mary had a more valid claim to the English throne than had either the illegitimate Elizabeth or the heretic Edward.

23 The New Church was not without its critics. The finest were Abbot Quintin Kennedy of Crossraguel and the Maister of Linlithgow Parish School, Ninian Winyet, who had vehemently criticised the corruption of the Old Church. They and others now poured forth superbly eloquent tirades against the 'pretendit ministeris of the deformit Kirk'. Winyet, indeed, was in no doubt that John Knox was an agent of England as much as of Satan, and attacked him and the Reformers for betraying their country, as later Catholics would continue to do.

24 See Alexander Scott's poem *Ane new Year Gift to the Queen Mary, when she come first hame, 1562*, in *Poems by Alexander Scott* (ed. A Scott), The Saltire Classics, Oliver & Boyd, Edinburgh, 1952, pp 12–20.

25 See John McQuaid, *Scottish Musicians of the Reformation*, Edinburgh, 1949, p 61 and p 80.

26 In the Ruthven Raid of 1582, James was kidnapped by the Earls of Gowrie and Mar, but when he escaped the following year, he saw to the execution of Gowrie and the exile of his accomplices. During his imprisonment, his captors had failed to pay the salaries of the court musicians, an omission which James promptly made good.

27 These circumstances are by no means unique to England. The Spanish composer Manuel de Falla was well acquainted with his country's early music, both Mediaeval and Renaissance, through Felipe Pedrell, and was no more a 'folksong composer' than was Vaughan Williams.

28 The poem appears in *The New Makars: The Mercat Anthology of Contemporary Poetry in Scots* (ed. Tom Hubbard), Mercat Press, Edinburgh, 1991, pp 162–3.

CHAPTER 1

1 J A Fuller-Maitland, '*A Scottish composer of the 16th Century*', Gedenkenboek aangeboden aan Dr D F Schleurkeer op zijn 70sten verjaardag', s-Gravenhage: Nijhoff, 1925, p 119–122. Though very much of their time, his studies of the contents of the *Carver Choirbook* reveal an acute awareness of the quality of Carver's music and its performance potential. The notes to his scholarly edition of *O bone Jesu*, Dean and Sons, London, 1926, contain the following enlightened observation: 'There is of course no indication as to light and shade, and to introduce nuances after the modern fashion would spoil the effect, since if all the voices sing with even tone, the addition of extra parts at important points will carry with it the effect of crescendos.'

2 A list of relevant writings by Dr Elliott appears in the Bibliography.

3 Woods, op.cit, Vol. I.

4 For a more detailed treatment see Ibid., p 19.

5 See Ibid., pp 14–17.

6 See p 31.

7 Dr Durkan informed me in 1991 that he had handed his findings on to Dr Kenneth Elliott, who eventually intends to publish an article in the *Innes Review*.

8 See Dr Kenneth Elliott and Professor Frederick Rimmer, *A History of Scottish Music*, BBC Publications, London, 1973, p 15.

9 It was not uncommon for composers in the sixteenth century to adopt the names of their principal benefactors. The tradition continued into the seventeenth century with the Italian composer Pier Francesco Bruni (1602–1676) adopting the name Cavalli in deference to a generous patron. The use of aliases in Scotland was extremely common; an instance of direct interest is Carver's contemporary William Lamb, author of *Ane Resonyng of Ane Scottis and Inglis Merchand* (1549) whose alias was Paniter, referring to his uncle Patrick Paniter, Abbot of Cambuskenneth and James IV's secretary. Lamb dropped the alias immediately after Paniter died.

10 See Woods, op.cit., Vol. I, p 19.

11 Ibid., pp 22–3. It is perhaps significant that Dr Durkan's research suggests that the young Robert Carver was staying with an uncle in Aberdeen at a time when, as we have seen, two major religious buildings were undergoing expansion involving extensive building and joinery work.

12 Quoted in Jim Inglis, *The Organ in Scotland before 1700*, De Mixtuur, Schagen 1991, p 57.

13 See Woods, op.cit., pp 26–38.

14 Here and elsewhere in the text the term 'motet' is used to indicate an independent piece of choral church music, distinct from a setting of the Mass, *Magnificat* or *Te Deum*.

15 A fuller discussion of these composers and their style can be found in David Wulstan, *Tudor Music*, Dent, London, 1985, pp 250–278.

16 See Woods, op.cit., Vol. I, p 110.

17 Here and elsewhere I have applied the implications of Dr Durkan's research to the dating of Carver's music.

18 For a full treatment see Ibid., p 91.

19 See Elliott, op.cit., pp 8–9.

20 For a fuller discussion of this and other aspects of *The St Andrews Music Book* see John Purser, *Scotland's Music*, Mainstream Publishing, Edinburgh & London, 1992, pp 49–56.

21 John Purser, op.cit., p 55.

22 See Farmer, *A History of Music in Scotland*, Hinrichson, London, 1947, p 67.

23 See Woods, op.cit., Vol. I, p 211.

24 Judson Maynard, *An Anonymous Scottish Treatise on Music from the Sixteenth Century, British Museum, Additional Manuscript 4911, Edition and Commentary*, Indiana University, 1961. In two volumes, Vol. I Commentary, Vol. II Edition. For a full treatment of this MS see p 94.

25 On the other hand, the utter silence of contemporary written records with regard to Carver's artistic achievement may suggest that he was simply one of many gifted Scottish polyphonists at this time, all of whom were taken for granted, musicians being all too often regarded merely as servants until the late eighteenth century.

CHAPTER 2

1 As most modern readers will be acquainted with modern western concepts of tonality, I have endeavoured to explain modality using modern concepts of key, tonal centres, tonic, dominant etc. On the whole they are terms which would have been alien to Carver. I also use the accepted names and numbers for the modes

developed from the Gregorian system and formulated by Henricus Glareanus in 1547. Throughout the book, when discussing examples, I have used standard English organ pitch notation (C, c, c', c" – where c' is 'middle c' between bass and treble clefs). Where pitch is irrelevant, as for example when discussing tonal centres, I have consistently used the capital letter. For a full discussion of performance pitch see pp 58–59. I have also used modern terminology for concepts of rhythm, such as simple and compound time.

2   For a full treatment of *musica ficta* see Wulstan, op.cit., pp 164–7.

3   In a letter to the author, dated 19/2/85. Readers who wish to hear the extent to which the application of *musica ficta* changes the complexion of Carver's music should compare Capella Nova's performance of Muriel Brown's edition of Carver's Mass *Dum sacrum mysterium* with their performances of the other Masses in Kenneth Elliott's editions. For further details see Discography.

4   Rapid scales of this type were a feature of some of the Scottish works in *The St Andrews Music Book*.

5   As has already been observed, *The St Andrews Music Book* was noted for its demands on extremes of vocal range.

6   The *Kyrie* in the Sarum Rite was often troped with extra text, and as such was viewed as forming part of the 'proper' of the Mass, i.e. what was proper or specific to the liturgical celebration in question.

7   See Woods, op.cit., Vol. I, pp 87–89. (The plainchant melodies used by Carver in his Masses *Dum sacrum mysterium* and *Pater Creator omnium* differ slightly from the standard versions in the Sarum Gradual which may indicate an alternative plainchant tradition in Scotland.) For a fuller treatment of plainchant see pp 62–63.

8   For a fuller treatment see Ibid., Vol. I, p 186–9.

9   The Burgundian Dukes' interest stemmed from two sources: first, the need to steal a march on the French monarchy, with which they had a complex and uneasy relationship, and attract Europe-wide attention as the premier force of chivalry in Christendom, and secondly, as Jim Reid Baxter has pointed out, to blot out the memory of the humiliation of the capture of John the Fearless, Duke Philip's father, by the Turks at Nicopolis in 1396. The evidence for Charles using his image as the 'armed man' to enlist support for a crusade is overwhelming. The most spectacular collection of *L'Homme Armé* settings, an encyclopaedic set of thirty Mass movements, each concentrating on different aspects of the *cantus*, preserved in a manuscript in the Biblioteca Nazionale in Naples (B.N. Ms VI. E. 40), bear an inscription stating that they were enjoyed by Charles before being presented to Beatrice of Aragon, daughter of Ferdinand I of Naples and wife of Matthias Corvinus. Charles is known to have approached both these powerful rulers with a view to convincing them of the need for a crusade.

Both the glittering Philip and the warlike Charles served as models for James IV, in whose policies England played the rôle France had played vis-à-vis Burgundy. There are many striking parallels between Charles and James, down to their apparent shared enthusiasm for Alexander the Great and Judas Macabeus. Ironically, though, it was in his death that James would come closest in his emulation of his Burgundian rôle model; in both cases the monarch's mutilated body was only identified on the day following his violent death in battle.

10   David Fallows in *Dufay* points out that although he can find no substantiation for the tradition that Regis was actually Dufay's clerk for a time, he did in fact hold Dufay's curacy at Soignie and clearly knew the Cambrai master, who actively sought but failed to obtain his services as choirmaster.

11 For a full treatment of the use of the *Fera pessima cantus firmus* by Machaut and Compère, see Jeffrey Dean, 'The Occasion of Compère's *Sola caret monstris:* a Case Study in Historical Interpretation', *Musica Disciplina*, 1986, Vol.40, pp 99–133. Compère's body of work also includes a Mass *L'Homme Armé*.

12 For a fuller treatment of the events surrounding the formation of the Holy League, see the Introduction.

13 Isobel Woods' suggestion that the *fera pessima* of the *cantus* may refer to the plague seems little more than a last vestige of her mistaken reading of the first part of the second word of the inscription as 'pest'.

14 See Margaret Sanderson, *Cardinal of Scotland*, John Donald, Edinburgh, 1986, especially p 116.

15 The 'Rough Wooing', ostensibly a reaction on the part of Henry VIII to Scotland's rejection of his son Edward in favour of the French Dauphin as a spouse for Mary, was in fact merely a continuation of the English pursuit of sovereignty over Scotland, which had led to the Battle of Solway Moss on 24 November 1542 and the death of James V. Scotland's suffering was again a result of the Auld Alliance. Henry had concluded a treaty with the Holy Roman Emperor against France and in a situation similar in many ways to that preceding Flodden, Scotland was forced to choose between England and France. The choice of France, which triggered the 'Rough Wooing' as an immediate consequence, would also colour events in Scotland until the end of the sixteenth century.

16 Instructions of Henry's Privy Council to Hertford in 1544. Quoted in William Dickinson, Gordon Donaldson, Isabel Milne (ed.), *A Source Book of Scottish History*, vol II, Thomas Nelson, London 1953, pp 126–7.

17 Quoted in Ibid., pp 127–8.

18 See pp 5–6. If Carver was studying in Louvain in Brabant in the period following 1503/4, he would have been geographically close to Compère, who seems to have spent these years in Douai in the northern part of France.

CHAPTER 3

1 Kenneth Elliott's edition of this work is published in *Musica Britannica*, Vol. XV, Stainer & Bell, London, 1975, pp 30–57 and Muriel Brown's edition is available from Bardic Edition (see Bibliography).

2 Elliott, op.cit., p 17.

3 Maynard, op.cit., vol II p 18.

4 *Ritson's MS* (BL Add. 5665) was compiled between 1480 and 1530 and contains carols, ballades and earthy secular songs. *Henry VIII's Manuscript* (BL Add. 31922) was compiled in the early sixteenth century and contains a selection of canons, three-part songs and lively music for consort.

5 Carver would of course have heard a lot of ceremonial trumpeting at James IV's court. See John Purser, *Scotland's Music*, Mainstream Publishing, Edinburgh 1992, pp 86–7.

6 The hocket or *hoquetus* is a compositional device which involves the rapid alternation in two voices of bursts of notes and rests, so that each voice 'fills in the spaces' for the other and the result is a continuous texture.

CHAPTER 4

1 A complete edition of this work is available in Woods, op.cit., Vol. II, pp 137–175. Muriel Brown's edition is available from Bardic Edition (see Bibliography).
2 For a full treatment see Woods, op.cit., Vol. 1, p 214.
3 I have used the term 'treble' here and elsewhere to denote the upper voice part(s), intended for performance by boy trebles, irrespective of the upper limit. This would appear to be the way in which the term was used in sixteenth century Scotland.
4 Quoted in Jim Inglis, op.cit., p 90. Interestingly, Squire Meldrum would appear to have sailed on board the *Great Michael* when the ship attacked Carrickfergus.

CHAPTER 5

1 A complete edition of this work is available in Woods, op.cit., Vol II, pp 62–136 and Muriel Brown's edition is available from Bardic Edition (see Bibliography).
2 For a full treatment of Alesius see Wormald, op.cit., pp 102–103. As an Augustinian canon of St Andrews, Alexander Alane (which he latinised to Alesius) conducted a disputation with Patrick Hamilton before Hamilton's execution, and as a result he became first a reformer inside the Old Church and from 1533 a Protestant, writing from exile on the continent.
3 Farmer, op.cit., p 113. Hamilton studied Hebrew at Louvain University. Alesius mentions that Hamilton 'composed a Mass for nine voices for the office of the missal which begins, *Benedicant Dominum omnes angeli eius*' (quoted in Purser, op.cit., p 94).
4 Woods, op.cit., Vol. I, p 209.
5 See notes by Hugh Keyte to the Taverner Consort recording on CDC 7 495552.
6 Carver does not set the *Kyrie*. The Sarum *Kyrie* for St Michael's Day is *Kyrie Rex splendens*.
7 Jim Reid Baxter has observed that Brumel's choice of *cantus*, the first seven notes of the Easter antiphon *Et ecce terrae motus*, provides a further connection with Carver's Mass. The earthquake, referred to in the antiphon and so graphically illustrated by Brumel, announces the descent from heaven of the Angel of the Lord, traditionally supposed to be St Michael: 'Et ecce terrae motus factus est magnus: angelus enim Domini descendit de caelo. Alleluia.' Another of Brumel's Masses uses the associated *L'Homme Armé* tune as *cantus*.
8 Woods, op.cit., pp 14–15.
9 See footnote 6 above.
10 Jim Reid Baxter's research into the liturgical context of Carver's ten-part Mass has featured in programme notes for a number of performances of the work which he instigated in 1988 and 1991.
11 For a full treatment of the subject of performance pitch in general and the vocal ranges that Carver uses see pp 58–60.
12 The circumstances of the 1513 performance of the Mass *Dum sacrum mysterium* lend a poignant relevance in retrospect to the words of the section that Carver makes reference to:

To recall your former joys now all turned to grief.

13 Both Carver and Cornysh anticipate the English technique of gymel which involved the division of the treble part to permit interplay between two high voices of equal

range. One of the finest examples of gymel is in John Taverner's Mass *Corona spinea*. It is double gymel with both trebles and altos divided—in effect the same scoring as that used by Carver—and it is perhaps not insignificant that it too occurs in the 'qui tollis' section of the central *Agnus Dei*.

CHAPTER 6

1 A complete edition is to be found in Denis Stevens (Ed.), *Opera Omnia: Corpus Mensurabilis Musicae*, Vol. XVI, American Institute of Musicology, Rome, 1959. Muriel Brown's edition is available from Bardic Edition (see Bibliography).

2 A complete edition is to be found in Kenneth Elliott (Ed.), *Music in Scotland 1500–1700, Musica Britannica*, Vol. XV, Stainer & Bell, London, 1975, pp 87–102. Muriel Brown's edition is available from Bardic Edition (see Bibliography).

3 See Woods, op.cit., Vol. I, pp 202–208. Four of the *Magnificat* settings and the four-part *Salve Regina* have not so far been found in any other source, leading to speculation that they may have been composed in Scotland in emulation of the work of the *Eton* masters. While much of the music seems to be standard *Eton* fare, sections of the anonymous *Salve Regina* were revealed as intriguingly Carveresque in its first modern performances in Aberdeen and Edinburgh in 1989.

4 See Wulstan, op.cit., p 251.

5 For a full treatment of the subject of performance pitch and vocal ranges see pp 58–60.

6 However, given that this archaic sounding music refers to 'heavenly joys', it may not be irrelevant to note that the angels of heaven, in 'All sons of Adam' sing in archaic faburden (see pp 125–126).

7 The *Choirbook* gives no clue as to why Carver chose nineteen voices, or for that matter precisely when he composed the motet, but it is interesting to note that James III was murdered on 11 June 1488 and so in 1506/7 his son, James IV, was in the nineteenth year of his reign. This would tie the piece in with the overwhelming guilt which James IV is known to have felt about his part in the death of his father and the circumstances of his accession to the throne and would help to explain the amendment of text (paralleled in the Litany *Vos quoque sancti patriarche*) first noted by Isobel Woods from the normal first person plural to the singular, giving this monumental work the character of a fervent private prayer of deep contrition. A composition date of 1506/7 would also place it nearer in chronology to the Mass *Dum sacrum mysterium* with which it shares material. However, there is no independent evidence, and the *Carver Choirbook* copy seems to date from around 1513.

8 Further reference to this practice is made in Wulstan, op.cit., p 258.

9 Maynard, op.cit., Vol. II, p 135.

CHAPTER 7

1 An edition which restores the missing tenor part, but does not reconstruct the top line, is available in Woods, op.cit., Vol. II, pp 238–247. My own fully reconstructed performance edition remains unpublished but has been recorded by Musick Fyne (CMF 004) as part of a liturgical reconstruction of a Scottish Mass of 1546, which also includes the Inverness setting of *Laudate pueri*. (For full details see Discography.) Muriel Brown's reconstructed edition is available from Bardic Edition (see Bibliography). Kenneth Elliott's edition is unpublished but has been recorded by Capella Nova. (See Discography.)

2 Woods, op.cit., Vol. I, pp 191–192.

3 Woods, op.cit., Vol. I, p 35. Isobel Woods speculates that this Mass was written for the Stirling Parish Church on the occasion of its elevation to collegiate status, which is known to have taken place around 1546, but as 1543 is now the most likely date for the Mass, this seems unlikely.

4 See Inglis, op.cit., p 20.

5 See Woods, op.cit., Vol. I, p 140.

6 Maynard, op.cit., Vol. II, pp 281–331.

7 Woods, op.cit., Vol. I, p 141.

8 There is the further consideration that in the *Credo* the polyphony begins only with 'factorem celi', the words 'Credo in unum Deum, patrem omnipotentem' unusually all being sung to plainchant; this was a feature of Benedictine practice, and may indicate some link with the Benedictine Abbey of Dunfermline, or even Paisley, a Cluniac (Reformed Benedictine) house, whose Abbot John Hamilton was instrumental in his half-brother Arran's return to Catholicism.

9 For a full treatment of Richardson see Wormald, op.cit., p 84. Like his relative Alexander Alesius, Robertus Richardinus eventually gave up the struggle for reform from within the Old Church. After a period of exile on the Continent and in England, in 1543 he was sent back to Scotland by Henry VIII as a Protestant preacher and English agent, like George Wishart.

10 This work is dealt with more fully in Woods, op.cit., Vol. I, pp 81–92.

11 Translation from Latin quoted in ibid., p 85.

12 A complete edition of this work appears in Maynard, op.cit., Vol. II, pp 310–324 and pp 330–331.

13 A complete edition of this material and a full discussion of its significance is to be found in Stephen Allenson, 'The Inverness Fragments: Music from a Pre-Reformation Scottish Parish Church and School', *Music & Letters* Vol. 70, No. 1, 1989, pp 1–45. The timeless nature of faburden makes Allenson's dating of the material to the second or third quarter of the sixteenth century rather speculative, and as he points out himself, 'the archaic consonant style of much of it might suggest a date of 50 or more years earlier'. I have collaborated with Fr. Mark Dilworth on a paper for publication in the *Innes Review* which reconsiders the *Fragments* in the light of recent research into the practice of faburden in sixteenth century Scotland. In this item I have speculated that we should perhaps reinterpret the apparent and short-lived triumph of faburden over freely composed polyphony at the Chapel Royal as the temporary overwhelming of the urbane courtly taste by the provincial. My performance edition of the *Laudate pueri*, which alternates verses in the three-part first kind of faburden (K2—version 3) with verses in the four-part second kind of faburden (L1r, K1-2r and K4v—version 6) published by CMF music, is performed by Musick Fyne on CMF 004. For full details see Discography and Bibliography.

14 If this was the task Carver was asked to fulfil he was only partially successful—while Arran's conversion proved not to be the nine days' wonder many must have feared (or hoped), by contrast the Earl of Lennox defected to the English cause immediately after participating in the coronation.

CHAPTER 8

1 A complete edition of this work is to be found in Woods, op.cit., Vol. 11, pp 248–286. Muriel Brown's edition is available from Bardic Edition (see Bibliography).

2 See pp 42–44.

3 Kenneth Elliott, 'Robert Carver', *The New Grove Dictionary of Music and Musicians*, Macmillan, London, 1980, Vol. III, p 842.
4 See p 17.
5 Quoted in Lionel Pike, 'Tallis—Vaughan Williams—Howells', *Tempo*, No.149, 1985, p 2.
6 For a treatment of the link between this motet and Carver's Mass see p 17.
7 Both *The Art of Music* and Thomas Wode's notes to his *Part-books* cite Fayrfax as a touchstone of creative greatness.
8 Jim Reid Baxter has pointed out that the *Agnus Dei* was the obvious place for composers to display their accomplishments because 'they were, after all, directly addressing the Godhead present on the altar at this point in the liturgy'. He has also observed that Carver's emphasis on the final petition with its plea for peace may reflect the personal influence of James IV, a view confirmed by recent scholarship which reveals him as a man who saw himself primarily as a warrior—after all, the ultimate goal was the peace of God, to be achieved by crusading.
9 Wulstan, op.cit., pp 49–51.
10 If this concluding section was added later, the presence of a similar chime imitation in the 'et homo factus est' section of the *Credo* may have some implications for current perceptions of Renaissance compositional method.

CHAPTER 9

1 A complete edition of this work is to be found in *Musica Britannica*, Vol. XV, pp 1–8.
2 Woods, op.cit., Vol. I, pp 110–111.
3 Kenneth Elliott's transcription in *Musica Britannica*, Vol. XV for three altos is an unacknowledged editorial liberty, for which the manuscript provides no justification, and which is dismissed by Isobel Woods, op.cit., Vol. I, pp 165–166.
4 Woods, op.cit., Vol. I, p 151.
5 See Woods, op.cit., Vol. I, pp 145–150 (commentary) and Vol. II pp 223–238, pp 287–297 and p 299 (editions). The opening pages of the (as yet unidentified) Litany are missing, and the setting commences with the text *vos quoque sancti patriarche*, which, by default, provides the piece with its provisional title. The psalm setting is dealt with on pp 104–105.
6 The *Dowglas/Fischar Part-books* are discussed on pp 75–76.
7 Dr Elliott's edition of this work remains unpublished, but a performance using his edition has been recorded by Paisley Abbey Choir on ACA532.

CHAPTER 10

1 See Farmer, op.cit., p 113.
2 Recently the Dutch group Capella Pratensis has attempted to work out the full implications of authentic performance of the works of Ockeghem by restaging the illustrated performance down to the last detail. The performers use a single large choirbook with no barlines and maintain contact within the ensemble by resting a hand on the singer in front as the choir appear to be doing in the illustration. The resulting performances have a convincing sense of flow and forward momentum (although sadly tuning inaccuracies, incidental to the reconstruction process, make them less than satisfactory).

3 Maynard, op.cit., Vol. II, p 67.

4 Wulstan, op.cit., pp 207–210.

5 Woods, op.cit., Vol. I, pp 154–166.

6 Not bass and alto as Isobel Woods states (ibid., pp 161–162) as this presupposes an upward transposition in line with Wulstan's theories which probably do not apply.

7 Quoted in Woods, op.cit., Vol. I, pp 69–70.

8 Quoted in C Rogers, *History of the Chapel Royal of Scotland*, Edinburgh, 1882, p xli. As the Abbey of Scone was involved in this expansion of the Chapel Royal and we know that Carver was working there by 1506, having completed his studies at Louvain in 1504/5 (see pp 5–6), it is not unreasonable to assume that the young composer was part of this intake.

9 See Wulstan, op.cit., pp 223–5.

10 See Leslie MacFarlane, *William Elphinstone and the Kingdom of Scotland 1431–1514*, Aberdeen University Press, Aberdeen, 1985, p 224.

11 Dr Jim Reid Baxter in a programme note for the first complete performance in modern times of Carver's Mass *L'Homme Armé*, St Machar's Cathedral, Aberdeen, 1982.

12 See Woods, op.cit., Vol. I, p 89.

13 Decree of the Lords of the Council in support of Chepman and Millar's monopoly 1507, quoted in Dickinson, Donaldson and Milne, op.cit., pp 117–8.

14 'that forsamekill as oor lovittis servitouris Walter Chepman and Andro Millar burgess of our burgh of Edinburgh, has at our instance and request, for our plesour, the honour and proffit of our realme and leigis, takin on thame to furnis and bring hame ane prent with al stuf belangand tharto and expert men to use the samyne . . . and because we understand that this can nocht be perfurnist without rycht greit cost, labour and expens, we have grantit and promittit to thame that thai sal nocht be hurt nor preventit thairin be ony utheris to tak copyis of any bukis furtht of our realme, to ger imprent the samyne in utheris cuntreis to be brocht and sauld agane within our realme to caus the said Walter and Androu tyne thare greit labour and expens.'

    Decree of the Lords of the Council in support of Chepman and Millar's monopoly 1507, quoted in Dickinson, Donaldson and Milne, op.cit., p 118.

15 John Purser's recent discovery that the thirteenth-century *Sprouston Breviary* in the National Library of Scotland contains music as well as text relevant to a number of services for Scottish saints, including St Kentigern, indicates that Elphinstone was trying to reconstruct rather than fabricate services for Scottish Saints. The music also neatly confirms Scotland's early adoption of the Sarum Rite. The older Celtic chant, apparently exemplified in the thirteenth-century *Inchcolm Antiphoner* in Edinburgh University Library, was gradually overtaken by the new Sarum chant, and notwithstanding a few surviving pockets, seems to have been largely marginalised by the sixteenth century.

16 This performance by the Ensemble Organum and the Ensemble Clément Janequin is available on HMC 901239.

17 The standard text on this subject is Harold Copeman, *Singing in Latin*, Published by the author, Oxford 1990.

18 An interesting source of information on the pronunciation of Latin is John Hart's *Orthographie*, written in 1551 and published in London in 1569. Referring to pronunciation practice in England, it largely corroborates the idea that Latin was given a standard vernacular pronunciation.

CHAPTER 11

1 An authoritative commentary on the *Wode Part-books* is Hilda Hutchison, *The St Andrews Psalter, Edition and Commentary*, Vol.I, Edinburgh University, 1957, while the second volume of her dissertation provides a complete transcription of the *Part-books'* contents. This information about David Peebles is quoted on pp 75–6.

2 It is not clear whether the inclusion of some of Peebles' pre-Reformation music was part of a deal struck between Wode and the composer to help overcome the latter's reluctance to set the psalms, or whether it was entirely Wode's own idea. Indeed, while the blots on Wode's record of service to the Reformed Church seem to have been sins of omission resulting probably from the additional demands made on his time by his work on the *Part-books*, he seems, like Peebles, to have retained certain attitudes from his pre-Reformation years as a monk. His obvious love of polyphony was hardly in line with current Reformed thinking and it is perhaps also significant that he never married.

3 In the face of such lamentable lack of interest in Scottish archival material, one can only echo John Purser's wry observation on discovering that the *Sprouston Breviary* in the National Library of Scotland contained a great deal of music, a fact no commentator had even mentioned: 'It remains to be seen whether there are not other manuscripts . . . lurking in libraries or, perhaps known to all except the people of Scotland and the musicologists who should be working on their behalf.' Op. cit. p 48.

4 See Wormald, op.cit. pp 113, 124 and 135. In the period immediately preceding Wode's compilation of the *Part-books*, both John Knox and Christopher Goodman were resident in St Andrews. Goodman, an Englishman and the author of *How Superior Powers ought to be Obeyed*, was Knox's right-hand man and as a reward for his loyalty was appointed minister in Ayr in 1559. In *Scottish Musicians of the Reformation*, Edinburgh University, 1949, John McQuaid makes the point that Wode and his patron James Stewart, together with Knox and Goodman, may well have played a leading rôle in defining the sort of music which would be suitable for Reformed services, namely very simple syllabic settings of the Psalms and Canticles. The understandable misgivings of musicians in St Andrews at the same time, such as David Peebles and Andrew Kemp (both of whom harmonised psalm tunes under varying degrees of duress), seem to have been largely ignored, although subsequent events suggest that in practice Wode does not seem to have been able to stick to the fundamentalist party line either.

5 Published in *Musica Britannica*, Vol.XV, pp 103–105.

6 Ibid., pp 111–114.

7 Similar observations have been made by a number of scholars studying a range of Scottish arts of this period. In his study of Robert Henryson in the Scottish Writers series (pp 30–5), Matthew McDiarmid identifies and tries to account for these same qualities in the poetry of the fifteenth and sixteenth centuries.

8 *Musica Britannica*, Vol.XV, pp 106–110.

9 Wulstan, op.cit. p 298. This idea was first mooted by Henry Farmer, op.cit., pp 112–3.

10 Most of the information we have about Johnson's early life stems from Wode, who comments that he fled to England 'lang before reformation . . . for accusation of heresy'. Exactly when this was is not clear. There was a major burning of heretics in August 1534, the year of Henry VIII's final break with Rome, at which time many churchmen fled to England. This mass emigration was counterpointed by an equivalent immigration of English clerics escaping Henry's anti-Catholic mea-

sures, which culminated the following year in the executions of Dr Richard Reynolds (4 May), Bishop John Fisher (25 June) and Sir Thomas More (6 July), whose martyrdom sent reverberations up and down Europe.

In *Scottish Musicians of the Reformation*, Edinburgh University, 1949, John McQuaid makes the point that Thomas Wode may well be mistaken in stating accusation of heresy as Robert Johnson's reason for fleeing to England, confusing him with the Protestant Andrew Johnson, convicted of heresy in 1535. If Robert Johnson fled for purely political reasons, it would help to explain why he preserved the 'Catholic' music written before his flight and apparently continued to set Latin texts, including Psalm 21, *Domine in virtute tua*, of which Wode records a substantial five-part setting by Johnson, which he notes was 'set in ingland in tyme of papistry, IX or X yeiris before reformation', i.e. in the early 1550s and during the reign of Mary I. The apparent references to a likeness of Mary ('formam Mariae' – possibly a religious effigy of the Virgin) in a splendid five-part setting of *Omnes gentes, attendite* (See Bibliography) recorded by Wode between the two pieces by Johnson may indicate that it shares a similar provenance.

11 *Musica Britannica*, Vol.XV, pp 115–119.
12 Robart Stewart was actually to all intents and purposes an Anglican; he even held a prebend of Canterbury Cathedral, for he spent many years in English exile. It seems possible that he emulated Elizabeth I in her tolerance of those with Catholic sympathies. It may be pertinent to recall that 1575 saw the fanatical Calvinist Andrew Melville and the General Assembly criticising the Regent Morton's court for its luxury and display; Morton was no Presbyerian, also having spent much time in England. *Quam multi Domine* may have suggested itself to Robart Stewart as a suitable response to the fiery Melville, with his anti-episcopalism and his claims of Kirk supremacy. Although the composition of the piece may have been the result of some such temporary alliance of convenience, Peebles' music tells us what it meant to him.

CHAPTER 12

1 Kenneth Elliott, 'Church Music at Dunkell', *Music & Letters*, Vol. XLV, No. 3, 1964, p 232.
2 Published in *Musica Britannica*, Vol. XV, pp 58–86 in Kenneth Elliott's edition, which reconstructs the missing second Bass part.
3 For a fuller treatment see Wulstan, op.cit., p 108.
4 Farmer, op.cit., p 114.
5 The so-called English dissonance was a device which caused a passing clash of a sharpened leading note with its unsharpened counterpart, a jarring of adjacent semitones which sounds daring even to modern listeners. The clash was the result of the application of *musica ficta* in the case of the one note but not of the other, because of the differing melodic contexts of each. It arises in Continental music of the fourteenth and fifteenth centuries, but earned its name from the fact that it became a hallmark of Tudor composition. For a full treatment of English dissonance and of *musica ficta* see Wulstan, op.cit., p 164–7.
6 See p 40.
7 The *Benedictus* trope 'Mariae filius' may have been felt to have had a personal rather than liturgical significance on such an occasion. I describe later how Alexander Scott, poet, composer and member of the Chapel Royal would appear to have been involved in the arrangements surrounding Mary's departure and may even have accompanied her to the French court (see p 127).

8 See W C Dickinson (revised A A M Duncan), *Scotland from the Earliest Times to 1603*, Oxford University Press, Oxford 1977, p 348.
9 It is not outwith the realms of possibility that the setting was composed specially for this occasion, which would have taken place in Mary's private chambers at Holyrood, and indeed these circumstances may explain a couple of unusual features of the Mass *Felix namque*. The limited space may well have necessitated the use of only six solo voices, accounting both for the lack of contrasting density of ornamentation between solo and full choir sections and for the low range of the second bass part. I have made the point (p 59) that the use of unusually low bass notes may indicate that the work in question was intended for an intimate domestic context, and while the second bass part of the Mass *Felix namque* is missing, Kenneth Elliott is undoubtedly justified in his assumption that it descends frequently to an E.

CHAPTER 13

1 Act anent heresy 1525, quoted in Dickinson, Donaldson and Milne, op. cit., p 108.
2 Quoted in John McQuaid, *Scottish Musicians of the Reformation*, Edinburgh University, 1949, p 17.
3 Account by Thomas Randolph quoted in Purser, op.cit., p 100.
4 See pp 65–57. Wode's attempts to preserve music have a literary parallel in the Maitland and Bannatyne Manuscripts, collections of poetry gathered with the intention of saving Scottish culture. Clearly Wode's fears were shared by a number of contemporaries. See Wormald, op.cit., p 189 on Kirk censorship. See also footnote 13 below.
5 For a fuller treatment see Elliott, op.cit., p 25.
6 This poem is printed in Iain Ross (ed.), *The Gude and Godlie Ballatis*, The Saltire Classics, Oliver and Boyd, London, 1940, pp 43–46.
7 Robert Carver may well have been the son of a priest (see p 5), and Isobel Woods suggests that he may have registered illegitimate children of his own. Woods, op.cit., Vol. I, pp 31–2.
8 This poem is printed in Iain Ross (Ed.), op.cit., p 54.
9 Ibid., pp 60–63. The branding of the Pope as a pagan has an interesting parallel in *Ane Prayer* recorded in the *Wode Part-books*, where the Pope acquires the same bogey-man status that the infidel had enjoyed since the reign of James IV.

> Preserve us Lord by thy deare worde
> from Turke and Pope defend us Lord,
> which both would thrust out of his throne,
> O Lord, Jesus Christ, thy deare Sonne.

10 Ibid., pp 13–14.
11 Four of these harmonisations are printed in *Musica Britannica*, vol. XV, p 132, p 133, p 135 and p 138.
12 Luther's comment on the musical prowess of Josquin, 'He is master of the notes; others are mastered by them', was no isolated expression of enthusiasm for polyphony. In his foreword to the *Wittemberg Gesangbuch* of 1524 he writes even more explicitly in support of music,

> Because I am not of the opinion that all the arts shall be crushed and perish through the Gospel, as some bigoted persons pretend, but would willingly see

them all, and especially music, servants of him who gave and created them. So I pray that every pious Christian may bear with this and, should God grant him an equal or a greater talent, help to further it.

13 The Reformers also abandoned the Scots language in favour of English, native to some such as Goodman, and the preferred tongue of Knox himself, who was attacked by the Catholic counter-Reformer, Ninian Winyet (c 1518–92) in these uncompromising terms:

Gif ye, throw curiositie of novationis, haif forget our auld plane Scottis quhilk your mother leirit ye, in tymes cuming I sall wryte to you my mynd in Latin, for I am nocht acquyintit with your Southeroun.

The effects of choosing 'Southeroun' as the language of the soul were disastrous for Scottish intellectual life: a Scots prose literature failed to develop (the effect of the Word of God being read in English to Scots-speaking congregations can scarcely have enhanced Scottish self-esteem). Scots continued to be used by the court, but King James VI's departure for London in 1603 sealed the fate of literary Scots until the pioneering work of Allan Ramsay (1684–1758) and Robert Fergusson (1750–1774) a century and a half later. Indeed Ramsay republished the great makars of the sixteenth century in 1724.

CHAPTER 14

1 Published in *Musica Britannica*, vol. XV, pp 128–9.
2 Elliott, op.cit., pp 30–31.
3 Published in *Musica Britannica*, vol. XV, pp 120–3. Although Wode dates the piece 1575, the wedding that he associates it with took place in 1573. Clearly here, as occasionally elsewhere during his taxing enterprise, he slipped up.
4 Ibid., pp 124–7.
5 In her commentary on the *Part-books*, Hilda Hutchison points out that Wode's statements that the psalm was written in 1575 and 'set & send be blakhall to my l. mar at his first mariadge with my l. of Angus sister' are unaccountably inaccurate in almost every respect. Perhaps it was a similar error in the publishing of banns of marriage that caused him to fall foul of the St Andrews Presbytery in July 1587. At any rate, we can surely afford Wode the sort of magnanimity he demonstrates so frequently himself, putting his errors down to overwork as he toiled to complete his remarkable labour of love. See Hilda Hutchison, *The St Andrews Psalter, Edition and Commentary*, Vol. I (Commentary), Edinburgh University, 1957, p 171 and p 14.
6 Jim Reid Baxter's research into the provenance of Blakhall's psalms, on which this account draws heavily, exposes considerable credibility gaps in the assumption, initiated by Kenneth Elliot (op.cit., pp 31–2) and widely promulgated since, that *Judge and revenge my cause* was part of Morton's attempt to obtain a fair hearing of his case against implication in the murder of Darnley. As Dr Reid Baxter points out, in February 1579 (called 1578 by Wode, still conforming to the sixteenth century Scottish calendar according to which the year changed at Annunciation) Morton was at the peak of his powers, and no-one in the kingdom would have dared to accuse him of murder. Dr Reid Baxter is currently preparing a paper for *The Innes Review* on this subject.
7 The Protestant poet, Robert Sempill (c. 1530–1595), spent some time in Paris,

returning to Scotland in 1572 after escaping the St Bartholomew's Eve Massacre. He was pressed into service by Morton and the pro-English party as a propagandist.

8 The Carberry Banner is illustrated in Purser, op.cit., p 114.

9 Quoted in Dickinson, Donaldson and Milne, op.cit., vol III p 430. Jim Reid Baxter has proposed that as Blakhall's other two five-part polyphonic psalms would seem to have been cynical attempts by Morton to manipulate the young James VI through his greatest love, music, we should perhaps regard *Of mercy and of judgement both* in the same light. Dated 1569, it could have been written after the murder of Moray in January 1570 (remembering that the sixteenth century Scottish year turned on 25 March) and may mark Morton's very earliest attempt to prepare the ground at court for a counter-strike against the Hamiltons. The choice of text would certainly seem to bear this out.

> As for the proude and wicked man
> I will with force expell
> Whoso his nyghtboure doth backbyte
> That man will I distroy.
> And whoso hath ane proude highe luke
> This sam will I anoy . . .
> The ungodly sonne [soon] I will distroy
> Which dwell the land about
> And from the Citye of the Lord
> All wicked men rute out.

10 See p 44.

11 Published in *Musica Britannica*, vol. XV, p 134.

12 See Isobel Woods, 'A note on "Scottish Anonymous"', *Research Chronicle*, vol. 21, 1988, pp 37–9.

13 For a fuller treatment see Allenson, op.cit., pp 9–13.

14 Quoted in Hutchison, op.cit., p 79.

15 It is worth pointing out that in 1584 the same monarch published his *Essays of a Prentice to the Divine Art of Poesie*, and in 1585 *The Reulis and Cautelis of Poesie*, in which he advocated the use of Scots and encouraged native traditions such as alliteration. Unfortunately the splendid psalm translations produced by Montgomerie were rejected by the English-speaking Kirk of Scotland in favour of 'lesser men and metres' as R D S Jack puts it in his informative study of Montgomerie in the Scottish Writers series (pp 71–4). The great makar's *Twenty-third Psalm* has had to wait to our own times to receive a musical treatment worthy of its literary merit. In the course of his setting, the modern composer, Ronald Stevenson, evocatively spans the centuries by using various psalm tunes 'in reports'.

16 Quoted in Maynard, op.cit., vol I, p 170.

17 See p 133.

18 Quoted in C. Rogers, *History of the Chapel Royal of Scotland*, Edinburgh 1882, Introduction p lxxxiii. While Psalm 21, *Domine in virtute tua*, had been set in Latin some forty years previously by Robert Johnson and recorded by Thomas Wode (see p 162), this is unlikely to have been the setting used on this occasion unless with a vernacular underlay. There can be little doubt that James would have commissioned a special setting, perhaps from Andro Blakhall, whose polyphonic psalm settings the King had known from his own childhood. And although Alexander Montgomerie was in disgrace by 1594, he had already demonstrated exceptional facility in translating psalms into Scots. Sadly, neither the Scots text nor the music has

survived and we can only guess what a Castalian collaboration might have made of the highly apposite text,

> The King shall rejoice in thy strength, O Lord;
> exceeding glad shall he be of thy salvation.
> Thou hast given him his heart's desire;
> and hast not denied him the request of his lips.

As the Tudor line neared its end in the person of the aged Virgin Queen, Elizabeth, the King of Scots must indeed have rejoiced that his heart's desire, the succession (to both thrones), now seemed secure.

CHAPTER 15

1 A full treatment of this topic may be found in Jim Inglis, *The Organ in Scotland before 1700*, De Mixtuur, Schagen, 1991.
2 Quoted in Inglis, op.cit., pp 52–3.
3 See p 6.
4 A performance edition of this piece is available in D James Ross (ed), *Two Anonymous Scottish Counters on* 'Pater Creator omnium', CMF Music, Inverness 1992. It uses as *cantus* the same plainchant melody as Carver uses in his Mass *Pater Creator omnium*.
5 Maynard, op.cit., Vol. II, p 83.
6 In referring to the rôle of organs in the celebration of special feast days in his *Commentary on the Rule of St Augustine*, Robert Richardson recommends the use of 'more outstanding ornaments and *with the addition of organs.*' (Editorial italics.) Quoted in Woods, Vol. I, op.cit., p 86.
7 For a full treatment of Fethy's career see John MacQueen's fascinating introduction to *Ballatis of Luve*, Edinburgh University Press, Edinburgh, 1970.
8 It is unlikely to refer to the use of the thumbs, which only came into play in the early seventeenth century.
9 Quoted in Inglis, op.cit., p 90.
10 This piece is published in *Musica Britannica*, vol. XV, pp 198–9.
11 Ibid., pp 194–5.
12 Quoted in Inglis, op.cit., p 72.
13 Ibid., p 73.
14 Ibid., p 74.
15 Ibid., p 76.
16 See p 111.
17 See Inglis, op.cit., p 79.

CHAPTER 16

1 Quoted in Inglis, op.cit., p 91.
2 'Propter carnales autem, non propter spirituales consuetudo cantandi, et psallendi in ecclesia inducta est.' Quoted in Woods, op.cit., Vol. I, p 83.
3 The entire issue of the use of instruments in the context of church music of the fifteenth and sixteenth centuries is an extremely contentious one (other than in Spain and Spanish America, where it was undoubtedly standard practice). The Clemencic Consort of Vienna have clearly demonstrated that a combination of voices and a

variety of period instruments produces a plausible performance of the music of masters such as Dufay, Ockeghem and Isaac, and their ideas have been taken up and developed by continental consorts such as the Huelgas Ensemble. With few exceptions, English performers, steeped in the 'English cathedral tradition', have proved reluctant to combine instruments with voices in performances of fifteenth and sixteenth century church music. As usual, historical reality probably lies somewhere between these two poles. To cite accounts of services where instruments are mentioned as participating and illustrations showing combined groups of vocalists and instrumentalists as evidence for standard practice is to ignore the many exceptions. It is likely that instruments were used on a largely casual basis, when they were available or when the status of the occasion demanded their presence.

4 See p 27.
5 Quoted in Inglis, op.cit., p 57.
6 Quoted in ibid., p 20.
7 My performance edition of both these pieces is available: see p 166, notes to Chapter 15, 4.
8 A transcription of this piece is available in Maynard, op.cit. Vol II, pp 264–5
9 Letter from Randolph to Cecil, 29 April 1565. Quoted in Inglis, op. cit., p 72.
10 Waldegrave, *A true reportarie of the most triumphant and royal Accomplishment of the Baptisme of Frederick-Henry, Prince of Scotland.* Quoted in Purser, op.cit., p 117.
11 A transcription of this piece is available in Woods, op.cit. Vol II, p 299.
12 In this respect, too, the Scottish Reformers were at odds with the views of Luther. In his foreword to the *Wittemberg Gesangbuch* of 1524 he cites 'the example of the prophets and Kings in the Old Testament who praised God with singing and with playing, with hymns and the sound of all manner of stringed instruments,' as evidence that instruments are just as pleasing to God as voices and deserve a part in church music.
13 Published in *Musica Britannica*, vol. XV, pp 195–6.
14 Ibid., pp 196–7.
15 A performance edition of these pieces is available in D James Ross (ed), *Four Anonymous Scottish Consorts on Psalm Tunes*, CMF Music, Inverness 1992.
16 A transcription of this piece is available in Maynard, op.cit. Vol II, pp 256–7.
17 Preserved in *Duncan Burnett's Music-book* of 1610 in the Library of the Earl of Dalhousie, Panmure MS 10.

CHAPTER 17

1 See pp 62–64.
2 For a full treatment of this issue, see Mairi Robinson, 'Language Choice in the Reformation', *Scotland and the Lowland Tongue*, (ed. D J McClure), Aberdeen University Press, 1983, p 59.
3 See p 99.
4 In a letter of 1631 to Charles I (quoted in Inglis, op.cit., p 77) the Director of the Chapel Royal, Edward Kellie, mentions that among 'English, French, Dutch, Spaynish, Latin (and) Italian . . . musick, vocall and instrumental' in the Chapel library there was also intriguingly some 'old Scotch music'. Presumably the Chapel Royal instruments also mentioned in this letter, 'two flutes, two pandores with violls and other instruments' perished along with the organs and the music.
5 See Elliott, op.cit., p 32.

CHAPTER 18

1 Gawain Douglas, *Palice of Honour*, 490–507, quoted in Maynard, op.cit., vol. I, p 103. Similar lists of musical instruments occur in a number of other mediaeval poems including a famous example in the Orcadian Richard Holland's *Book of the Howlat* of around 1450, which Douglas seems to have drawn upon.

> All thus our lady lovit with lyking and lyst,
> Menstralis and musicianis mo than I mene may:
> The psaltery, the sytholis, the soft sytharist,
> The croude and the monycordis, the gittyrnis gay,
> The rote and the recordour, the ribupe, the rist,
> The lilt pype and the lute, the fydill in fist,
> The dulset, the dulsacordis, the shalme of assay,
> The amyable organis usit full oft,
> > Claryonis lowde knellis,
> > Portativis and bellis,
> > Cymbaclavis in the cellis
> > That soundis so soft.

A copy of Holland's poem is available in Priscilla Bawcutt & Felicity Riddy (ed.), *Longer Scottish Poems, vol. I 1375–1650*, pp 43–84.

CHAPTER 19

1 Barbour's poem even contains an intriguing reference to the fact that the anecdotes he is relating may have been sung on occasion.

> 'Young women when thai will play
> Syng it amang thaim ilk day.' (XVI 529–30)

Hary, the author of *Wallace*, was formerly thought to be the 'Blin Hary' mentioned by Dunbar in his *Lament for the Makaris*, but this is now considered unlikely.

2 Purser, op.cit., p 66.
3 See pp 145–146.
4 See Farmer, op.cit., p 73.
5 Published in *Musica Britannica*, vol. XV, p 150.
6 Ibid., pp 141–7.
7 See Elliott, op.cit., pp 13–15.
8 For a fuller definition of these terms see Mairi Robinson (ed.) *The Concise Scots Dictionary*, Aberdeen University Press, Aberdeen, 1985.
9 Is this line, which appears twice in Lindsay's play (lines 1703 and 2561), an indication that *The Pleugh Sang* was performed as part of the action? Although the song predates the play, it was still current at the time of the first performance.
10 A performance edition of this piece is available in D James Ross (ed.), *An anonymous Scottish Fantasia on 'L'Homme Armé'*, CMF Music, Inverness, 1992.

CHAPTER 20

1 Kenneth Elliott's performance edition of this piece remains unpublished, but it has been recorded by the King's Singers on SRCM111.
2 See Farmer, op.cit., p 77.
3 See Ibid., p 77.
4 Ibid., p 77.
5 This piece is published in *Musica Britannica*, vol. XV, pp 158–9.
6 Ibid., p 151.
7 Ibid., p 160.
8 Ibid., pp 154–6.
9 Ibid., pp 152–3.
10 See Maynard, op.cit., Vol. II, p 281.
11 The text of *All Sons of Adam* contains a number of parallels with Carver's Mass *Dum sacrum mysterium* including the presence of St Michael and St John, as in the *Magnificat* Antiphon which Carver uses as a *cantus*, and the picture of mankind joining the angels in praising God, implicit in Carver's ten-voice texture.
12 See p 9.
13 Purser, op.cit., p 119.
14 This piece is published in *Musica Britannica*, vol. XV, p 163.
15 See Elliott, op.cit., p 22.
16 Quoted in Woods, op.cit., Vol. I, p 240.
17 See Elliott, op.cit., p 22.
18 This account draws heavily on John MacQueen's introduction to *Ballatis of Luve*, Edinburgh University Press, Edinburgh, 1970, where he puts forward some convincing arguments for Alexander Scott poet and musician being one and the same man. He also suggests that Scott may well have prepared and participated in elaborate masques while resident in Paris in 1540. See also his 'Biography of Alexander Scott' in *Scotland and the Lowland Tongue* (ed. D J McClure), Aberdeen University Press, Aberdeen, 1983.

CHAPTER 21

1 Quoted in Farmer, op.cit., p 78.
2 The court accounts mention payments to viol players called John Feldie, Moreis Dow, William Hay, John Dow and John Hay. Quoted Ibid., p 123.
3 See Ibid., p 77.
4 It is not clear whether the 'base' refers to its pitch or its social status! In the event of the latter it is probably a rebec, in the event of the former, a bass viol (rather than a violone), which would tend to confirm the suggestion made in the previous chapter that by this time in Scotland the bass viol was treated as a solo instrument with its own distinctive repertoire.
5 See Elliott, op.cit., p 34. Lauder was a friend of Alexander Montgomerie, who wrote a sonnet which refers punningly to James Lauder's loyalty to the captive Mary, 'James Lawder, I wald se Mare'. The interchangeable I and J meant that the second half of the first line is an exact anagram of the first.
6 Published in *Musica Britannica*, vol. XV, p 192. Here and elsewhere I use 'paven', the spelling of the word consistently used by Wode, rather than the alternatives 'pavane' or 'pavan'.

7 Ibid., p 193.

8 Ibid., p 198.

9 The alto part is in the Georgetown University Library copy of the Altus *Part-book* (see pp 66–7), and it has allowed Kenneth Elliott to reconstruct the piece in four parts. His edition is published in *The Innes Review*, Volume XXXIX, No. 2, Autumn 1988. The result is impressively close to a speculative reconstruction completed without the help of this additional source by Charles Foster of Aberdeen.

CHAPTER 22

1 See Elliott, op.cit., p 36. The Hudsons' father, William the elder, who had known Robert Johnson in England, was also present at the Scottish court. This mass influx of English musicians, who quickly secured influential positions and soon controlled much of the musical patronage associated with the court, caused some resentment among their Scots counterparts, who viewed them as interlopers and referred to them dismissively as 'the Inglis rabble'.

2 The tunes of *Black called fyne musick* and *Blak major* are preserved in the *Tolquhon Cantus* of 1611 and *William Stirling's Cantus* of 1639, while the former also features in *Robert Edwards' Commonplace-book* 1630–65. The basses of both are in *David Melvill's Bassus Part-book* of 1604. I am grateful to Charles Foster for this information and for the use of his edition of these pieces.

3 Published in *Musica Britannica*, Vol. XV, p 170. Eyewitness accounts of the celebrations in Edinburgh include references to music and to Bacchus, whose 'blissing' is mentioned in the text of *Nou let us sing*.

4 Ibid., p 189.

5 See Elliott, op.cit., p 36.

6 Published in *Musica Britannica*, Vol. XV, p 176.

7 Ibid., p 177.

8 Ibid., p 173.

9 Ibid., p 174.

10 Ibid., p 170.

11 Ibid., p 175.

12 It was named after probably its first and certainly its most famous example, *The Banks of Helicon*, probably also by Montgomerie. It is an elaborate fourteen line stanza, rhyming AAB CCB DEDE FGHG, but further complicated by an internal rhyme in the F and H lines. Extensive alliteration and an equally complex pattern of stressed and unstressed syllables make this an extremely daunting form to maintain. Montgomerie's *The Cherrie and the Slae* with its one hundred and fourteen Helicon stanzas is an extraordinary *tour de force*.

13 Discussed briefly in Elliott, op.cit., p 38 and at greater length in Purser, op.cit., pp 109–10.

14 Kenneth Elliott (ed.), *Early Scottish Keyboard Music*, Stainer and Bell, London, 1967, pp 4–8. Kinloch's entire surviving output has been edited by John Purser and while it remains unpublished it is performed by John Kitchen (harpsichord) on *The Music of William Kinloch and Duncan Burnett* (ASV Gaudeamus). See Discography for details.

15 Ibid., pp 9–10.

16 Maynard, op.cit., vol. II p 17.

17 It is a touching tribute to the magnanimity of James VI and to the high regard in which he held Montgomerie, 'beloved Sanders maistre of our art', that he braved the fury of the Presbytery of Edinburgh to attend the funeral of the greatest of the Castalians, and arguably the most accomplished of the Scottish courtly poets of this whole era. He also composed a fitting epitaph for his friend in the medium in which he had excelled.

> What drowsie sleepe doth syle your eyes allace
> Ye sacred brethren of Castalian band
> And shall the prince of poets in our land
> Goe thus to grave unmurned in anie cace?
> No: whett your pens ye imps of heavenlie grace
> And toone me up your sweete resounding strings
> And mount him so on your immortall wings
> That ever he may live in everie place.

The elegance of the King's verses is itself an eloquent tribute to his mentor. (Research by John Durkan into the circumstances of Montgomerie's death and burial, as well as James VI's epitaph, are quoted in R D S Jack's study of the poet in the Scottish Writers series.)

CHAPTER 23

1 See Howard Mayer Brown, *Embellishing 16th Century Music*, Oxford University Press, New York, 1976.
2 This mode of performance is lent a degree of authority by the fact that the appendix to the *Wode Part-books* includes underlay for only the treble part in several of the part-songs. In my examples I have supplied bracketed speculative underlay for the other parts, although readers will notice that this often presupposes the subdivision of longer notes in these parts.
3 The Scottish Poetry Library, Tweeddale Court, 14 High Street, Edinburgh, EH1 1TE, are delighted to help with enquiries regarding pronunciation of Scots texts.
4 R Waldegrave, *A true Reportarie of the most triumphant and royal Accomplishment of the Baptisme of Frederick-Henry, Prince of Scotland*, Edinburgh, 1594. Quoted in Purser, op.cit., p 119.
5 Ibid., p 117.

CHAPTER 24

1 For a fuller treatment see Elliott, op.cit., p 46.
2 Maynard, op.cit., vol. II, p 28.
3 *Basilikon Doron* 1599, quoted in Dickinson, Donaldson and Milne, op. cit., vol III, p 261.
4 As yet none of these pieces has been published, but two selections of pieces from the main lute manuscripts (including all the tunes discussed above) have been recorded by Jakob Lindberg on BIS-CD 201 and Ronn McFarlane on DOR-90129. For further information see Discography.
5 Alison Kinnaird and Keith Sanger's *Tree of Strings*, Kinmore Music, Shillinghill

(Scotland), 1992, pp 174–91 provides an informative account of the rôle of Celtic harper-minstrels in the wider context of Scottish music.

6 Ibid. p 177.

7 For a fuller treatment see Elliott, op.cit., p 45.

Select Bibliography

The secund part of music beand dressit and formalie put in ordour, it is now expedient to proceid fordwart with the process of the thrid part quhilk is the gardin of music quhairin habundance of concordis and semeconcordis plesantlye ar plantit, furth of the quhilkis all kind of wyld weydis, that is to say, all barbur and onformall puyntis ar utterly exterminat and repellit so that musicianis, amang the plesand plantis of concordance, may find and gadder dyvverss punctis rethoricall to the decornig of harmony and amphian of the samyn.

(*The Art of Music*: transcribed Judson Maynard.)

A. PRINTED EDITIONS

Muriel Brown (ed.), *The Complete Works of Robert Carver*, Bardic Edition, Aylesbury, 1989
Muriel Brown's excellent edition, which embodies her respectful approach to the original manuscript in her very limited application of *musica ficta*, is available from Bardic Edition, 6 Fairfax Crescent, Aylesbury, Bucks., HP22 ES.

Gabor Darvas (ed.), *Robert Carver: Mass L'Homme Armé*, Editio Musica, Budapest, 1975
This Hungarian edition was part of a projected complete edition of all the surviving *L'Homme Armé* Masses.

Kenneth Elliott (ed.), *Music of Scotland 1500–1700: Musica Britannica*, Vol. XV, Stainer & Bell, London, 1975
This is quite simply the definitive collection of Scottish Renaissance music for church and court. Seminal to the wider popularity of the music of this period, it contains a wealth of part-songs, consort music and church music, including Carver's Mass *L'Homme Armé*, *O bone Jesu*, the Mass in three parts, and the anonymous Masses *Felix namque* and *Rex virginum*, as well as selections of High Renaissance motets and music of the Reformed Church. With the recent completion of his work on the ten-part Mass, Dr Elliott has now edited the complete works of Robert Carver but these remain unpublished.

Kenneth Elliott (ed.), *Early Scottish Keyboard Music*, Stainer & Bell, London, 1967
This collection constitutes an appendix to the above, presenting a selection from the music books of the early seventeenth century for keyboard and for solo stringed instruments, including a selection of works by William Kinloch.

Kenneth Elliot (ed.), *Fourteen Psalm Settings of the Early Reformed Church*, Oxford University Press, London, 1960
This less than user friendly edition bafflingly underlays with ('modernised') text only the psalm tune, which is printed above the textless four-part harmonisations. Disappointingly, given the number of surviving psalm settings which remain unpublished, four of the settings are already available in *Musica Britannica* XV.

Charles Foster (ed.), *4 Scottish Partsongs c. 1545*, London Pro Musica Edition, London, 1990
This collection contains editions of *O lusty May*, *Wo worth the tyme*, *How suld my febill body fure*, and *Depairte, depairte*.

Hilda Hutchison (ed.), *The St Andrews Psalter, Edition and Commentary*, Vol. II (Edition), Edinburgh University, 1957
The second volume of this dissertation consists of a complete transcription of the contents of the *Wode Part-books.*

John Alexander Fuller-Maitland (ed.), *Robert Carver, O bone Jesu*, Dean and Sons, London, 1926
This edition, now out of print, is of largely historical interest as one of the earliest attempts to edit Carver's music.

Judson Maynard (ed.), *An Anonymous Scottish Treatise on Music from the Sixteenth Century, British Museum, Additional Manuscript 4911, Edition and Commentary*, Vol. II (Edition), Indiana University, 1961
The second volume of this dissertation consists of a complete transcription of the text and musical examples, which include native pieces.

D James Ross (ed.), *Two anonymous Scottish Counters on 'Pater Creator omnium*, CMF Music, Inverness, 1992
D James Ross (ed), *Four anonymous Scottish Consorts on Psalm Tunes*, CMF Music, Inverness 1992
D James Ross (ed.), *An anonymous Scottish Fantasia on 'L'Homme Armé'*, CMF Music, Inverness, 1992
D James Ross (ed.), *A Faburden Processional from the Inverness Sang Schule (c. 1550)*, CMF Music, Inverness, 1992
D James Ross (ed.), *Omnes gentes, attendite*, CMF Music, Inverness, 1993
Copies of these editions by the author are available from Coronach, 'Cullaggan', 18 Sunnyside, Culloden Moor, Inverness, IV1 2EE.

Denis Stevens (ed.), *Opera omnia: Corpus Mensurabilis Musicae*, Vol. XVI, American Institute of Musicology, Rome, 1959
Carver's *Gaude flore virginali* and *O bone Jesu* appear in this edition.

Isobel Woods (ed.), *The Carvor (sic) Choirbook*, Vol. II, Princeton University, 1984
The second volume of this dissertation contains transcriptions of all the unpublished material from the *Choirbook*: Carver's Masses *Dum sacrum mysterium*, *Pater Creator omnium* (not reconstructed), *Fera pessima*, the Mass in six parts, four anonymous *Magnificats*, an anonymous *Salve Regina*, the anonymous Mass *Deus Creator omnium*, and various fragments.

B. BOOKS

Kenneth Elliott & Frederick Rimmer, *A History of Scottish Music*, BBC Publications, London, 1973
A stylish and enjoyable account, based on impeccable scholarship.

Henry Farmer, *A History of Music in Scotland*, Hinrichsen, London, 1947 (second impression, Da Capo, New York, 1970)
A work of towering scholarship whose stature sets it above changing fashions in prose style. Enthusiastic and very readable.

John Purser, *Scotland's Music*, Mainstream Publishing, Edinburgh & London, 1992
An ambitious attempt to chart the history of both traditional and classical music in Scotland from the earliest times to the present day. Generously illustrated, informative, persuasive and stylishly written, with recourse to both scholarship and intuition.

Helena Shire, *Song, Dance and Poetry of the Court of Scotland under James VI*, Cambridge University Press, Cambridge, 1969
Despite its idiosyncratic literary style, a useful study which goes far beyond the scope promised by its title.

Jenny Wormald (ed.), *Scotland Revisited*, London, 1991
A superb collection.

C. ARTICLES/DISSERTATIONS

Stephen Allenson, 'The Inverness Fragments: Music from a Pre-Reformation Scottish Parish Church and School', *Music & Letters* Vol. 70, No. 1, 1989, pp 1–45

Kenneth Elliott, 'The Carver Choirbook', *Music & Letters*, Vol. XLI, No. 4, 1960, pp 349–357
Kenneth Elliott, 'Church Music at Dunkell' (sic), *Music & Letters*, Vol. XLV, No. 3, 1964, pp 228–232
Kenneth Elliott, 'Another of Thomas Wode's Missing Parts', *The Innes Review*, Vol. XXXIX, No. 2, pp 151–154

Hilda Hutchison, *The St Andrews Psalter, Edition and Commentary*, Vol. I (Commentary), Edinburgh University, 1957

John McQuaid, *Scottish Musicians of the Reformation*, Edinburgh University 1949
John McQuaid, 'Music and the Administration', *The Innes Review*, Vol. III, 1952, pp 14–21

J.A.Fuller-Maitland, 'A Scottish composer of the 16th Century', *Gedenkenboek aangeboden aan Dr D.F. Schleurkeer op zijn 70sten verjaardag.* 's-Gravenhage: Nijhoff, 1925, p 119–122

Judson Maynard, *An Anonymous Scottish Treatise on Music from the Sixteenth Century, British Museum, Additional Manuscript 4911, Edition and Commentary*, Vol. I (Commentary), Indiana University, 1961

James Ross, 'Robert Carver, A Quincentenary Celebration', *Brio*, Vol. XXIV, No. 1, 1987, pp 14–25

James Ross, 'Robert Carver, A 16th Century Scottish Master of Polyphony', *The Consort*, No. 43, 1987, pp 1–12
James Ross, 'Robert Carver, Quincentenary of a Neglected Genius', *Musical Opinion*, No. 1320, Vol. 110, 1987, pp 358–360

Isobel Woods, *The Carvor* (sic) *Choirbook*, Vol. I (Commentary), Princeton University, 1984
Isobel Woods, 'A Note on Scottish Anonymous', *Research Chronicle*, Vol. 21, 1988
Isobel Woods, 'Towards a Biography of Carver', *Music Review*, May 1989

2. CULTURAL BACKGROUND

David Daiches (ed.), *A Companion to Scottish Culture*, Edward Arnold, London, 1981
Gordon Donaldson & Robert Morpeth, *A Dictionary of Scottish History*, John Donald Publishers Ltd., Edinburgh, 1977
Mairi Robinson (ed.), *The Concise Scots Dictionary*, Aberdeen University Press, Aberdeen, 1985
Three indispensable reference works.

John & Winifred MacQueen, *Scottish Verse 1470–1570*, Faber, London, 1972
A subjective but enjoyable selection of the poetry of this period.
John MacQueen, *Ballatis of Luve, The Scottish Courtly Love Lyric 1400–1570* Edinburgh University Press, Edinburgh, 1970
This exquisite collection is enhanced by Professor MacQueen's scholarly commentary.

R D S Jack, *Scottish Prose 1550–1700*, Calder and Boyars, London 1971
This invaluable collection of Scots prose includes extracts from James VI's essay *Reulis and Cautelis of Poesie*, and one of the few surviving works in Scots by George Buchanan, his political satire *Chameleon*.
Since 1884 the Scottish Text Society has been issuing scholarly editions of the work of most of the greatest Scots writers of the sixteenth century, and the serious student may wish to consult these for a fuller picture of the literary wealth of the period.

Jenny Wormald, *Court, Kirk and Community: Scotland 1470–1625*, Edward Arnold, London, 1981
The most approachable and comprehensive of a number of recent accounts of the history of the period. Its treatment of music is derivative and occasionally inaccurate, but the book provides a very colourful and detailed picture of Renaissance Scotland and its culture.

Norman Macdougall, *James IV*, John Donald, Edinburgh, 1989
Those interested in a more detailed account of the history of the period covered by the present book will wish to consult the relevant parts of a projected nine volume series to be published by John Donald of Edinburgh, covering the entire Stewart dynasty in Scotland 1371–1603. If the standard of excellence achieved by Norman Macdougall in the inaugural volume is maintained through the series it should prove an epoch-making publication.

3. GENERAL MUSICAL BACKGROUND

Howard Brown, *Music in the Renaissance*, Prentice-Hall, New Jersey, 1976
A full treatment of the church and secular music of the period. Probably the most comprehensive and certainly the most readable account available (but don't blink or you will miss Carver and Johnson on p 247).

Howard Brown, *Embellishing Sixteenth Century Music*, Oxford University Press, Oxford, 1976
An authoritative and lucid description of a complex area of performance. Essential reading for singers and instrumentalists alike, which clarifies the treatment of graces and *passagi* in various Continental authorities and suggests practical applications.

Jeremy and Elizabeth Roche (ed.), *A Dictionary of Early Music*, Faber, London, 1980
A very useful compendium, which sadly perpetuates the customary cursory treatment of Robert Carver and ignores David Peebles altogether.

David Wulstan, *Tudor Music*, Dent, London, 1985
A beautifully written and comprehensive account of the sacred and secular music of Tudor England, including the research and insights gleaned over a lifetime of practical experience.

DISCOGRAPHY

(Where a recording is available in different formats, these are all listed as LP, MC and CD.)

'*The King's Musick, 1250–1550*', *A History of Scottish Music, Vol. I*, (Scottish Records, LP SRSS1, MC SRCM111)
This recording includes performances by the King's Singers of *The Pleugh Sang, All Sons of Adam, Trip and go, hey*, the *Sanctus* from Carver's six-part Mass and the *Credo* from the anonymous Mass *Felix namque*. The collection is now rather dated in terms of performance practice and editorial liberties (e.g. sections of the Carver are transposed to place them within the vocal range of the performers and in other works vocal lines are moved up or down an octave for the same reason), but it still represents the only recording so far of some of the material.

'*Musick Fyne, 1550–1625*', *A History of Scottish Music, Vol.II*, (Scottish Records, LP SRSS2, MC SRCM112)
This recording includes a selection of part-songs, performed by the Saltire Singers, and solo songs, performed by Clifford Hughes, interspersed with works for harpsichord performed by Kenneth Elliott. These performances are also rather dated.

Scottish Lute Music, Jakob Lindberg, (Grammofon A B BIS, LP BIS-LP201, CD BIS-CD201)
A polished and sympathetic performance of items from a number of Scottish lute manuscripts.

The Scottish Lute, Ronn McFarlane (Dorian CD DOR-90129)
A generous selection of tunes imaginatively performed by this leading American lutenist on the lute and mandora.

On the Banks of Helicon, Early music of Scotland, The Baltimore Consort, (Dorian CD DOR-90139)
Ronn McFarlane is joined by an able consort, well versed in folk conventions, for inspired renditions of consort and vocal music, much of it recorded for the first time.

Mary's Music: Songs and Dances from the time of Mary Queen of Scots, The Scottish Early Music Consort (Chandos, LP ADRD1103, MC ABTD1103, CD CHAN1103)
Performances of English, French and Scottish music for consort and voices, which take into account the latest research into performance practices. Some curious eccentricities, such as bizarre pronunciation and annoying recorder vibrato, but on the whole very impressive.

Mediaeval and Renaissance Music, The Kincorth Waits, (MC CVF13345)
Early Scottish Music, The Kincorth Waits, (MC HRT0010)
Two interesting selections from this enterprising amateur group, using a wide variety of period instruments and a distinctive naive vocal style.

Coronach: Early Scottish Music, Coronach, (MC CMF001)
Coronach: Celtic Heritage, Coronach, (MC CMF002)
Coronach: O Lustie May, Coronach, (MC CMF003)
A wide selection of Early Scottish Music performed on period instruments and directed by the author. All three recordings are available from Coronach, 'Cullaggan', 18 Sunnyside, Culloden Moor, Inverness, IV1 2EE.

Coronach: Whip my Towdie: Coronach (CD CMF 005)
A collection of popular music from Renaissance Scotland including the *Pleugh Sang* and realisations for mixed consort of tunes from the Scottish lute books. Available from Coronach, 'Cullaggan', 18 Sunnyside, Culloden Moor, Inverness, IV1 2EE.

Carver: Mass L'Homme Armé, The Renaissance Group of the University of St Andrews (Abbey, LP ACA518, MC CACA518)
The first complete recording of this Carver Mass, distinguished by fine articulation from the choir and a radiant tonal quality from the soloists, and in particular from Alison Bleasby, soprano.

Cantate Domino: Scottish Sacred Music of the 16th and 20th Centuries, Paisley Abbey Choir (Abbey, LP ACA 532, MC CACA532)
An impressive rendition of the hitherto neglected Mass *Cantate Domino* from the *Dowglas/Fischar Part-books*, which may well be the work of Carver. Also on this crowded disc are an anonymous *Report upon the sixth psalm* and Andrew Kemp's forthright setting of Psalm 124.

Music from Sixteenth Century Scotland and England, Edinburgh University Renaissance Singers, (LP EURS1)
This useful collection of motets, raw at times and rather aggressive but enthusiastic throughout, includes Peebles' *Quam multi Domine*, the anonymous Scottish setting of *Descendi in hortum meum* and the *Gloria* of the Mass *L'Homme Armé* and *Gaude flore virginali* by Carver.

Robert Carver: Mass for Five Voices, The Carver Choir, (MC TD8720)
Robert Carver: Mass for Six Voices, The Carver Choir, (MC TD8801)

Both these recordings, directed by the author, are available from Donselco Ltd, Rose House, 27 Rose Street, Aberdeen.

Robert Carver: Mass for Ten Voices, The Renaissance Group of the University of St Andrews, (Abbey, LP ACA 582, MC CACA582)
Another fine recording from this enterprising ensemble. Some tempi are rather impetuous but the overall performance is very pleasing.

Popular music from the time of Henry VIII, The Hilliard Ensemble, (Saga, LP SAGA5444 CD SCD 9003)
Includes *The Pleugh Sang, O Lusty May, Begone, sweit night* and *Absent I am*. The album title and notes would make James IV turn in his grave. These are engaging performances marred by curious pronunciation.

Masterworks from late-medieval England and Scotland, The Taverner Choir, (EMI, CD C7 49661 2)
Superb performances of *O bone Jesu* and *Gaude flore virginali* and of other treasures by Taverner and Browne, including the latter's beautiful eight-part setting of *O Maria Salvatoris mater.*

The Music of Robert Johnson, Paisley Abbey Choir, (Abbey, LP ACA 558)
A rich selection of the work of this neglected master, including *Deus misereatur, Ave Dei Patris filia, Benedicam Domino, Dicant nunc Judei*, both settings of *Dum transisset, Gaude Maria virgo* and *Jubilate.*

Scottish Renaissance Polyphony: Robert Carver: Capella Nova (ASV Gaudeamus LP/ MC/CD 124, 126 and 127)
Following their presentation of the complete works of Carver in liturgical reconstructions at the 1990 Glasgow Chorus International Festival, Capella Nova have recorded the two motets and the five signed Masses in a three volume set for ASV. This superb professional ensemble perform at a consistently high level throughout in recordings which deserve worldwide recognition.

A Scottish Mass of 1546: Musick Fyne & Coronach (MC CMF 004)
Carver's Mass *Pater Creator omnium* in the author's performance edition performed by Musick Fyne, directed by the author, in the context of a partial liturgical reconstruction, which also incorporates *Laudate pueri* from the *Inverness Fragments*, David Peebles' two motets, the anonymous faburden *Deo Gratias* from *The Art of Music*, appropriate Sarum plainchant and contemporary Scottish consort music by John Blak and Robert Johnson. Available from Coronach, 'Cullaggan', 18 Sunnyside, Culloden Moor, Inverness, IV1 2EE.

A Scottish Mass of the High Renaissance: Musick Fyne (CD CMF 006)
The Mass *Felix namque* (anon. possibly the work of Robert Carver) with appropriate motets and plainchant, performed as a liturgical reconstruction of the Mass sung in Holyrood Palace in August 1561 to celebrate the return from France of Mary, Queen of Scots. Available from Coronach, 'Cullaggan', 18 Sunnyside, Culloden Moor, Inverness, IV1 2EE.

Scotland's Music: Selected works from the history of Scottish music: (Various Artists) (2CD Linn CKD 008)

These companion discs to the book of the same name consist of a compilation of recorded material already available on discs mentioned above, with several recordings specially made for the *Scotland's Music* radio series, including the anonymous faburden setting of *Salve festa dies* from *The Art of Music* and Robert Johnson's two-part setting of *Dicant nunc judei.*

The Music of William Kinloch and Duncan Burnett: John Kitchen (Harpsichord) (ASV Gaudeamus CD GAU 134)
The complete verifiable keyboard music by these two great Scottish masters performed by Scotland's leading early keyboard player in editions by John Purser.

Thes Art of Musick is richt dry
Of all the seavine the mirriest.
Deame, ye are sweir that lets us cry
Once fill the stoop and let us rest.

(*Nou let us sing*)

Index

MERCAT PRESS

A SELECTION OF IMPORTANT ACADEMIC TITLES

Building for Books
IAIN GORDON BROWN
The architectural evolution of the Advocates' Library, Edinburgh, 1689-1925. "A fitting tribute to its subject" **Library Assoc. Record**
294pp new pbk 008 0379680 £14.95

The Campaigns of Montrose
STUART REID
A detailed study of the Civil War period in Scotland from a military point of view, reconstructing the battles of the charismatic general, Montrose.
208pp hbk 0901824 925 £14.95

Castellated and Domestic Architecture of Scotland
MACGIBBON & ROSS (eds)
"One of the most important and complete books on Scottish architecture that has ever been published" **The Scotsman**
5 vol set hbk 0901824 186 £125.00

Cereal Science and Technology
G H PALMER (ed.)
The standard work on the uses of cereals in brewing, distilling, baking, malting, animal nutrition, farming etc. Fully illustrated.
"Highly recommended" **Journal of Experimental Botany**
544pp hbk 008 035064X £40.00

Deprivation and Health in Scotland
V CARSTAIRS & R MORRIS
The health of Scots and the link between poor health and poverty. Here is the evidence on which future policy will have to be based.
350pp pbk 008 0303749 £19.95

The Dictionary of Scottish Business Biography
A SLAVEN & S CHECKLAND (eds.)
The story of Scottish enterprise as seen in the lives of its leading figures. "A massive work: massive in scholarship, comprehensive in scope" Business History
Volume 1: The Staple Industries
512pp hbk 008 0303986 £48.00
Volume 2: Processing, Distributing, Services
462pp hbk 008 0303994 £48.00

The Ecclesiastical Architecture of Scotland
MACGIBBON & ROSS (eds)
The standard work of reference for the architect, the historian and all who are interested in things Scottish.
3 vol set hbk 1873644 000 £100.00

The Edinburgh History of Scotland
GORDON DONALDSON (Gen ed)
The most important project in Scottish historical writing for more than half a century
Vol 1 The Making of the Kingdom
A A M DUNCAN
706pp pbk 0901824 836 £13.95
Vol 2 The Later Middle Ages
RANALD NICHOLSON
696pp pbk 0901824 844 £13.95
Vol 3 James V to James VII
GORDON DONALDSON
450pp pbk 0901824 852 £13.95
Vol 4 1689 to the Present
WILLIAM FERGUSON
470pp pbk 0901824 860 £13.95

Gaelic Dictionary
Gaelic-English / English-Gaelic
M MACLENNAN
The leading Gaelic dictionary, invaluable to learners and native speakers alike.
630pp pbk 1873644 116 £11.95

The Greig-Duncan Folk Song Collection
P SHULDHAM SHAW & E B LYLE (eds)
The largest and most important manuscript collection of Scottish ballads and folksongs.
Vol 1: Nautical, military and historical songs
590pp hbk 008 0257593 £35.00
Vol 2: Narrative songs
624pp hbk 008 0284833 £35.00
Vol 3: Songs of the countryside, of home and social life
800pp hbk 008 0303919 £35.00
Vol 4: Songs of courtship, night visiting songs, songs about particular people
620pp hbk 008 0365736 £35.00
Vols 5 & 6 due 1993--orders can be recorded now.

A Guid Cause: the Women's Suffrage Movement in Scotland
LEAH LENEMAN
The suffrage movement in Scotland was as strong as that in England. Dr Leneman describes the tremendous battle that women fought and won at the turn of the century.
250pp pbk 008 0412017 £9.95

The History of the Highland Clearances
ALEXANDER MACKENZIE
"It has been and will remain a book to be read, an essential part of any study of the Clearances" **John Prebble**
560pp pbk 0901824 968 £9.95

The History of Scottish Literature: in four volumes:
CAIRNS CRAIG (gen ed)
The major reference-work.
Volume 1 (Origins to 1660)
editor R D S JACK
322pp hbk 0080350542 £19.50
pbk 0080377254 £12.50
Volume 2 (1660-1800)
editor ANDREW HOOK
hbk 0080350550 £19.50
pbk 0080377262 £12.50
Volume 3 (nineteenth century)
editor DOUGLAS GIFFORD
474pp hbk 0080350569 £19.50
pbk 0080377270 £12.50
Volume 4 (twentieth)
editor CAIRNS CRAIG
416pp hbk 0080350577 £19.50
pbk 0080377289 £12.50

A Linguistic Atlas of Late Medieval English
A MACINTOSH, M L SAMUELS, M BENSKIN, M LAING, & K WILLIAMSON
A wide-ranging and detailed survey of English dialects in the Middle Ages. In four volumes.
2084pp hbk 008 0324371 £335.00

Memorials of His Time
HENRY COCKBURN
A lively portrait of the Scotland of his time. The reader is introduced to many of the most interesting people of the day.
470pp hbk 0901824 119 £9.95

Middle English Dialectology
M LAING (ed)
Essays on some principles and problems. An indispensible work of reference.
272pp hbk 008 0364047 £24.90

Musick Fyne
D JAMES ROSS
The achievement of Robert Carver and his contemporaries is examined in this groundbreaking study of music and culture in Renaissance Scotland.
176pp hbk 1873644 175 £15.95

The New Makars: the Mercat Anthology of Contemporary Poetry in Scots
TOM HUBBARD (ed)
"A lively collection which should entice new readers" **The Scotsman**
230pp pbk 0901824 95X £7.95

Poems and Fables
ROBERT HENRYSON
(ed HARVEY WOOD)
This complete edition of his poetry contains a wealth of personal observation, simple pathos and lively humour.
304pp pbk 0901824534 £5.95

Patronage and Principle: a Political History of Modern Scotland
MICHAEL FRY
"One of the most stimulating and provocative books ever written on Scottish politics" **Paul Scott**
256pp hbk 008 0350631 £19.95
pbk 008 0414079 £9.95

Poems of William Dunbar
W MACKAY MACKENZIE (ed)
The fifteenth century poet William Dunbar remains a major literary force in Scotland today.
272pp pbk 0901824941 £6.95

Alexander Pope
C NICHOLSON (ed.)
"essays which will interest the bibliographer, the sleuth and the art historian" Choice
278pp hbk 008 0363946 £14.90

The Road to the Never Land
Professor R D S JACK
A Reassessment of J M Barrie's dramatic art. A totally new outlook on Barrie's work, for the general reader, student and academic.
250pp hbk 008 0377424 £25.00

Rural Life in Victorian Aberdeenshire
WILLIAM ALEXANDER
A matchless account of the countryside and agriculture of the region.
176pp pbk 1873644 06X £6.95

The Romans in Scotland
GORDON MAXWELL
"A splendid book which brings together the wealth of detail we now possess about Roman Scotland, including much that will be new to the general reader." **TLS**
200pp hbk 0901824 763 £16.95

Scotichronicon
WALTER BOWER
D E R WATT (Gen ed.)
The remarkable medieval chronicle, available for the first time in a page-for-page translation opposite the Latin text.
Vol 2 (400 – 1150)
432pp hbk 008 0364101 £35.00
Vol 5 (1214 – 1286)
570pp hbk 008 0379850 £35.00
Vol 6 (1286 – 1319)
450pp hbk 008 041222X £35.00
Vol 8 (1390 – 1430)
430pp hbk 008 0345271 £35.00
Volume 1 in preparation - due May 1993

Scottish Archaeology: New Perspectives
W S HANSON & E A SLATER (eds)
A richly illustrated collection of essays on Scottish archaeology.
192pp pbk 008 0412122 £14.95

Sociability and Society in Eighteenth Century Scotland
J DWYER & R B SHER (eds)
Aspects of thought and experience in the age of the Enlightenment. "A delight to read" **Paul H Scott**
272pp pbk 1873644 205 £9.95

Scottish Handwriting 1150-1650: an introduction to the reading of documents
G G SIMPSON
148pp pbk 008 0345166 £9.95

Scott's Interleaved Waverley Novels
IAN GORDON BROWN (ed)
An introduction and illustrated commentary of Sir Walter Scott's **Magnum Opus,** the forty-eight volume edition published between 1829 and 1833.
142pp hbk 008 0350828 £19.50

Scottish Writers Series
Concise critical guides to leading Scottish writers: invaluable primers for students.
1 **Walter Scott** T CRAWFORD
140pp pbk 07073 03052 £4.95
2 **Hugh MacDiarmid** K BUTHLAY
150pp pbk 07073 02079 £4.95
3 **Robert Henryson** M MCDIARMID
132pp pbk 07073 03060 £4.95
4 **Robert Fergusson** D DAICHES
136pp pbk 07073 03133 £4.95
5 **John Galt** P H SCOTT
136pp pbk 07073 03648 £4.95
6 **Lewis Grassic Gibbon** I CAMPBELL
138pp pbk 07073 03566 £4.95
7 **Alexander Montgomerie** R D S JACK
70pp pbk 07073 03672 £4.95
8 **Robert Burns** D LOW
144pp pbk 07073 03680 £4.95
9 **John Davidson** M O'CONNOR
146pp pbk 07073 03664 £4.95
10 **J M Barrie** L ORMOND
154pp pbk 07073 05047 £4.95
11 **George MacDonald** D S ROBB
136pp pbk 07073 05233 £4.95

Social Services in Scotland
JOHN ENGLISH (ed)
The standard textbook for social administration and social work students, also of use to professionals in those fields.
208pp pbk 1873644086 £10.95

Social Work and Criminal Law in Scotland (2nd ed)
MOORE & WOOD
The new edition of the standard work for students and practitioners in law and social work.
336pp pbk 1873644 078 £14.95